D1034785

ALEXEI SOKOLSKY

YOUR FIRST MOVE

CHESS FOR BEGINNERS

Raduga Publishers
Moscow

Translated from the Russian by *Arthur Krivovyaz*
Designed by *Alexander Salnikov*

Алексей Сокольский

ВАШ ПЕРВЫЙ ХОД

На английском языке

REQUEST TO READERS

Raduga Publishers would be glad to have your opinion of this book, its translation and design and any suggestions you may have for future publications.

Please send all your comments to 17, Zubovsky Boulevard, Moscow, USSR.

First printing by Progress Publishers 1981
Second printing by Raduga Publishers 1984

Printed in the Union of Soviet Socialist Republics

С $\frac{4202000000 - 370}{031(01) - 84}$ без объявл.

CONTENTS

I. RULES OF THE GAME

THE BOARD AND NOTATION

Chess is a game for two players. One uses *chessmen* of a light colour while those of the other are usually black. The board is a square divided into 64 smaller alternating white and black squares.

Diagram 1

There exists a system of *notation* describing the situation on the board and the movement of pieces and Pawns.

In this system the vertical rows of squares called *files* are lettered from left to right: a, b, c, d, e, f, g and h. The horizontal rows of squares are called *ranks* and are numbered from

1 to 8 (1st rank, 2nd rank, etc.). Each square has its own letter and number (for instance, the e4 square).

The names of the squares are shown in Diagram 2.

Diagram 2

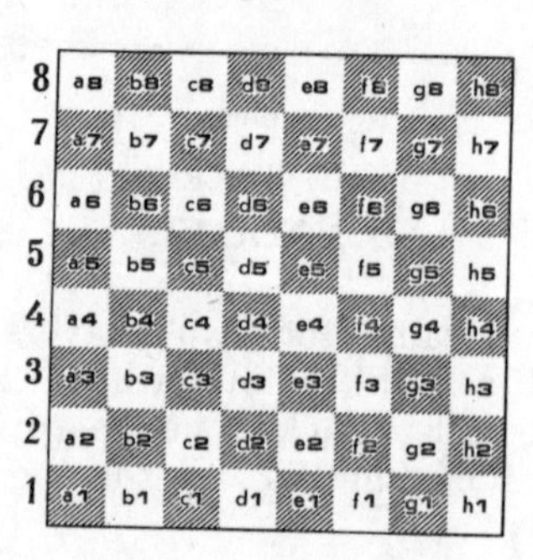

The slanting rows of squares, called *diagonals*, are designated by their end squares, for instance: the a2-g8 and h4-d8 diagonal. Whereas the colours of the squares on the ranks and files alternate, the diagonals consist of squares of the same colour, either white or black. For example, the b1-h7 diagonal is white and the c1-a3 is black. The two diagonals consisting of eight squares (a1-h8 and h1-a8) are called *long diagonals*.

Exercise.

For the purpose of this exercise the squares in Diagram 3 have been numbered at random. Give their correct names, guiding yourself by the letters and numbers on the sides. Start at square 1 (which is really h1) and go all the way up to 64 (which is really h2). After a while try giving the correct names without referring to the letters and numbers on the sides, in other words, by covering up with slips of paper. Write the answers as you go along, and when you finish check them with the solution*.

Diagram 3

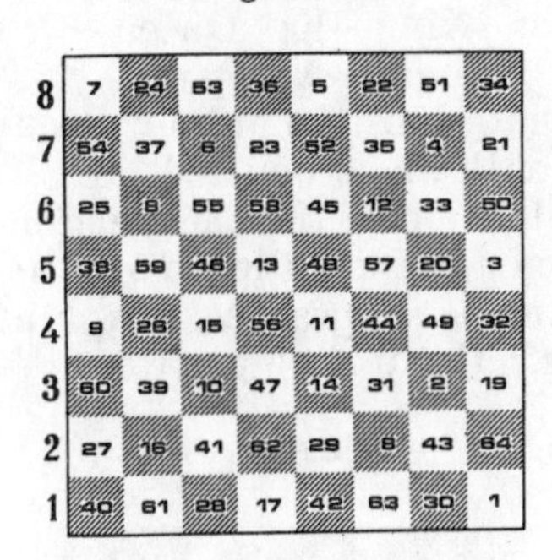

INITIAL POSITION

At the start of the *game* each side has:

a King ♔ ♚
a Queen ♕ ♛
two Rooks ♖ ♜
two Bishops ♗ ♝
two Knights ♘ ♞
eight Pawns ♙ ♟

The pieces and Pawns as a whole are called *material*. When the game starts the two sides

---

* See p. 293 for the solutions of this and other exercises.

have *material equality*. The aim of the game is to capture the opposing King. This is called to *checkmate* the King.

The Queen and Rooks are *major* pieces. The Bishops and Knights are *minor* pieces.

The chessmen are designated by the following contractions: King—K; Queen—Q; Rook—R; Bishop—B; Knight—N; Pawn—P.

In game notations the abbreviation "P" which stands for a Pawn is omitted.

The distribution of the chessmen on the board at any given time is called a *position* or *situation*. Diagram 4 shows the board at the start of play, i.e., the initial position.

Diagram 4

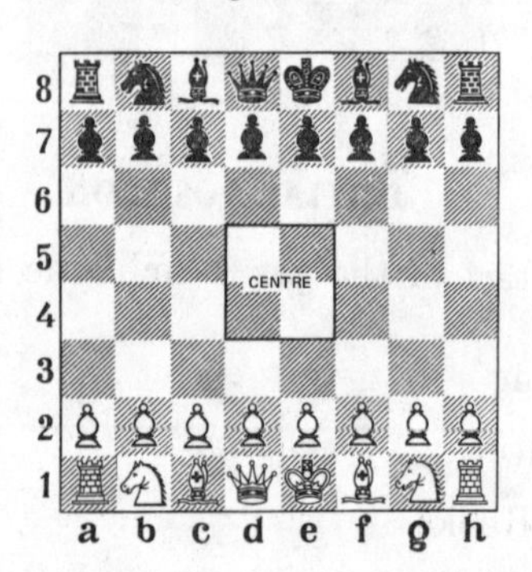

White occupies the first and second ranks, Black the seventh and eighth. The board should be placed in such a way that there is a white corner square on each player's right-hand side (h1 for White and a8 for Black). In the initial position the White Queen is on a white square (d1) and Black's Queen on a black square (d8).

The left half of the chess board (from *a* to *d*) is called the *Q-side* and the right half (from *e* to *h*) the *K-side*.

The four midboard squares (d4, d5, e4, e5) are called the *centre*. This is a very important section of the board. We will talk about its significance later on.

MOVES

Any shift of a piece or Pawn on the board is called a *move*. The players take turns in making moves, with White always starting the game.

A player cannot move a piece or Pawn to a square occupied by one of his own pieces or Pawns. The Knight is the only piece that can leap over a square occupied by another piece or Pawn.

The *Rook* can move any number of squares along a file or rank.

Diagram 5

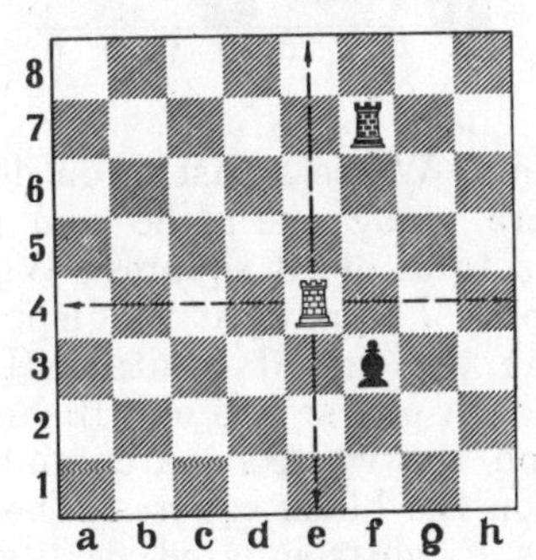

In Diagram 5 White's Rook can move to any square on the e-file or on the 4th rank, that is, to any one of 14 squares.

Exercises.

1. Name the squares in Diagram 5 to which Black's Rook can move.

2. Name the squares of the f-file to which Black's Rook cannot move in this position.

The *Bishop* can move any number of squares along a diagonal.

Diagram 6

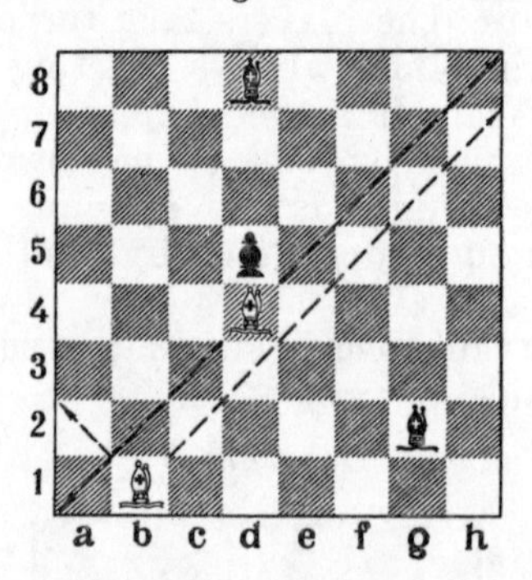

In Diagram 6 White's Bishop on d4 can move to any square along the a1-h8 and g1-a7 diagonals, i.e., a total of 13 squares. White's other Bishop has only 7 squares at its disposal.

Looking at the initial position (Diagram 4) we see that each player has one Bishop that can move only on the white squares and one that moves only on the black squares. They are often spoken of as a white-squared or black-squared Bishop.

Exercises.

1. To which squares in Diagram 6 can Black's black-squared Bishop move?

2. Which squares on the h1-a8 diagonal are inaccessible to Black's white-squared Bishop?

The *Queen* can move any number of squares along a file, rank or diagonal as indicated on Diagram 7.

Diagram 7

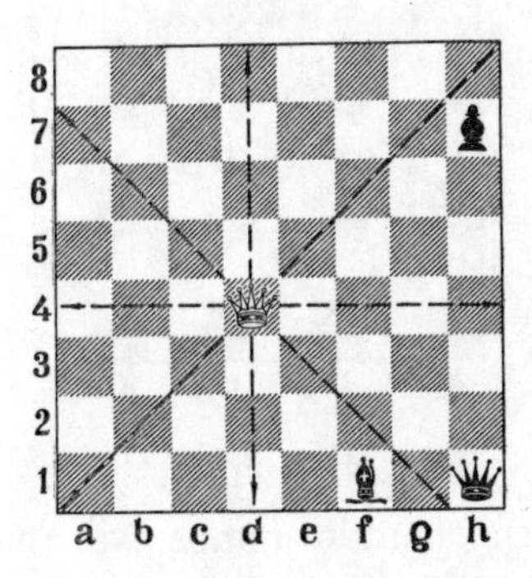

The Queen thus combines the merits of the Rook and Bishop and, besides, can move along both the white and black diagonal. The diagram shows all the 27 squares the Queen standing on d4, in the centre of the board, can reach. This tremendous mobility makes the Queen unquestionably the strongest piece.

Exercises.

1. Which squares are accessible to Black's Queen?
2. Can it move to h8?

The *Knight* moves in a very distinctive way (see Diagram 8).

From e5, a black square, White's Knight can move to any of the eight white squares marked by dots. The Knight moves from the square on which it stands over a neighbouring square on the file or rank onto a square that is opposite

Diagram 8

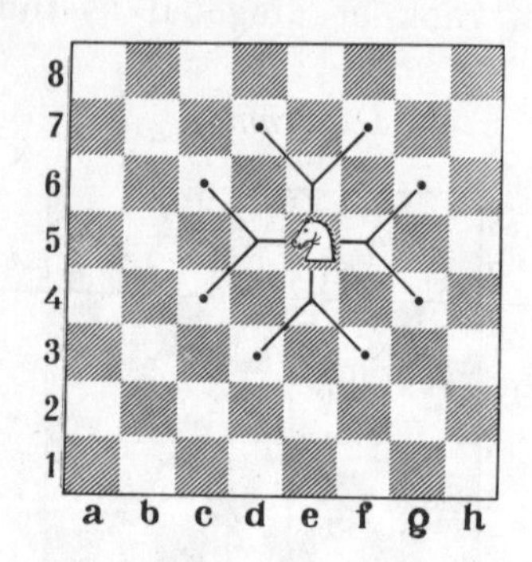

in colour to its initial position. The diagram shows how the Knight jumps over the d5-square to c6 or c4; over the e6 square to d7 or f7; over the f5 square to g6 or g4, and over e4 to d3 or f3. It may be said that the Knight moves one square vertically or horizontally and one more square along the diagonal. The Knight always moves from a white square to a black square, or vice versa. It is the only piece that can leap over its own or opposing chessmen, which remain in their places (see Diagram 9).

Though White's Knight is surrounded on all sides by his own and black pieces and Pawns, this does not prevent him from reaching any of the marked squares.

Exercises (see Diagram 9).

1. To which squares can Black's Knight move?
2. Take another look at Diagram 3 and determine the method used in numbering its squares.

The Knight is distinguished by its exceptional maneuvrability.

Diagram 9

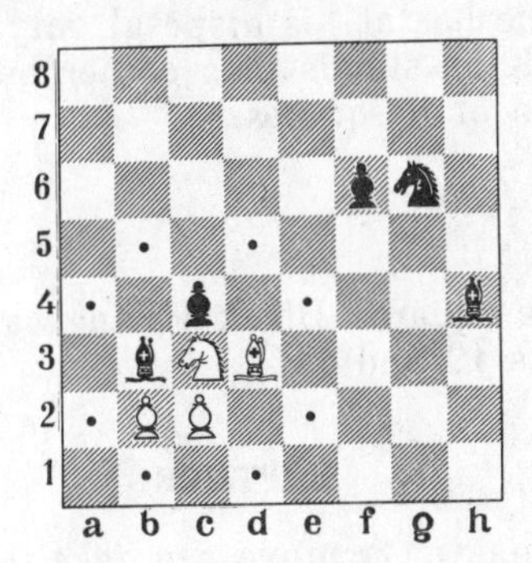

A well-known chess riddle is to lay out a route across the board in such a way that a Knight lands on each square only once. Mathematicians have established that more than 30 million such routes are possible. Although some great minds have worked on this problem over the centuries, so far no one has determined the exact total number.

The *King* can move only one square in any direction on a rank, file or diagonal.

The squares to which the Kings in Diagrams 10 and 11 can move are indicated by dots.

Diagram 10

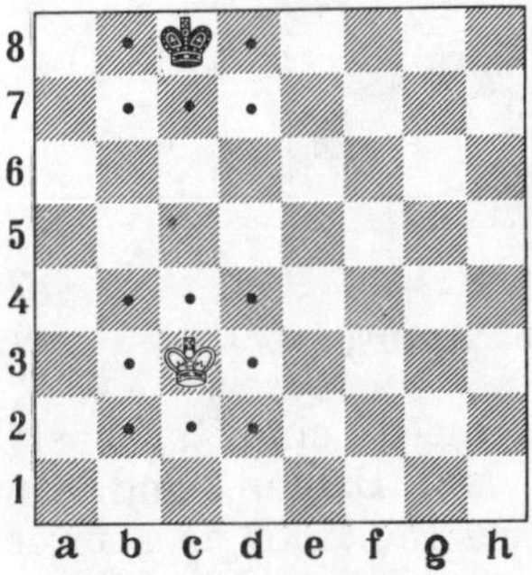

Diagram 11

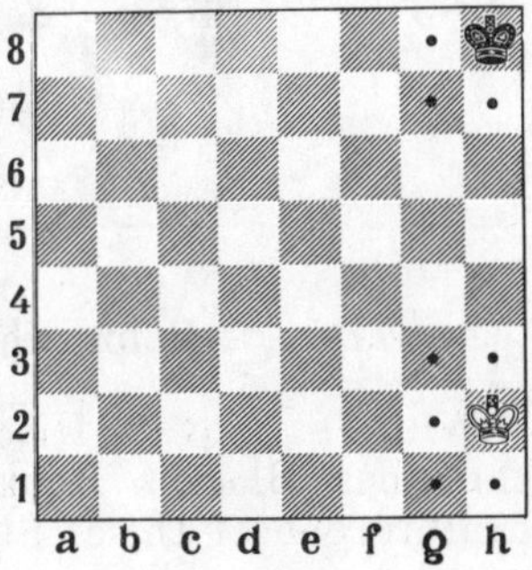

8
7
6
5
4
3
2
1
a b c d e f g h

8
7
6
5
4
3
2
1
a b c d e f g h

On the edge of the board the King's mobility decreases: he has at his disposal only 5 squares. When the King stands in a corner he can move to only one of 3 squares.

Exercise.

Name the squares Black's King can move to in Diagrams 10 and 11.

CAPTURE

A piece making a move can *take* (*capture*) an enemy piece or Pawn standing in its way. That piece or Pawn is removed from the board and its square is occupied by the piece making the move. The move is then considered finished. A piece can only capture a piece or Pawn standing on a square to which it can move.

Diagram 12

Before the capture

White's move. His Queen simultaneously threatens Black's Rook and Bishop, and can capture one of them. Since the Rook is a more valuable piece than the Bishop, White takes the Rook on d4. The following position arises:

Diagram 13

After the capture

A player is not obliged to make a capture.

PAWNS

To single out any particular Pawn we name the file or square on which it stands: the f-Pawn the g4-Pawn, etc. The Pawns are also named according to the pieces in front of which they stand in the initial position: the Q-Pawn (d-Pawn), K-Pawn (e-Pawn), R-Pawn (a- or h-Pawn), N-Pawn (b or g), B-Pawn (c or f).

Unlike the pieces, which can move in any direction, the Pawn goes only one square ahead on its file at a time. From its initial position, i.e., a White Pawn from the second rank and a Black Pawn from the seventh rank, it can move two squares ahead at once.

A Pawn moves only along a file, but it captures obliquely, only one square along a diagonal, to the left or right.

In the diagrams the White Pawns move only upwards, and the Black Pawns downwards.

Diagram 14

Let us examine the Pawn moves that can be made in the position in Diagram 14. White's a4-Pawn can move only one square: 1. a5. Since White's c-Pawn is on its initial position, both 1. c3 and 1. c4+ are possible. White's d4-Pawn does not threaten Black's King but it can capture either one of two Black pieces: 1. dxc5 or 1. dxe5. Black can make the following Pawn moves: 1. ... a5; 1. ...axb5; 1. ... e6; 1. ... g2.

Besides its usual capture a Pawn can take an enemy Pawn (but not a piece) *en passant* (in passing).

Diagram 15

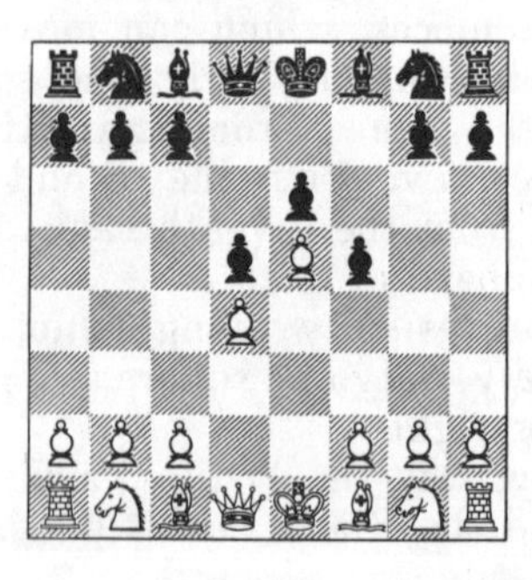

The situation in Diagram 15 arose after the moves 1. e4 e6 2. d4 d5. 3. e5 f5. Now White has the right to take Black's f-Pawn *en passant* of its e-Pawn. To do this White removes the Black Pawn from the board and places its e-Pawn on f6. In notation: 4. exf6.

Diagram 16

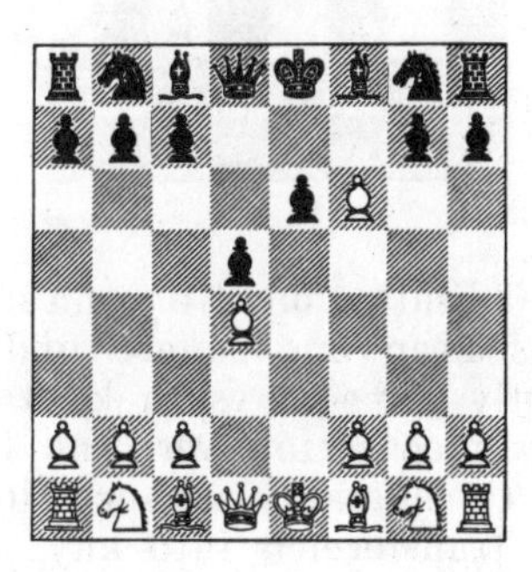

The same situation could arise if Black played 3. ... f6 instead of 3. ... f5. Hence an *en passant* capture is the term used for taking a Pawn that makes from its initial position a move of two squares and finds itself horizontally next to an enemy Pawn. If, in the situation in Diagram 15, White does not play 4. exf6, he loses the right to capture the Pawn. Only a White Pawn on the fifth rank and a Black Pawn on the fourth rank can take an opposing Pawn *en passant*.

Exercise (see Diagram **17**).

Is an *en passant* capture possible in the case of the following moves?
a) 1. d4; 1. ... d5
b) 1. Bd4; 1. ... Nd5
c) 1. f4+?

Diagram 17

The Pawn's limited mobility and striking power (R-Pawns keep one square under fire and the others only two squares) make it much weaker than any piece. However, the Pawn has a feature that considerably enhances its value: the right to be transformed into any piece except the King. When a player moves a Pawn to the last rank (the eighth rank for White and the first rank for Black) he can transform it at once into a piece (a Queen, Bishop, Rook or Knight) of the same colour irrespective of whether he still has pieces of this type. This is called *Pawn promotion* or *queening*.

Thanks to Pawn promotion a player may have more pieces of the same kind than in the initial position, several Queens, for instance. Most frequently the Pawn is transformed into the most powerful piece, the Queen.

When the Pawn reaches the last rank, after the usual notation the abbreviated name of the new piece is given. In the position in Diagram 18 the notation 1. d8Q means that White advanced his d-Pawn to d8 and transformed it into a Queen. This Pawn can also queen by taking the Bishop on e8: dxe8Q. White can transform its Pawn

Diagram 18

into any other piece. In this case, for instance, it would be advantageous for White to take the Bishop and promote the Pawn to a Knight, which could immediately attack Black's King and Queen at the same time (1. dxe8N+).

NOTATION

Diagram 19

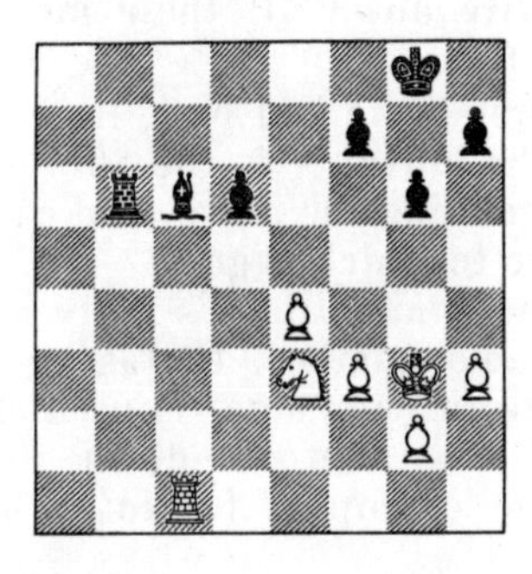

In this situation White moves his Knight from e3 to c4, attacking simultaneously Black's Rook on b6 and Pawn on d6. Such an attack is called also a *double blow*. Black moves the Rook to b8, and White wins the Pawn on d6.

Now a new danger hangs over Black: White threatens the Bishop on c6.

Diagram 20

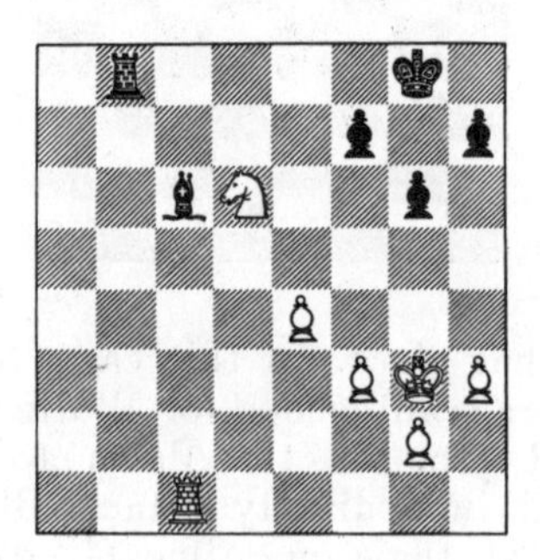

To avoid this threat Black moves the Bishop to d7.

Let us write down all these moves with the aid of notation.

White's first move is 1.Nc4, in which 1 is the number of the move, N is the abbreviated name of the piece making the move, and c4 is the name of the square to which it goes.

White's move and Black's reply are designated by the same number. In taking a piece the sign x (multiplication sign) is used, for instance 2. Nxd6. Now we can put down all the moves in the above example: 1. Nc4 Rb8 2. Nxd6 Bd7.

Three dots are used if it is not necessary to include White's or Black's move in the notation. For instance, in the following position Black is to move.

Diagram 21

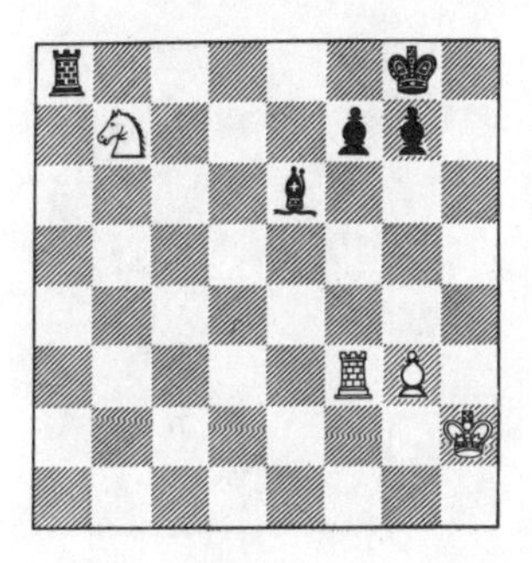

Black's Bishop delivers a double blow, winning a piece. Here is the notation: 1. ... Bd5.

Diagram 22

Exercise.

White's move: list all the captures he can make in this situation.

Exercise (see Diagram 23).

Black to move: list the double attacks he can make in this position.

Diagram 23

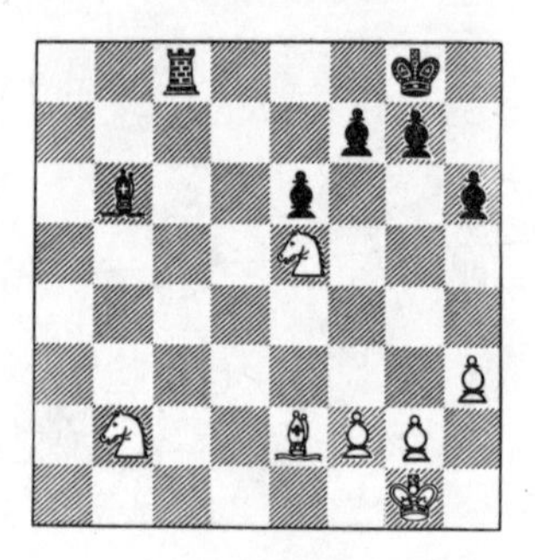

THE KING'S SPECIAL FEATURES. CHECK

The King is the only piece that has no right to move to a square attacked by an enemy piece or Pawn, and it cannot be placed under attack.

Diagram 24

Here White, having the move, can play 1. Bxb2 or 1. Kxb1, but 1. Kxb2 is impossible since the King would come under attack from Black's

Bishop on c3. Neither is 1. Kxc3 possible since the c3 square is under the control of Black's Knight on b1. The b3, d3, d2 and d1 square are tabu for the King, all of them being under Black's control.

Another special feature of the King is that in the case of an attack he has to be defended immediately. An attack against the King is called *check*, designated in notation by a plus sign (+).

In Diagram 25 White has just played 1. Ne5+, attacking simultaneously Black's King and Rook.

Diagram 25

According to the rules of the game the King cannot be left under attack or, in chess terminology, under *check*. No matter how highly Black values his Rook, he is compelled to leave it to its fate, because the King's safety comes first. After 1. ... Kf6 (Black takes the King away from attack) White plays 2. Nxd7+ and soon wins.

There are three methods of defence against check, and all are possible in the situation in Diagram 26:

1) *to capture the piece* (*Pawn*) declaring check (1. ... Qxd7);

Diagram 26

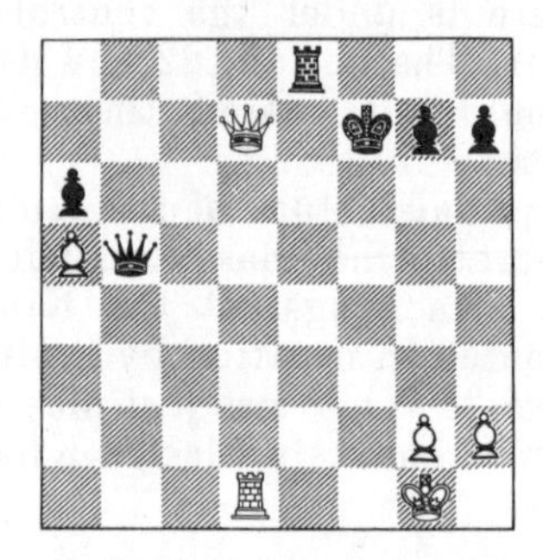

2) *to move away from check*, i.e., to shift the King to a square not attacked by the opponent, for instance 1. ... Kg8;

3) *to cover oneself from check*, i.e., to place one's own piece or Pawn between the King and the piece declaring check: (1. ... Re7). However, it is impossible to cover the King from a check declared by a Knight.

Diagram 27

In Diagram 27 Black's Knight has declared check 1. ... Nc5+. White has only two methods of defence: to move the King to another square, for instance, 2. Ka2 (b2, c2, c3, c4, b4), or to capture the Knight (2. Bxc5) since the King cannot be placed on a square under attack or left under check. The King is the only piece that cannot be captured. In the course of a game all the pieces and Pawns can be taken but the Kings remain on the board to the very end of the game.

Finally, as distinguished from all the other pieces and Pawns, a King cannot check the opposing King. Indeed, it cannot attack the opposing King because it could do this only from a square adjoining the former. That square is under attack by the opposing King and is forbidden by the rules. The Kings must always be separated by at least one square.

Diagram 28

An impossible situation

Diagram 29

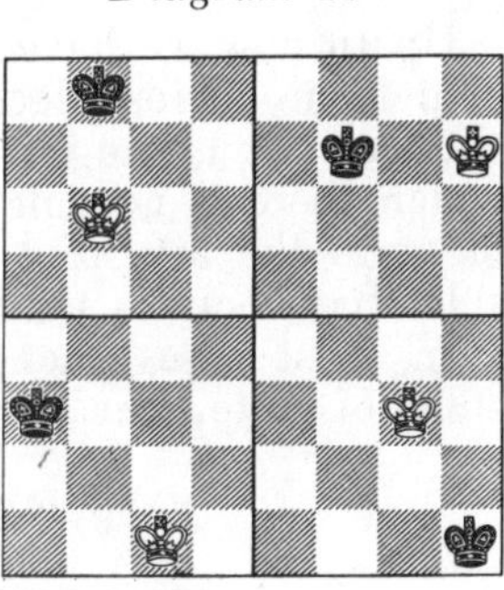

Fully possible situations

Exercise.

In Diagram 30 discover and write down how, with the aid of a double attack and having the move:

Diagram 30

a) White wins the Queen
b) Black takes the Knight.

CHECKMATE

Up to now we have been looking at examples of defence against declared check. *Checkmate* or simply *mate* is the term used for a check against which there is no defence. With the declaration of mate the aim of the game is achieved. The side that declares mate wins the game.

In most cases the game does not reach the stage of mate. One of the opponents; seeing that

Diagram 31

mate is inevitable, resigns, admitting his defeat.

In notation the sign for checkmate is++.

Diagram 31 shows a typical example of a mate by the Queen under the defence of the King. Black's King cannot capture the Queen that declared mate since it would fall under the attack of White's King. At the same time the White Queen on the d7 square deprives the opposing King of all the squares for retreat (c8, c7, e7, e8).

Diagram 32

In Diagram 32 we see a typical example of mate on the last rank. Black has nothing with which to take the Rook or hide from its lethal check, and his own Pawns hamper the King from getting away.

Exercise (see Diagram on p. *30*).

Mate in one move:
a) with White to move
b) with Black to move.

CASTLING

A simultaneous move of the King and Rook is permitted once in the course of play.

Diagram 33

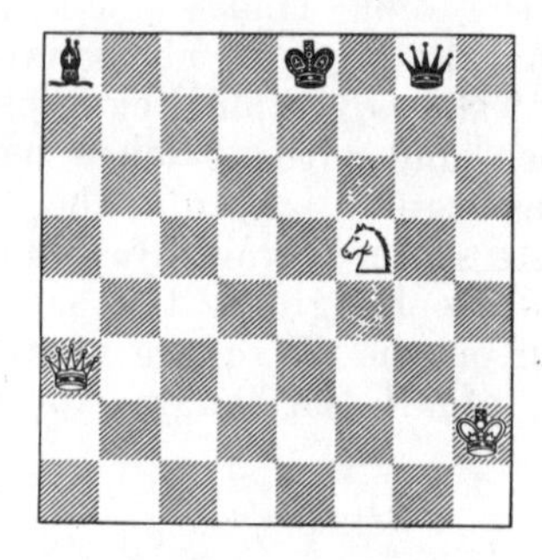

It is considered one move and is called *castling*. Here is how it is done: the King moves two squares in the direction of the Rook, after which the Rook passes above the King and occupies the square adjoining the King. Castling on the side of the Queen's flank is called *castling long*, and on the side of the King's flank *castling short*.

Diagram 34

In Diagram 34 White castled long and Black castled short.

Castling is impossible in the following cases: a) the King or the Rook have already made a move; b) the King is under check; c) as a result of castling the King comes under check; d) a square the King has to pass across is under check by an enemy piece; e) other pieces stand between the King and Rook on the side the King has to be placed.

Thus, in Diagram 35 White can castle only short, and Black only long.

Diagram 35

Castling enables a player to transfer the King away to a safe place quickly and bring the Rook into play. This is a very important and necessary move for mobilising one's forces.

Castling short is designated in notation as 0-0, and castling long as 0-0-0.

STALEMATE

A situation in which the King of the side having the move is not under check but has no place to go, and none of that side's other pieces or Pawns can move, is called *stalemate*. A game in which stalemate occurs is considered a draw.

If it is White's move in Diagram 36 he plays 1. Rxf8++. However, if Black is to move then, despite White's huge advantage, the game ends

Diagram 36

in a draw, since Black is stalemated. Black's Pawns are blocked, the King cannot move because all the possible squares are under the control of White's Queen, and the Knight is prevented from moving by White's Rook on e8 (the Knight move would place Black's King in check).

In situations with a small number of pieces the side that has the advantage and is playing for a win has to take care that the opponent should not be stalemated. The weaker side is frequently very resourceful in seeking ways and means of sacrificing its pieces and forcing a stalemate.

Diagram 37

In Diagram 37, if it were Black's move he would take the Bishop and, with an extra Queen, easily win. But it is White's move, and with it comes the first surprise: 1. Bc2+, a double attack. White *sacrifices* the Bishop. Black cannot reject the *sacrifice* because he cannot win without his Queen. Hence, 1. ... Qxc2 is obligatory. Then there follows 2. Ne3+, another sacrifice and a double attack. Once more the Queen has to be saved, but after 2. ... Bxe3 White's King has nowhere to move. This is stalemate.

Diagram 38

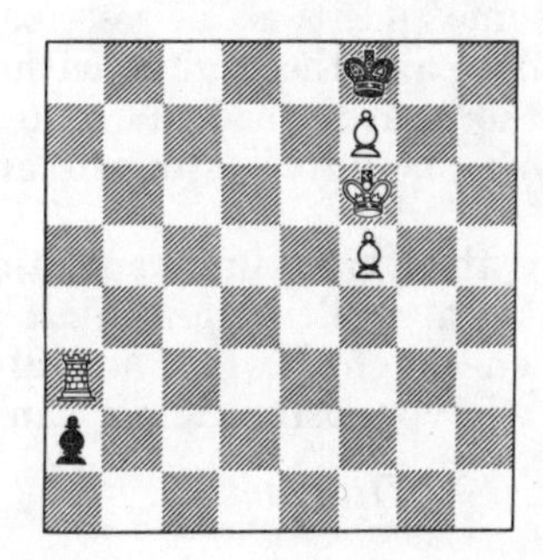

Exercise.

Discover and write down how:
a) White moves and wins
b) Black moves and draws.

OTHER KINDS OF DRAWS. PERPETUAL CHECK

A game is also drawn if:

a) neither side has sufficient material advantage to win (one of the players has only a King left while his opponent has only a King, or a King plus a Bishop or Knight, or each of them has only a King plus a Bishop or Knight, or both have a King plus a Bishop, both Bishops moving along squares of the same colour);

b) a player declares that in the last 50 (or more) moves there haven't been any captures and not a single Pawn has moved. He demands that the game be stopped and called a draw (the 50-move rule);

c) the same position occurs on the board three or more times in a row, with the first of the two moves made each time by the same player (recurrence). In this case the player after whose move the same position arises for the third (or more) time has the right, without making a move on the board, to declare to the umpire that the game should be stopped and declared a draw.

Frequently the three-time repetition of a position arises as a result of *perpetual check*, i. e., a series of checks following one after another from which the opposing King cannot escape.

Diagram 39

After the situation shown in Diagram 39 there followed 1. ... Kg8 2. Qg5+ Kh8 3. Qf6+ (the position on the board is repeated) Kg8 4. Qg5+ Kh8, and now White, without making his move, asked the umpire to declare the game a draw following the third recurrence of the position after 4. Qf6+.

Diagram 40

In the position in Diagram 40 Black declares perpetual check, continuously attacking White's King with the Rook from the a1 and a2 squares. White has at his disposal many more squares than in the preceding example but he has nowhere to hide from the checks. A draw is unavoidable.

In practice, the two players agree to a draw without appealing to the umpire to establish the three-time recurrence of a position or to apply the 50-move rule.

THE METHOD OF NOTATION

A system of naming the squares and moves of pieces which has been described so far is known as a system of *notation*. In putting down a capture by a Pawn all that is indicated is to what file the Pawn passes. In positions where two pieces of the same kind can go to the given square additional information is provided. For instance, 12. Rhe1 means that of the two Rooks that could have occupied the e1 square, it is the Rook on h1 (and not the Rook on d1) that did it. For greater precision the number of the rank is also employed. For instance, if White's Knights stand on e2 and e4, then the move N4g3 should be written.

Further on the main moves are given in full notation, and annotation (comments) in short.

The following signs are used in annotation for economy of space:

! a good move
!! a very good (beautiful) move
? a weak move
?? a bad mistake
?! a risky, questionable move
∽ any move
= even position
± White's position is superior
⩲ White's position is somewhat preferable
∓ Black's position is better
⩱ Black's position is somewhat preferable.

Up to now we have written down the moves linearly. But there is also a columnar form. As an example, here is one of the shortest games ever played in a tournament.

GIBAUD — *LAZARD*

Paris, 1924

1. d2-d4	Ng8-f6
2. Nb1-d2	e7-e5
3. d4xe5	Nf6-g4
4. h2-h3??	...

Clearly White lacks thoughtfulness and deliberation. He impatiently wants to drive away the approaching Knight, though actually it is not a danger to him. He could have played 4. Ngf3 Bc5 5. e3 Nc6 6. Nc4 b5 7. Nd2 a6 8. a4±.

5. ... Ng4—e3!

White resigns because the loss of the Queen is inevitable. In the case of 5. fxe3 there follows 5. ... Qh4+ 6. g3 Qxg3++. This miniature game was played in the championship of Paris.

For the sake of comparison here is that game in the condensed style of notation:

A. Gibaud—F. Lazard (Paris, 1924) 1. d4 Nf6 2. Nd2 e5 3. dxe5 Ng4 4. h3?? Ne3! White resigns.

In recording the position on the board we designate the location of the chessmen in the following order: King, Queen, Rooks, Bishops, Knights and then Pawns. For example, the position in Diagram 15 appears thus. *White*: Ke1, Qd1, Ra1, Rh1, Bc1, Bf1, Nb1 g1. Pawns a2, b2, c2, d4, e5, f2, g2, h2 (16); *Black*: Ke8, Qd8, Ra8, Rh8, Bc8, Bf8, Nb8, Ng8, Pawns a7, b7, c7, d5, e6, f5, g7, h7 (16).

The position is described from left to right, from the Q-side to the King's flank. First the location of White's black-squared Bishop (c1) is given, then that of the white-squared (f1); the first to be put down is the a2 Pawn, and the last the h2 Pawn. The total number of pieces and Pawns is given in brackets.

Exercises (see Diagram 41).

1. Record this position.
2. Find the way to mate in two moves:

a) with White to move
b) with Black to move
(in both cases mate is declared on the last rank).

Diagram 41

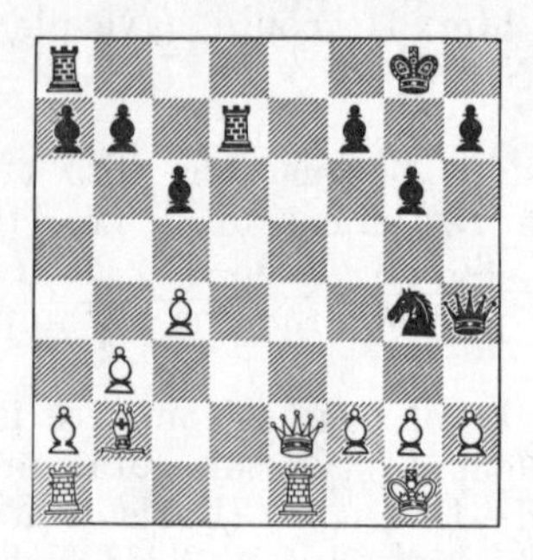

COMPARATIVE VALUE OF THE PIECES

In playing the game, especially in exchanges, it is necessary to know the value of the pieces and Pawns.

The Queen, as mentioned above, is the most powerful piece. It is approximately equal to two Rooks, or to a Rook, a minor piece and two Pawns. However, a Rook and two minor pieces are stronger than the Queen.

The Rook is the second strongest piece. It is more valuable than a Bishop or Knight. The exchange of a light piece for a Rook has a special term: *winning the Exchange*, or for the other side *losing the Exchange*. Usually the Exchange is worth two Pawns, i.e., the Bishop or Knight plus two Pawns are approximately of the same value as the Rook. Depending on the position even one Pawn can compensate the loss of the Exchange.

The Rook is weaker than two minor pieces, which may be equal in strength to a Rook and two Pawns.

The Knight is of the same strength as the Bishop. A minor piece is equal to three Pawns.

The Pawn is the weakest unit of the chess troops, but it should not be scorned. The importance of Pawns increases at the end of play, when there is not enough strength on the board to declare mate, and victory is achieved by the side which manages to promote a Pawn to a Queen.

The King is the most valuable piece since the outcome of the game depends on his fate. It is worthwhile sacrificing pieces and Pawns in order to achieve mate. However, the King differs from all the other pieces in that his value is not equal to his strength. At the start of the game—the opening, as well as in the middle game, this is a weak piece that has to be safeguarded in all possible ways, but in the end, when there is no danger of being mated by the few pieces remaining on the board, the King's strength increases sharply between that of a minor piece and a Rook.

These appraisals are a result of the experience gained by generations of chess players. But they should not be treated as absolute rules that hold true always and under all circumstances. Experienced players know that not a single piece or Pawn has a constant value. Their value changes depending on the position (see Diagram 42).

Diagram 42

Here Black has an overwhelming superiority in forces: a Queen versus a Bishop. White, however, is in no hurry to lay down his weapons.

1. Bc7!

Threatening 2. Bg3++.

1. ... Qf2

Black loses in the case of 1. ... g4 because then follows 2. Bd8++ and in the case of 1. ... Qe1 2. g3++.

2. Bd6!

Waiting move. That is the term used for a move marking time in order to hand over the move to the opponent. Now Black finds himself in *zugzwang*, i.e., a situation in which any move leads to the disadvantage of the player whose turn it is to move. Indeed, Black's Queen cannot leave the f2 square, otherwise there will follow 3. g3++ or Bg3++. Neither can Black's Pawn on g5 move because of 3. Be7++.

2. ... Qf4+

The Queen has to be sacrificed to achieve, after 3. Bxf4 gxf4, at least a draw, but ...

3. g2-g3+! Qxg3 4. Bxg3++.

Thus, in the position in Diagram 42 the unhappy situation of Black's King makes the Queen weaker than the Bishop. This example is not intended to shake your faith in the comparative values of chessmen set forth above. They are correct and you can boldly depend on them in play. But rules have their exceptions. While gradually perfecting your play you will learn to see the special features of every position more clearly, evaluate the strength of the pieces and Pawns with greater finesse, and discover remarkable exceptions like the one just cited.

ADDITIONAL RULES

If a player whose turn it is to move touches one of his chessmen he is obliged to move it, and if he touches an opposing piece of Pawn he must capture it. This does not apply, of course, to a chessman that cannot move or the opponent's one that cannot be captured.

An opponent touching simultaneously his own and the opponent's chessman is to take the latter (by the piece he touched, and if that is impossible, then by any other piece), and if according to the rules that is impossible, then he has to make a move with his piece he touched.

On wishing to adjust one or more pieces on his squares, the player whose turn it is to move has to *notify* his opponent. (It is customary to use the expression "I adjust"). The adjustment can be made only in the presence of his opponent, and if the latter has left the table, then in the presence of the umpire.

A move is considered finished when the player has put the piece or Pawn on a new square and removed his hand from it. As long as the player keeps his hand on the chessman he can make any move with it.

A player may suggest a draw only after completing a move. The opponent may accept the draw or refuse it either by saying so or by making his next move. A player may repeat the offer of a draw only after his opponent, in turn, has made use of his right to suggest a draw.

It is not obligatory to declare check or mate verbally.

Now you should be sufficiently acquainted with the rules to play your first game. Sit down at the table, decide, by drawing lots, who is to have the white and who the black chessmen, and *Make Your First Move!* But you still have a lot to learn about the game. Combine playing chess with a study of the following chapters.

II. THE SIMPLEST ENDINGS

THREE STAGES IN CHESS PLAY

The play in chess is divided into three stages: the *opening*, the *middle game* and the *endgame*.

In the opening mate is possible only as a result of a crude blunder and is very rare in the practice of strong players. After the opponents mobilise their forces in the opening, play usually enters the middle game stage, where the main aim is to mate the opponent or, having achieved an overwhelming advantage, compel him to resign. Quite often, however, one fails to mate the opposing King in the middle game, when there are many pieces on the board. When few chessmen remain on the board after exchanges the endgame stage arises. Here the main aim is not to mate the opponent, for neither of the sides usually has enough forces for this, but to promote Pawns. After that it is not so difficult to achieve mate.

In this chapter we will look at some of the simplest endgames. The beginner should first learn to play endings where the stronger side has a big *material advantage* and the opponent only a King.

MATING A LONG KING

Queen Mates

When one side has only the King and the other side only the King and Queen the latter side can mate only on the edge of the board, to which he pushes the King by the coordinated actions of his King and Queen. Here are two typical positions of this kind:

Diagram 43

Diagram 44

In both cases the Kings face each other with one square between them on the rank or file. Such a position of the Kings is called *opposition.* In one case (Diagram 43) it is a *vertical* opposition, and in the other (Diagram 44), a *horizontal* opposition. In opposition White's King is in a more favourable situation, depriving Black's King of three squares. In the case of a vertical or horizontal opposition no less than six different mating positions can be created (in Diagram 43 the Queen can stand also on the a8, b8, f8, g8, d7, and in Diagram 44 on a2, a6, a7, a8, b4 squares).

The Queen can also achieve mate by making use of *diagonal opposition.*

Diagram 45

In this case, however, White's King deprives the opposing King of only one square, and White must drive Black's King into a corner in order to win.

No matter what the position is, mate is achieved by the Queen within 9 moves. In such endings superfluous checks should be avoided. Most frequently it is a useless waste of time and attention should be paid to avoiding an accidental stalemate.

Diagram 46

1. Kg7 (approaching Black's King to push him out of the centre) 1. ... Kd4 (Black strives to keep his King as long as possible in the cen-

tre, where it is impossible to be mated) 2. Kf6 Ke4 3. Qd8 (depriving the Black King of half the board) 3. ... Kf4 4. Qd3 Kg4 5. Qe3 Kh4. (The aim is achieved: Black's King is pushed back to the edge of the board. Note that this was done without a single check.) 6. Kf5 (but not 6. Qf3? stalemate!) 6. ... Kh5 7. Qh3(g5)++.

Black could have played differently but by using the same methods White can always push the Black King to the edge of the board.

Exercise.

White starts and mates in two moves.

Diagram 47

Mate by Two Rooks

In the ending where the King and Queen opposed the King, mate was achieved with the aid of the stronger side. Here, however, two Rooks, without the help of the King, push the opposing King to the edge of the board and mate him.

1. Rh3 (the third rank is cut off to Black's King) 1. ... Kf4 2. Ra4+ Kg5 3. Rh4 Kf5 (or 3. ... Kg6 4. Ra5!) 4. Rh5+ Kg6 5. Ra5 Kf6 6. Ra6+ Kg7 7. Rh6 Kf7 8. Ra7+ Kg8 9. Rh7 Kf8 10. Rh8++.

Diagram 48

This method is the simplest and easily remembered. However, mate can be achieved faster by pushing back Black's King in another direction and putting White's King into action: 1. Rh5 Kf4 2. Ra4+ Kg3 3. Ke2! Kg2 4. Rg4++.

Mate by Rook

Mate by the Rook is also achieved only on the edge of the board.

Diagram 49

Diagram 50

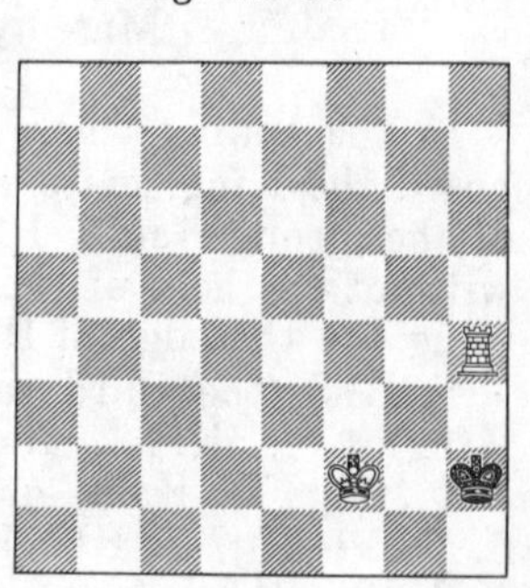

The methods of pushing the lone King to the edge of the board is the same as in the case of mating with the Queen, but since the Rook is weaker than the Queen, and the King can attack it along the diagonal, more time is required. However, no matter what the position is, the Rook can achieve mate within 16 moves. Let us consider a typical example.

Diagram 51

1. Re8 (cutting off half of the board) 1. ... Kd5 2. Kg2 Kd4 3. Kf3 Kd5 4. Ke3 (pushing back Black's King from the centre) 4. ... Kc4 5. Re5 (restricting the King's mobility even more) 5. ... Kc3 6. Rc5+! (when the Kings are in opposition such a Rook check from the side is especially effective: Black's King is now pushed farther back to the edge of the board) 6. ... Kb4 7. Kd4 Kb3 8. Rc4 Kb2 9. Rc3 Kb1 10. Kd3 (bringing the King nearer to create a mating situation) 10. ... Kb2 11. Kd2 Kb1 12. Rb3+ Ka1 13. Kc2 Ka2 14. Rh3! (a waiting move. Black is in zugzwang) 14. ... Ka1 15. Ra3++.

Exercise (see Diagram 52).

White to play and mate in three moves.

Diagram 52

Mate by Two Bishops

Two Bishops can declare mate by pushing the King into a corner.

Diagram 53

Diagram 54

By their concerted actions White's King and Bishops on joint diagonals create a barrier which Black's King cannot cope with.

1. Kf2 Kd4 2. Bd2 Ke4 3. Be3 Kd5 4. Kf3 Ke5 5. Bd3 Kd5 6. Kf4 Ke6 7. Be4 Kd6 8. Kf5 Ke7 9. Bf4 Kd7 10. Kf6 Ke8 11. Bf5 Kd8 12. Be6

Diagram 55

(Black's King finds himself on the last rank. Now White has to push him into the corner. However, the move 12. Kf7? is tabu because of stalemate) 12. ... Ke8 13. Bc7! Kf8 14. Bd7 Kg8 15. Kg6 (the King should not be allowed to get out of the last rank) 15. ... Kf8 16. Bd6+ Kg8 17. Be6+ Kh8 18. Be5++.

Diagram 56

Exercise.

White to play and mate in three moves.

Mate by Bishop and Knight

Mate by Bishop and Knight is possible only in the corners which the Bishop can attack.

Diagram 57 *Diagram 58*

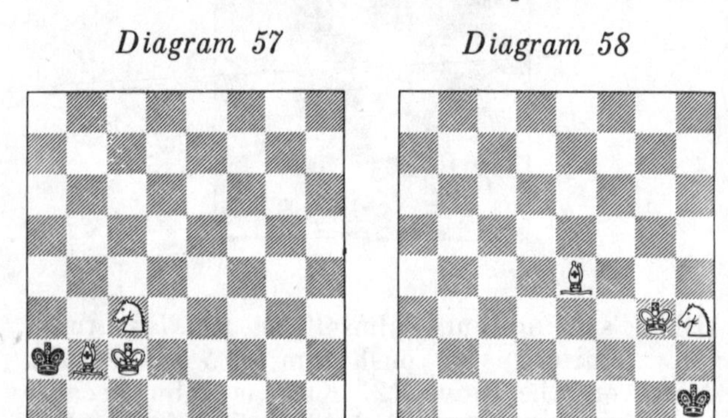

This ending is considerably more difficult than all the preceding ones. Achieving mate by Bishop and Knight without violating the 50-move rule calls for the most precise play. According to the theory of endings this can be done from the most unfavourable initial position of the pieces within 36 moves.

Since this ending is rarely met in practice we shall examine only one example: in which Black's King stands in the corner the Bishop cannot reach. White's job is to chase him to the corner of the same colour as the squares along which the Bishop moves (a8).

1. Nf7+ Kg8 2. Kf6 Kf8 3. Bh7 Ke8 4. Ne5! Kf8 (the King tries to keep away from the a8 square. In case of 4. ... Kd8, there follows 5. Ke6 Kc7 6. Nd7! Kc6 7. Bd3! Kc7 8. Be4, etc.) 5. Nd7+ Ke8 6. Ke6 Kd8 7. Kd6 Ke8 8. Bg6+ Kd8 9. Nc5 Kc8 10. Bf7 (waiting move) 10. ...

Diagram 59

Kd8 11. Nb7+ Kc8 12. Kc6 Kb8 13. Be6 Ka7 14. Nc5 Ka8 15. Kb6 Kb8 16. Na6+ Ka8 17. Bd5++.

Mate by Two Knights

Such a mate is impossible if the opponent defends himself properly.

Diagram 60

White achieves the maximum by pushing the King not only to the edge of the board but also almost to the corner. If now 1. ... Kh8?? then White declares mate: 2. Nf7++. After the correct reply, however, i.e., 1. ... Kf8!, the King breaks away to freedom, leaving White no winning chances.

King and Bishop (or Knight) Versus King

The King plus a minor piece cannot mate a lone King. In such endings continuation of play is senseless and the game ends in a draw.

Diagram 61

As an exception to the rule, here is a curious finale in which a lone Knight mates Black's King. This is because Black's Pawn prevents the King's escape from the trap.

White wins by continuing 1. Ng4+ Kh1 2. Kf1! h2 3. Nf2++.

King and Pawn Versus King

The capture of a Pawn in the middle game by no means ensures victory. But it is otherwise in the ending, where an extra Pawn is an important advantage. Frequently the player who wins a Pawn gradually exchanges all the pieces and transfers the play into a *Pawn ending*, in which the advantage of one Pawn is usually sufficient to win the game. The play quite often boils down to King and Pawn against a lone King.

Let us take a look at some different types of such endgames.

1. The opposing King is driven away and the Pawn queens all by itself.

If you want to know whether Black's King can catch up with the Pawn you do not have to count the moves. There is a special method for that, the *rule of the quadrate*. The King stops the Pawn if it is within a quadrate whose side is equal in length from the square on which the Pawn stands (b3) to the square of the Pawn's promotion (b8).

Diagram 62

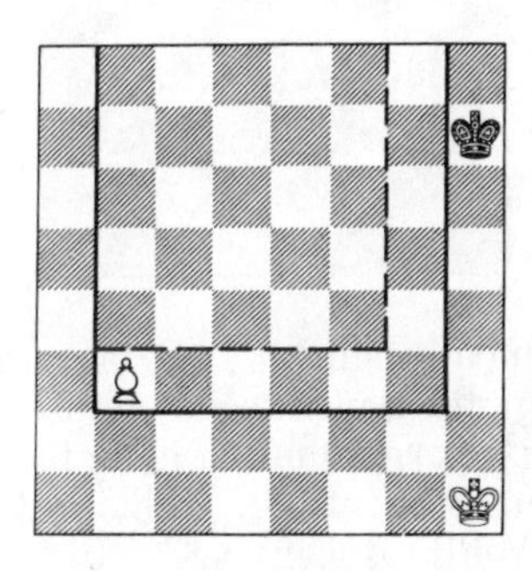

The quadrate formed by the Pawn on b3 is indicated in Diagram 62 by dotted lines (during play it can be easily imagined). If in this example it is Black's move then, by playing 1. ... Kg6 (as also 1. ... Kg7 or 1. ... Kg8), Black enters the quadrate and easily captures the Pawn.

With White to move, after 1. b4 a new quadrate is formed, as is shown by the dotted line.

Now Black's King is no longer capable of entering this quadrate on his move and, hence, cannot catch up with the Pawn. It should be borne in mind that the Pawn can move two squares ahead from its initial position. This should be taken into consideration in applying the rule of the quadrate.

2. The opposing King is too near for the Pawn to be able to queen by its own efforts.

The opposition of Kings has an important bearing on the outcome of such endings.

Diagram 63

In the situation shown in Diagram 63 the result of the game depends on whose move it is. If it is Black's turn to move he is forced to abandon the opposition: 1. ... Ke8, and after 2. e7 Kf7 3. Kd7 White queens and wins. If, however, it is White's move, he is compelled to pull back his King, losing the opposition, or to play 1. e7 Ke8 2. Ke6 and stalemate. Thus, if it is White's move the result is a draw, and if it is Black's move then White wins. This is a typical example of mutual zugzwang, in which it is disadvantageous for either side to move first.

Now let us examine a case when the Pawn is farther away from the last rank.

Diagram 64

In this position Black achieves a draw by occupying the opposition all the time: 1. d4+ Kd5 2. Kd3 Kd6! (Attention should be paid to this move. Black retreats in such a way as to be in opposition no matter where White's King goes.) 3. Ke4 Ke6! 4. d5+ Kd6! 5. Kd4 Kd7! 6. Kc5 Kc7! 7. d6+ Kd7 8. Kd5 Kd8! 9. Ke6 Ke8! 10. d7+ Kd8. A draw.

Employing the same tactics, the weaker side easily achieves a draw in the following positions as well, irrespective of whose move it is.

Diagram 65

Diagram 66

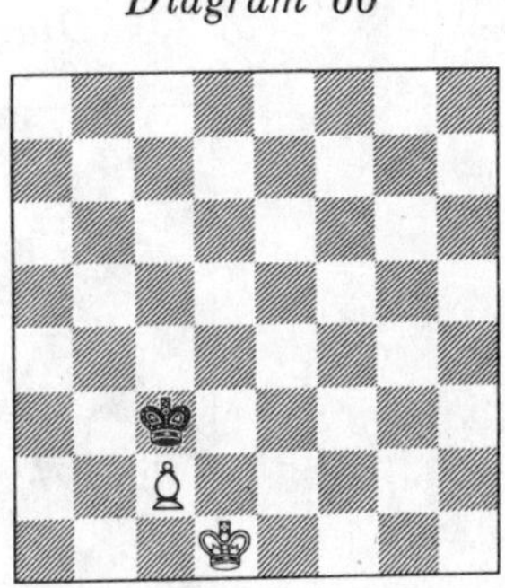

Diagram 67

Diagram 68

The following conclusion may be drawn: if the King of the stronger side is behind the Pawn or next to it, while the King of the weaker side is in front of the Pawn, not letting the opposing King through, the game ends in a draw.

3. The King stands in front of the Pawn.

If the King of the stronger side can pass ahead so as to pull the Pawn along behind himself the win comes quite easily as a rule.

White wins (Dia. 69) by pushing his King forward: 1. Ke3! (but not 1. f4? Kf7 2. Ke3 Kf6 3.

Diagram 69

Ke4 Ke6 with a draw) 1. ... Ke7 2. Ke4 Ke6 3. Kf4 Kf6 4. f3! (This important reserve move that White has at his disposal compels Black to give up the opposition) 4. ... Kg6 5. Ke5 Kf7 6. Kf5 (again not f4? because of 6. ... Ke7! 7. Kf7) 6. ... Ke7 7. Kg6! Kf8 (or 7. ... Ke6 8. f4 Ke7 9. f5 Kf8 10. Kf6! Kg8 11. Ke7, and White wins) 8. Kf6 Kg8 9. f4 Kf8 10. f5 Ke8 11. Kg7 Ke7 12. f6+, and White gueens.

Diagram 70

Diagram 71

In the position in Diagram 70 White's King stands in front of the Pawn on the sixth rank. White wins irrespective of whose move it is. Black is compelled to cede the opposition if it is his move, for instance, 1. ... Kd8 2. Kb7, and White wins.

With White to move the play proceeds thus: 1. Kd6 Kd8 2. c6 Kc8 3. c7 Kb7 4. Kd7, and on the following move White queens.

In the position in Diagram 71 the outcome depends on whose move it is. If it is Black's he has to retreat, losing the opposition: 1. ... Kg7 2. Ke6 Kf8 3. Kf6!, and White wins. If it is White's move the game ends in a draw: 1. Ke5 Ke7 2. f5 Kf7, etc.

All the above applies to Pawns on any file except those on the edges. In the case of a R-Pawn the King of the weaker side only has to reach the corner square to achieve a draw. It is easy to see that the stronger side cannot push the King out of the corner, while the advance of the R-Pawn up to the seventh rank leads only to a stalemate.

Diagram 72

Diagram 73

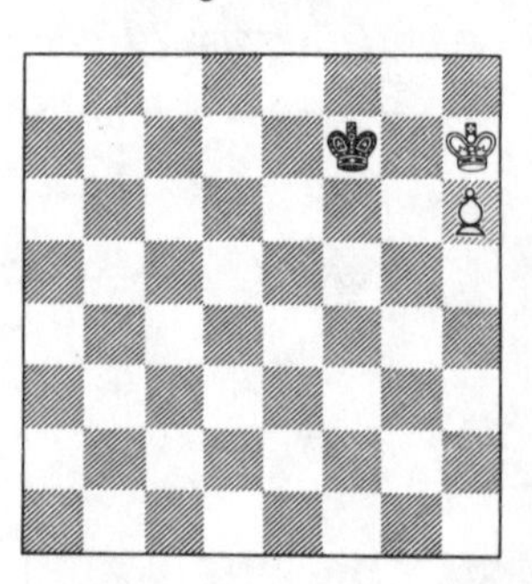

In both positions (Diagram 72 and Diagram 73) the result is a draw. The advance of the Pawn leads to a stalemate. For instance, in Diagram 72 after 1. Ka6 Kb8 2. Kb6 Ka8 3. a5 Kb8 4. a6 Ka8 5. a7—and stalemate. In Diagram 73 after 1. Kh8 Kf8 Black does not let out White's King, repeating the moves, while the advance of the Pawn to h7 results in a stalemate.

CONCLUSIONS

Victory is achieved in the following instances: a) the opposing King is far away, so that the Pawn itself queens (Diagram 62); b) the King of the stronger side occupies a square on the sixth rank, ahead of the Pawn (Diagram 70);

c) the King of the stronger side, with the opponent's turn to move, stands in front of the Pawn and is in opposition (Diagram 71).

A draw occurs in the following cases: a) when there is a R-Pawn, if the King of the weaker side gets into a corner square or locks the King of the stronger side in a corner (Diagrams 72 and 73); b) the King of the weaker side stands on the square in front of the Pawn and does not let the opposing King pass (Diagrams 65 to 68); c) the King of the stronger side, with White's turn to move, stands in front of the Pawn, but the opposition is maintained by the opponent and there is no alternative move for the Pawn (Diagram 71).

A REMOTE PASSED PAWN

In Diagram 74 there are no opposing Pawns in the path of the Pawns on e5 and h4 that could prevent their advancement. In this case the Pawns on e5 and h4 are called *passed Pawns*. Though there is material equality on the board and each side has a passed Pawn Black's position is a lost one since White has a *remote passed*

Diagram 74

Pawn on h4. That is what a passed Pawn standing far from the main mass of Pawns (here from the Pawns of the Q-side), is called.

The game proceeds thus: 1. h5 Kf6 2. h6 Kg6 (otherwise the Pawn will queen) 3. Kxe5 Kxh6 4. Kd5 Kg5 5. Kc5 Kf5 6. Kb6 Ke5 7. Kxa6 Kd6 8. Kb7, and White wins by queening the Pawn on a8.

The remote Pawn attracted the attention of Black's King. Taking advantage of that, White's King smashed the opponent on the other flank. Innumerable endings have been won by this standard method.

Diagram 75

Exercise.

In the attempt to transfer the play into a Pawn ending with an extra Pawn Black goes 1. ... Kc6+. What is your opinion of this move?

POSITIONAL ADVANTAGE

In the examples given in the Diagrams 74 and 75 White emerges victorious thanks to its remote passed Pawn. Such a Pawn is quite a weighty advantage. It enables one to achieve victory in the endgame when there is material equality (Diagram 74) or when the opposing side has superior forces (Diagram 75). Here we encounter another kind of advantage, *positional advantage*, i.e., a better distribution of pieces and Pawns.

We have already seen examples of positional advantage. In the position in Diagram 42 White's better distribution of pieces and Pawns brings victory despite Black's tremendous material advantage. A characteristic example of efforts to gain positional advantage is the struggle for opposition (i.e., for a better position for one's King) in endings where King and Pawn oppose the King.

Like material advantage, positional advantage may be of different degrees—small, considerable, overwhelming, etc. This is a very important factor in chess, and we will pay much attention to it further on.

III. SOME BASIC CONCEPTS

THE PIN

The pin is one of the most effective methods of restricting the mobility of your opponent's pieces.

Diagram 76

Diagram 77

In Diagram 76, after 1. ... c3, Black wins the Bishop, and with it the game. The move 2. Bxc3 is impossible since the Bishop is covering up White's King from the Black Rook's attack. In Diagram 77 White mates in two moves: 1. Qxh6+ Kg8 2. Qxg7++. The Pawn on g7 cannot capture White's Queen because it protects Black's King from the attack of the Bishop.

In both cases victory is attained thanks to a *pin.* The term *pin* is used for an attack by any chessman (with the exception of the Knight) on a Pawn or piece shielding the King or another piece more valuable than itself. In the examples given here the *pinning* pieces were the Rook and Bishop, and the *pinned* were the Bishop on b2 and Pawn on g7. If a pinned Pawn or piece protects the King, it becomes almost entirely immovable (it can move only along the line of attack). This is called a *full pin.*

Diagram 78

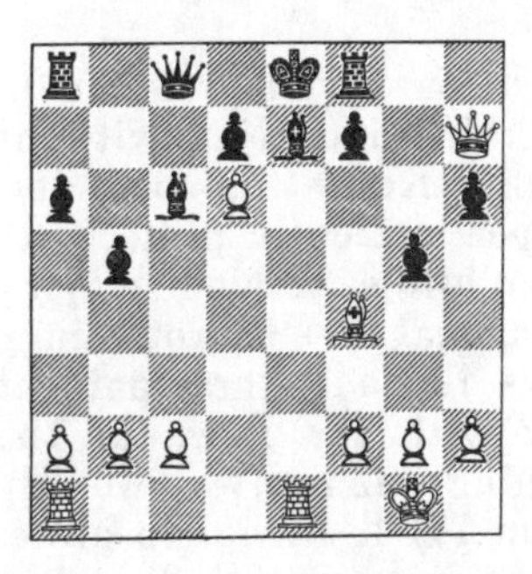

In the position shown in Diagram 78 Black has an extra Bishop and turn to move, but his situation is entirely hopeless due to the pin along the e-file. He does not have any satisfactory defence against the threatening move 2. dxe7, followed by the loss of the Rook and mate.

Note what a powerful influence White's Rook on e1 exerts on Black's position. This is because there are no Pawns on the e-file. A file that is free of Pawns is called an *open line.* White's Rook is in possession of the open line. Whoever holds an open line has an important positional advantage.

Diagram 79

In the position in Diagram 79 from a game between Alekhine and Nimzovitch in San Remo in 1930 Black's Knight on c6 is doubly pinned: along the open c-file (it protects the Rook on c7 against White's trebled major pieces and along the diagonal a4-e8 (protecting the Queen). There follows 1. Ba4! (threatening to deliver a mortal blow with the Pawn at the pinned—a typical pinning manoeuvre we already know from Diagram 77) 1. ... b5 (to protect the Rook by placing the King on d8) 2. Bxb5 Ke8 3. Ba4 Kd8 4. h4!! Black resigns. Alekhine said: "After several insignificant Pawn moves, Black is compelled to place the Queen on e8, and then the move b5 wins a piece."

If the King does not stand behind a pinned piece (or Pawn) such a pin is considered to be *incomplete*. You can sometimes get rid of an incomplete pin, or become unpinned, with the aid of a check or a sacrifice. For instance, after the moves 1. d4 d5 2. c4 (this opening is called *Queen's Gambit*) 2. ... e6 3. Nc3 Nf6 4. Bg5 Nd7 5. cxd5 exd5 the d5 Pawn cannot be taken by relying on the pin. The move 6. Nxd5? is followed by 6. Nxd5! 7. Bxd8 Bb4+ 8. Qd2

Bxd2+ 9. Kxd2 Kxd8, and Black has an extra piece.

Diagram 80

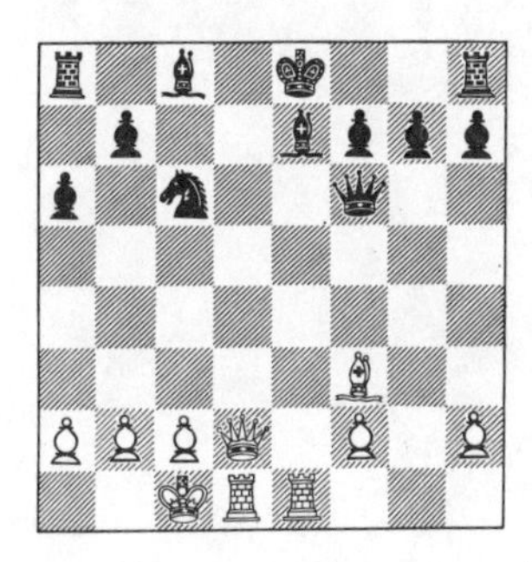

Exercise.

In this position there follows:

1. Bxc6+Kf8.

Explain:
a) why Black does not take the Bishop
b) how White wins.

DISCOVERED ATTACK

The term *discovered attack* is used to describe a move by a piece (or Pawn) that opens the way for a blow to be delivered by another piece, which stands in ambush as it were, behind the chessmen making the move. We have already come across this in Diagram 20.

If the receding piece or Pawn also joins in the assault the discovered attack becomes a double attack.

This position in Diagram 81 comes from a game between Vasyukov and Kholmov played in Moscow in 1965. 1. ... Nxc5! (compelling

Diagram 81

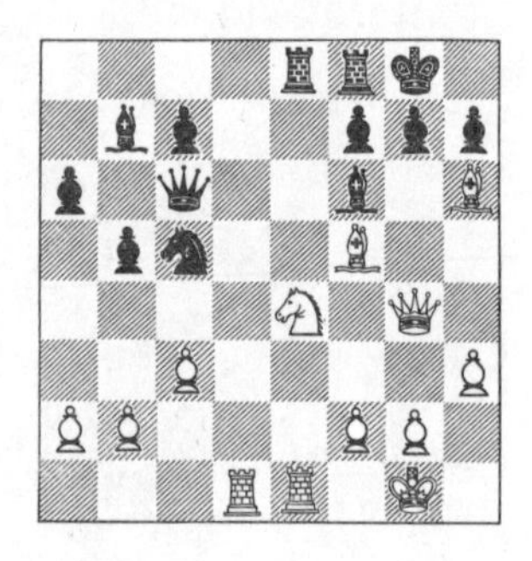

Black's Queen to occupy a square where it lacks protection) 1. ... Qxc5 2. Bxg7!! 3. Qh5 h6 (protecting himself against mate on h7) 4. Bh7+! (retreating with a check, the Bishop lays bare White's Queen, which delivers a blow along the rank) 4. ... Kxh7 5. Qxc5, and White wins.

Diagram 82

The position in Diagram 82 arose in the Capablanca-Alekhine world championship match in Buenos Aires in 1927. White played 1. Rd1, counting on winning back the pinned piece on the next move, but after 1. ... Nxe3! he was compelled to resign. Both the Queen and the Rook are under attack, and in the case of 2. Qxd5 Rxd5 3. fxe3 the issue is settled by one more discovered attack, 3. ... Bxe3+, winning the Rook.

Diagram 83

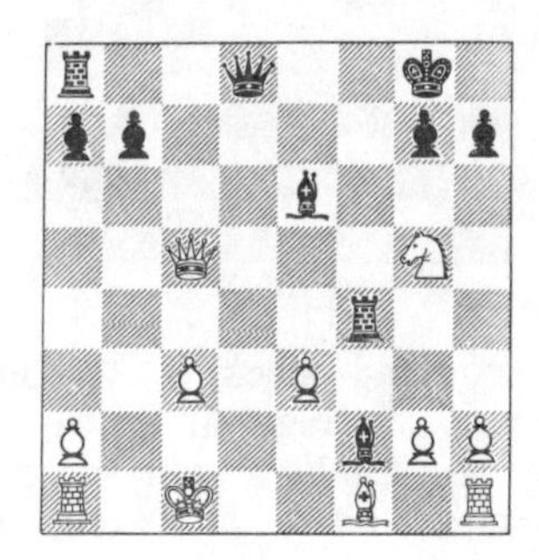

Exercise.

It is Black's move. In what way can he acquire material advantage through a Queen sacrifice and a discovered attack?

DISCOVERED CHECK

The *discovered check* is a particular case of a discovered attack: the piece making the move opens up the line of action for another piece to attack the King. A discovered check is very dangerous since the departing piece, being invulnerable, can capture any opposing piece or Pawn in its path, including strong pieces.

In Diagram 84 Black has an extra Queen and the exchange, but White skilfully employs a discovered check and wins: 1. Nxe8+! (but not 1. Nf5? Qe5!, and Black wins) 1. ... Kg8 2. Nf6+ (compelling Black's King to fall prey

Diagram 84

to another discovered check) 2. ... Kh8 3. Ng4+! Qe5 (but not 3. ... Kg8 4. Nh6++ or 3. ... Rg7? 4. Rf8++, taking advantage of the pinned Rook) 4. Bxe5+ Rxe5 5. Nxe5, and White wins.

Many a game has been lost because of a discovered check after the moves 1. e4 e5 2. Nf3 Nf6 (this opening is called Petroff's Defence) 3. Nxe5 Nxe4? (quite a natural but mistaken move. It is better to play 3. ... d6! 4. Nf3 Nxe4 5. Qe2 Qe7 6. d3 Nf6) 4. Qe2! Nf6?? (the lesser of two evils would be 4. ... Qe7 5. Qxe4 d6 6. d4, and Black loses only a Pawn) 5. Nc6+! (discovered check! Black loses the Queen).

DOUBLE CHECK

The *double check* is a variety of the discovered check. Here both the piece lying in ambush and the piece that moves declare check simultaneously. Quite naturally, the double check is an even more powerful weapon against which it is impossible to shield oneself. The King must retreat. And if that is impossible, as in the following example, the King is mated.

Diagram 85

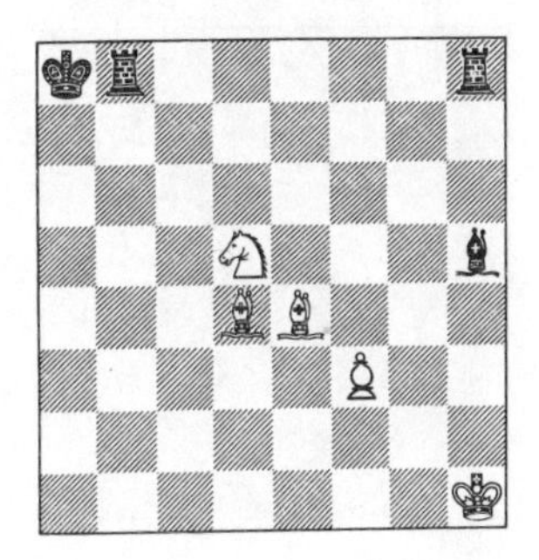

White, having the move, mates with the aid of a double check: 1. Nc7++! (but not 1. Nb6+? because of Ka7). If it is Black's move, he can declare a double check with advantage: 1. ... Bxf3 2. Kg1 Bxe4!, etc.

Note that, though Black's move 1. ... Bxf3+ places both of his pieces under attack, White cannot capture either of them and has to pull back his King.

This motif was employed in the famed *Réti-Tartakover* game (Vienna, 1910). Here is how the Soviet Grandmaster David Bronstein applied the double check in a simultaneous exhibition. Bronstein versus Amateur (1950): 1. e4 e5 2. d4 exd4 3. Qxd4 Nc6 4. Qa4 Nf6 5. Nc3 d5 6. Bg5 dxe4 7. Nxe4 Qe7? 8. 0-0-0 Qxe4 9. Rd8+ Kxd8 10. Qxe4. Black resigns.

Exercise (see Diagram 86).

Find the best continuation:
a) when it is White's move
b) when it is Black's move.

Diagram 86

VARIATION. COMBINATION

The term *variation*, which signifies a series of logically interconnected moves, is frequently used in chess literature. We have already come across it repeatedly in considering examples cited above.

Chess players also often employ such words as "to force" and "forced"; they talk of a "forced win", "forced variation", etc. Here "forced" means "compulsory". For instance, in Diagram 37 White compels Black to accept all the sacrifices and forces a draw by perpetual check, while in Diagram 42 a forced win is achieved with the aid of subtle Bishop manoeuvres. *Forced variation* is the term used for a chain of compelled moves. Whenever such a variation is played neither White nor Black can avoid it at any time, for to play otherwise threatens defeat or a clearly worsening position.

A special place among the forced variations is held by the *combination*. A combination is a forced variation through which a player achieves an advantage: he wins material, improves his position, brings about a draw, or mates his opponent. In a number of examples cited in this chapter combinations of different kinds were carried out. In some cases they helped to achieve mate (Diagrams 80, 86), and in others to win material (Diagrams 81-84). Various tactical methods were employed in carrying out the combinations: the pin, a double blow, discovered attack, and double check. Using these methods try to work out combinations in the following assignments (everywhere, with the exception of Diagram 90, it is White's move).

Diagram 87

Employing a discovered attack and double blow, White wins a piece.

Diagram 88

Employing a double check, White mates with the assistance of the Rook on h1.

Diagram 89

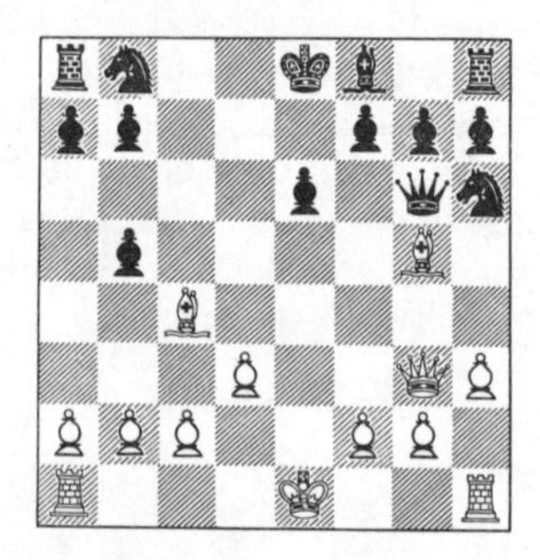

Sacrificing the Queen, White declares a double check and mate.

Diagram 90

Taking advantage of the pin along the open e-file, Black delivers a decisive double blow on the Queen's flank.

IV. HOW TO START A GAME

In the opening moves of a game both players mobilise their forces for the coming battle. To do this successfully and to ensure harmonious cooperation among your pieces and Pawns you must follow the three main principles of opening play. These are:

1) strive to gain possession of the centre;

2) develop (mobilise) your pieces as quickly as possible;

3) deploy your Pawns efficiently.

Let us examine these principles separately.

THE CENTRE

The centre of the chessboard is important because, as already stated, a piece standing there controls a maximum number of squares and can act effectively in all directions. On the contrary, the farther a piece is from the centre the weaker it becomes. When standing in the centre of the board the Queen can keep under attack 27 squares as compared to 21 squares when it stands in a corner; the Bishop, correspondingly, 13 and 7, the Knight 8 and 2. Also, a piece can be easier and faster transferred from the centre to any flank.

The centre is a sort of a commanding height dominating the chessboard. The side that holds the centre has a decisive advantage.

Diagram 91

The position in Diagram 91 is from the Sokolsky-Koblenz game (Kiev, 1944). White dominates the centre. After 1. Qf5! (transferring the Queen to the King's flank) Black resigns. Indeed, in the case of 1. ... 0-0 there follows 2. Bxh6. The sacrifice cannot be accepted: 2. ... gxh6 3. Be4, and mate is inevitable. There is no salvation in 3. ... Re8 4. Qh7+ Kf8 5. Qh8++. Simultaneously there threatens 3. Qg6! But Black cannot capture the Queen because the Pawn on f7 is pinned. It is bad to play 1. ... Rf8 2. Qh7 g5 3. Ne4, and if, for instance, 3. ... Qc8, then after 4. Bxc6 Bxc6 5. Nd6+! cxd6 6. exd6 there arises the already familiar hopeless situation for Black shown on Diagram 78.

Capture of the centre by Pawns, in other words, the creation of a *Pawn centre* is of special importance. The two sides fight for possession of the centre by attacking the central squares with their pieces and Pawns. The latter play a great role in this struggle. Indeed, any square attacked by a Pawn is closed to all the opposing pieces. The most effective way to attack the central squares is with Pawns. No wonder White's most common opening moves are 1. d4 or 1. e4 (to which Black replies with 1. ... d5 or 1. ... e5).

The following game convincingly illustrates the power of the Pawn centre.

1. e4 e5 2. Nf3 (2. Nc3 or 2. Bc4 is also possible but the next move is more powerful: White attacks the opponent's stronghold in the centre—the Pawn on e5) 2. ... Nc6 (The best defence. Also good is 2. ... Nf6, counter-attacking the K-Pawn, as well as 2. ... d6. But 2. ... Bd6? is a gross mistake. This move, like Bd3 in analogous cases on the part of White long delays mobilisation of the Queen's flank.) 3. Bc4 Bc5 (This opening can be met in books by Italian authors of the 16th and 17th centuries. Hence its Italian title Giuoco Piano, i.e., quiet game.) 4. c3 (White prepares the move d4 in order to seize the centre with the Q- and K-Pawns.) 4. ... Nf6 5. d4 exd4 6. cxd4 Bb6? A serious mistake. The correct move is 6. ... Bb4+, not giving White enough time to make use of the centre. For instance, 7. Bd2 Bxd2+ 8. Nbxd2 d5!, which is a typical method of struggle against a Pawn centre: its destruction with the aid of a Pawn. 9. exd5 Nxd5 and instead of the powerful Pawn duet on d4 and e4 White has merely the *isolated Pawn* d4. That is, a Pawn without any Pawns of the same colour on the adjoining files, as a result of which it cannot be protected by another Pawn.

7. d5! Ne7 (It is bad to play 7. ... Na5 8. Bd3, with the threat 9. b4, winning the Knight.)

8. e5 Ne4 (Black threatens 9. ... Nxf2, simultaneously attacking the Queen and the Rook.)

9. d6! (A powerful move paralysing Black's Q-side.)

9. ... Bxd6 10. exd6 Nxf2 11. Qb3 Nxh1 (The Pawn on d6 cramps Black to such an extent that even an extra Rook is of no avail.)

12. Bxf7+ Kf8 13. Bg5. Black resigns. (There is no defence against 14. Bxe7 with the capture

of the Queen and an annihilating attack.

This game shows that the Pawn centre is especially strong when it is mobile. It is the swift advance of the central Pawns that settles the outcome in White's favour. To prevent the formation of a *mobile Pawn centre* by his opponent, each player strives first of all to ensure himself a stable deployment of his Pawns in the centre. He continues to strengthen it, missing no chance of weakening and capturing the opponent's central Pawns.

FAST DEVELOPMENT OF PIECES

In the opening moves strive to put all the pieces into action as quickly as possible.

Here is an approximate outline of development to follow—unless your opponent hampers this plan: 1. advance the central Pawns, opening the way for the pieces; 2. put the minor pieces into action; 3. castle; 4. put the major pieces—Rooks and Queen—into action.

Naturally, the player who mobilises his forces faster will be able to start the attack first, carry out a successful combination and achieve success. And vice versa, the player who disregards development, who gets carried away by making Pawn moves on the edge of the board (a3, h6) and by striving to capture some of his opponent's chessmen while ignoring deployment of his own forces can soon find himself in serious trouble.

The following game is quite instructive.

1. e4 e5 2. d4 exd4 (Correct move, though thereby Black agrees to the elimination of his central Pawn. He counts on, after 3. Qxd4, White's Queen proving to be prematurely advanced. Then

Black will play 3. ... Nc6, the Queen will be compelled to retreat, and Black *gains a tempo* for further development. Tempo in chess is a time unit equal to one move. In this case Black, playing 3. ... Nc6, *gains a tempo* because he makes a favourable move for himself and compels White to *lose a tempo* by making an extra move with the Queen.

Moreover, it is not advantageous for Black to defend the Pawn on e5 by playing, let us say, 2. ... d6 since after 3. dxe5 dxe5 4. Qxd8+ Kxd8 he loses the chance of castling. Entirely bad is 2. ... f6? 3. dxe5 fxe5 4. Qh5+ g6 5. Qxe5+ with the loss of the Rook.

3. c3! (An unexpected reply. White sacrifices a Pawn in order to capture the centre.)

3. ... dxc3 (Better is 3. ... d5, continuing the battle for the centre. After 4. exd5 Nf6 5. Bb5+ Bd7 6. Bc4 dxc3 7. Nxc3 Bd6, the play is even.)

4. Bc4 cxb2 5. Bxb2 (This opening is called the Danish Gambit. The *gambit* is the name of an opening in which White sacrifices one or two Pawns, and sometimes even a piece, with the aim of capturing the centre and outstripping Black in development. In this case Black won two Pawns, but has not yet developed a single piece, whereas both of White's Bishops occupy excellent positions, with their sights set on the King's flank. Together with the Pawn on e4, White's Bishops fully control the centre.

5. ... Bb4+ (Though this check appears to be not a bad developing move the departure of the Bishop weakens Black's K-flank, creating a basis for dangerous threats. The move 5. ... d6 leads to a complicated struggle. Black could have simplified the play at once by returning both Pawns: 5. ... d5 6. Bxd5 Nf6 7. Bxf7+ Kxf7 8. Qxd8 Bb4+ 9. Qd2 Bxd2+ 10. Nxd2 c5 with even play.)

6. Nd2 (Now Black is threatened by 7. Bxg7, and also by 7. Bxf7+Kxf7 8. Qb3+ followed by Qxb4. White regains a Pawn while depriving Black of the chance to castle.)

6. ... Qg5? (It seems to Black that he discovered a happy move: there now threatens 7. ... Qxg2 with the gain of a third Pawn or the exchange of Queens on d2. The latter threat is especially dangerous for White. The attacking side usually avoids the exchange of Queens because it is rarely that one manages to attack successfully without the Queen. On the contrary, the exchange of Queens signifies, as a rule, an important success for the defence, the more so in the given case when, with two Pawns to the good, Black is interested in simplifications and in going over to the endgame.)

7. Nf3! (Not allowing the exchange of Queens and developing another piece.)

7. ... Qxg2 (Another extra Pawn and another tempo lost for development.)

8. Rg1 Bxd2+ (The first impression is that Black scores a success. On 9. Qxd2 there will follow 9. ... Qxf3; in the case of 9. Nxd2 the Rook on g1 is taken; and after Kxd2 Black takes the Pawn on f2 with a check. However, Black's calculations are not justified.)

9. Ke2! (White's advantage in development is so great that he can get along without castling.)

9. ... Qh3 10. Qxd2

White has developed all his pieces except the Rook on a1. Only Black's Queen is developed, and unsuccessfully at that. In other words, in the case of White the opening is already completed, while for Black it is only starting. How come? In the chase after Pawns Black made bad use of his time: out of nine moves four were with Pawns, three with the Queen, and two with the same Bishop. Black neglected both the centre and development. White, on the contrary, spent only one move on developing each piece.

Diagram 92

White has at his disposal a number of powerful threats, first of all 11. Bxg7 or 11. Bxf7+. Black's position cannot be defended.

10. ... Nf6 11. Bxf7+! Kd8 (The Bishop is immune: 11. ... Kxf7 12. Ng5+ with the capture of the Queen. 11. Kf8 is followed by 12. Qg5 with the inevitable loss of the Pawn on g7 and early mate.)

12. Rxg7 Nxe4 (There threatened 13. Bxf6++).

13. Qg5+! Ng5 14. Bf6++.

White quickly won this game because he gained time to develop the pieces, whereas Black lost a lot of time. A gain of time enables you to outstrip your opponent in development. The first to really understand the significance of time in the opening and to demonstrate how to take advantage of development was the outstanding American player Paul Morphy (1837-1884).

MORPHY *CONSULTANTS*

Paris, 1858

1. e4 e5 2. Nf3 d6 (This opening is called Philidor's Defence in honour of François Philidor (1726-1795), the strongest player in the second half of the 18th century.

3. d4 Bg4? (The correct move is 3. ... Nf6 or 3. ... Nd7.)

4. dxe5 Bxf3 (Otherwise While wins a Pawn: 4. ... dxe5 5. Qxd8+ Kxd8 6. Nxe5.)

5. Qxf3 dxe5 (Black's Bishop made two moves and disappeared from the board while White managed to get ahead in development.)

6. Bc4 (Threatening 7. Qxf7++.)

6. ... Nf6 (Defending himself against mate, Black does not notice another threat prepared by Morphy's last move. It is better to play 6. ... Qd7, although after 7. Qb3 8. Nc3 9. 0-0 and Rfd1, he still faces a by no means easy task.)

7. Qb3 (This double blow, both against the Pawn on f7 and b7 wins a Pawn.)

7. ... Qe7 (Relatively better. Black agrees to give up the Pawn in order after 8. Qxb7 Qb4+ to compel an exchange of Queens and thereby avoid an attack. It goes without saying that 7. ... Qd7? is a poor move because there follows 8. Qxb7 Qc6 9. Bb5, with the capture of the Queen).

8. Nc3! (In the opening the player should develop his pieces.)

8. ... c6 (Instead of development he is compelled to make another move with the Pawn to protect the b7 square.)

9. Bg5 (This move, which pins the Knight on f6, completes the development of White's minor pieces.)

9. ... b5? (Counting on playing Nd7 after the retreat of the Bishop and gradually developing the pieces. Preferable is 9. ... Qc7.)

10. Nxb5!

Diagram 93

A crucial moment: Morphy sacrifices the Knight so as to clear the lines along which his pieces will rush to attack the King. This is by no means an accidental sacrifice. It is in line with the chess law that the side which mobilises its forces quickly and outstrips the opponent in development should strive to open up the lines. On the contrary, the side that lags behind in development should avoid moves which might open the lines. His forces are not ready to take advantage of open lines. They will be captured by the opponent's pieces.

10. ... cxb5 11. Bxb5+ Nd7 12. 0-0-0 (There threatens 13. Bxd7+.)

12. ... Rd8. [If 12. ... Qb4, then 13. Bxf6 gxf6 (13. ... Qxb3 14. Bxd7++) 14. Bxd7+].

13. Rxd7! Rxd7 14. Rxd1. (White sacrifices the exchange to eliminate the Knight that is important for defence, and immediately puts into battle fresh forces—the Rook on h1. Black

plays the opening so poorly that he cannot now use either the Rook on h8 or Bishop on f8.)

14. ... Qe6 (Here too, after 14. ... Qb4, decisive was 15. Bxf6.)

15. Bxd7+ Nxd7 16. Qb8+! Nxb8 17. Rd8++.

A brilliant finale! This game was played in a box at an opera house during a performance of Rossini's opera *The Barber of Seville*. Morphy's opponents were Herzog von Braunschweig and Count Isouard.

SETTING UP A GOOD PAWN STRUCTURE

The Pawn is the weakest chessman but it plays a big role nevertheless. If a Pawn attacks a square, an opposing piece cannot occupy it. Thus, it is the Pawns that protect the important squares. By advancing your Pawns you can easily push back your opponent's pieces. A strong and mobile Pawn centre, as noted above, is important. The distribution of the Pawns often decides the location of all the pieces. The term "Pawn structure" is understood as the distribution of Pawns in the centre and its vicinity. The nature of the Pawn structure frequently determines the plans of the two opponents in the middle game.

The Pawns should be sufficiently advanced (space won for the pieces), mobile (not blocked by pieces) and unweakened.

In a game against G. Lisitsyn Grandmaster M. Botvinnik, playing Black, excellently distributed his Pawns and pieces.

Black's Pawns control the central squares. The pieces are very well placed behind them. White is cramped (see Diagram 94).

Diagram 94

MISTAKES IN THE OPENING

In this section we will deal with some typical mistakes in the opening made by beginners.

The first piece of advice is not to make many Pawn moves. A Pawn move as such is not a developing move; it only paves the way for developing the pieces. In the opening two or three Pawn moves are enough to ensure positions in the centre and open the way for the pieces. Indiscriminate movement of Pawns is always harmful and frequently leads to catastrophe. For instance, 1. f3? e5 2. g4?? Qh4++. Truly a "Fool's mate"!

Here is another example: 1. e4 e5 2. Nf3 d6 3. Bc4 Bg4 4. Nc3 g6? (4. ... h6? leads to the same combination. Better is 4. ... Nf6, developing the piece and defending the Bishop.)

5. Nxe5!! Bxd1? (Black should have played 5. ... dxe5, although after 6. Qxg4 White regains a piece and remains with an extra Pawn and a better position.)

6. Bxf7+Ke7 7. Nd5++.

Diagram 95

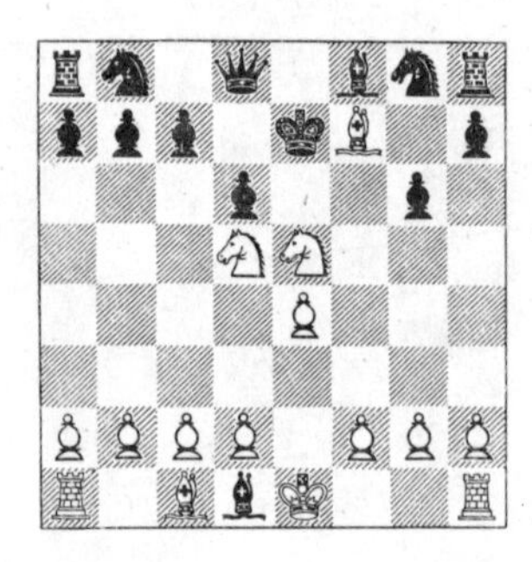

The beautiful finale in Diagram 95 has gone down in chess theory under the name of the *Légal mate.* The French chess player M. de Kermur, Sire de Légal (1702-1792) was Philidor's teacher and a good player until the end of his long life. At the age of 85 he defeated Saint-Brie in the following game that immortalised his name:

Légal vs. Saint-Brie: 1. e4 e5 2. Bc4 d6 3. Nf3 Nc6 4. Nc3 Bg4 5. Nxe5. (A mistaken move, of course, but evidently Légal knew his opponent well and was certain he would not resist the temptation of capturing the Queen.)

5. ... Bxd1?? (After 5. ... Nxe5 Black has an extra piece.)

6. Bxf7+ Ke7 7. Nd5++.

Since then the Légal mate has repeatedly appeared in the most diverse variations. Today too this combination is employed by strong chess players as a threat or trap.

In the following game the unnecessary advance of the Pawn on the flank places Black in a poor situation right on the second move.

1. e4 e5 2. Nf3 f6? (Black has several good replies at his disposal: 2. ... Nc6, 2. ... Nf6 and

2. ... d6. The movement of the f-Pawn weakens the King's position. If White wishes he can simply play 3. Bc4, and Black won't manage to castle for a long time. But White has a more powerful move.)

3. Nxe5!

Diagram 96

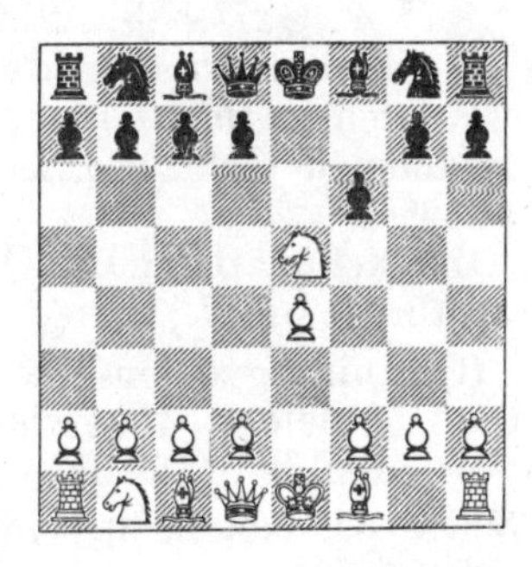

By sacrificing the Knight White gets an irrefutable attack:

3. ... e5? (Accepting the sacrifice, Black falls into a trap. Comparatively better is 3. ... Qe7 4. Nf3, but not 4. Qh5+? g6 5. Nxg6 because of 5. Qxe4+ 6. Be2 Qxg6, winning the Knight.)

4. ... Qxe4+ 5. Be2. (Black's position in this case too is worse as a result of the premature development of the Queen.)

4. Qh5+ Ke7. (In the case of 4. ... g6 5. Qxe5+, the Rook on h8 is lost.)

5. Qxe5+ Kf7 6. Bc4+ Kg6. (Not much better is 6. ... d5 after which there can follow 7. Bxd5+ Kg6 8. h4! h6 9. Bxb7! Bxb7 10. Qf5++.)

7. Qf5+ Kh6 8. d4+g5 9. h4! Be7. (This attempt at defence is also unsuccessful.)

10. hxg5+ Kg7 11. Qf7++.

The second piece of advice: don't be in a hurry to bring out your Queen.

Noticing that the f7 (or f2 in the case of White), protected only by the King, is the weakest point in his opponent's position, the beginner frequently tries in the initial moves to take advantage of this weakness with the aid of his strongest piece, the Queen. For instance, 1. e4 e5 2. Qh5 Nc6 3. Bc4 Nf6?? 4. Qxf7++. White wins by delivering a so-called childish mate. However, given a correct defence, that method of play in the opening is doomed to failure, as the following example shows.

1. e4 e5 2. Qh5 Nc6 3. Bc4 g6 4. Qf3. (Renewing the mating threat on f7.)

4. ... Nf6. (Combining defense with development—a method of defense that should be employed whenever possible in the opening.)

5. Qb3. (White persists in striving to attack the f7 square.)

5. ... Nd4! (Capturing with a tempo, i.e., with the gain of a tempo, the central d4-square with the Knight and indirectly protecting the Pawn on f7.)

6. Qc3. (It is bad to play 6. Bxf7+ Ke7 7. Qc4 b5 because White loses the Bishop. White has already become reconciled to the loss of the Pawn on e4. It is dangerous to play 6. Qd3 d5! 7. exd5 Bf5 followed by Nxc2+. However, Black has bigger intentions than winning a Pawn.)

6. ... d5! 7. Bxd5 Nxd5 8. exd5 Bf5 9. d3 Bb4! 10. Qxb4 Nxc2+.

And several moves later White resigned. Why did he lose so quickly? Because he has prematurely brought the Queen into play and is compelled to spend one tempo after another to protect it against attack by his opponent's minor pieces instead of developing his own pieces.

Meanwhile Black keeps on developing his pieces. Do not bring the Queen into play early. This almost always involves a lag in the development of the pieces.

Our third piece of advice concerns traps. Légal's fifth move Nxe5 was a typical trap. Saint-Brie succumbed to the temptation and lost, but in the case of the correct reply 5. ... Nxe6 Black, having an extra piece, wins. Don't follow Légal's example. Don't set a trap your opponent might see through. If he finds the correct reply he can gain an advantage. To become a good chess player you should respect your opponent and always proceed from the assumption that he might make the best possible reply.

Yet one should not underestimate the role of decoys in practical play. In a clearly lost position a trap frequently is the last chance of salvation. It is also good to know the traps employed in the opening.

V. THE OPENING

It is customary to divide chess openings into *open*, *semi-open* and *closed*, but this division is a conventional one. It arose long ago and today it frequently does not reflect the actual situation on the chessboard. In the Ruy Lopez, considered an open opening, there may arise a closed position, while in the Queen's Gambit, a closed opening, a position with numerous open lines often appears. The term "open" is applied to openings starting with the moves 1. e4 e5. The semi-open are those in which Black chooses in reply to 1. e4 any other move except 1. ... e5. In the closed openings White starts play with any move except 1. e4.

Throughout the centuries systems of openings designated by the terms "attack," "counter-attack," "defence," "system" and "variation" have developed. In the Ruy Lopez opening, for instance, there are the Rauzer Attack, the Marshall Counter-Attack, the Steinitz Defence, Strong Point (Tchigorin), the Exchange Variation and many other defences, variations, etc.

This chapter does not set out to describe all the existing openings. It merely gives a minimum amount of information on the theory of openings, an acquaintance with it will prove very useful for the beginner.

OPEN OPENINGS

Philidor's Defence

1. e4 e5 2. Nf3 d6. (In this old opening Black obtains a cramped, though quite firm, position.) 3. d4 Nf6. Black has to develop his K-flank faster. It is a mistake to play 3. ... Bg4. (See the Morphy versus Consultants game on page 80.)

More passive is 3. ... Nd7. After 4. Bc4 Black is obliged to play 4. ... c6! A bad move is to play 4. ... Nf6? because of 5. dxe5 (5. ... dxe5? 6. Ng5! and Black loses). 6. Nxe5 dxe5 7. Bxf7+ Kxf7 8. Qxd8 Bd4+ 9. Qd2 or 4. ... Be7? 5. dxe5 Nxe5 (5. ... dxe5? 6. Qd5, and White wins) 6. Nxe5 dxe5 7. Qh5 and White gains a Pawn, with a better position.

The move 3. ... f5? proposed by Philidor leads to difficult play for Black because of 4. exf5 e4 5. Ng5 Bxf5 6. Nc3 Nf6 7. f3.

4. Nc3. (If 4. dxe5 Nxe4 5. Nbd2, then comes 5. ... Nxd2 6. Bxd2 Nc6. White preserves a small advantage, but the play is simplified.)

4. ... Nd7 5. Bc4 Be7 6. 0-0 0-0 7. Qe2. (White frees the d1 square for his Q-Rook.)

7. ... c6 8. a4. (An important move that prevents the advance b5. White's position is freer. He takes the black-squared Bishop to e3, and moves the Rook on a1 to d1.)

V. TSESHKOVSKY *A. LUTIKOV*

USSR Championship (1968-1969)

1. e4 e5 2. Nf3 d6 3. d4 Nf6 4. Nc3 Nd7 5. Bc4 Be7. 6. 0-0 0-0 7. a4 c6 8. Qe2 exd4 9. Nxd4 Nxe4.

Black should not have carried out this combination. Though he regains the piece White gets a powerful attack.

10. Nxe4 d5 11. Nf5!

In the earlier played games White retreated his Bishop. White's move here is more powerful.

11. ... dxc4 12. Bh6!

Diagram 97

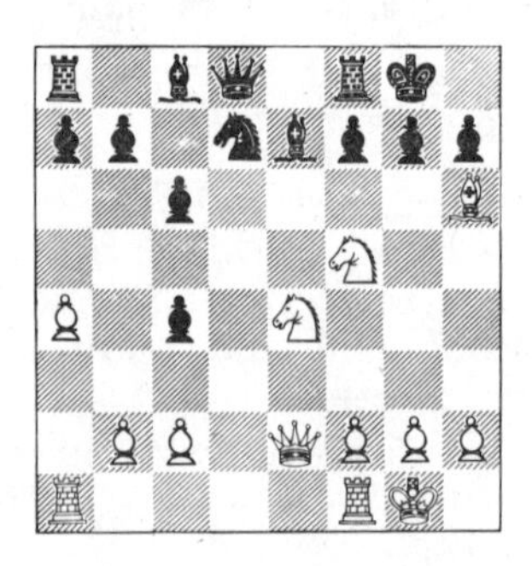

Superb play! Black has a hard time after 12. ... gxh6 13. Qg4+, and also after 12. ... Bf6 13. Bxg7 14. Qg4.

12. ... Nf6 13. Ng3 Bxf5 14. Nxf5 gxh6 15. Nxe7+ Kg7.

The move 15. ... Kh8 would be followed by 16. Qe5!

16. Nf5+Kg6 17. Ne7+ Kg7 18. Qe5! Qb8 19. Nf5+ Kg6 20. Nd6! Kg7 21. Re1 Rd8 22. Rd1 Rd7 23. Rd4 Qc7 24. Rg4+. Black resigns.

Petroff's Defence

1. e4 e5 2. Nf3 Nf6. (By counter-attacking the e4-Pawn Black simplifies the position in the centre and restricts White's possibilities in playing for a win. A big contribution was made to this opening by the outstanding 18th-century Russian chess player A. Petroff.)

3. d4. (This is a more active continuation. In the case of 3. Nxe5 Black, it goes without saying, has to respond with 3. ... d6, because Nxe4 is bad due to the move Qe2. After 3. ... d6 4. Nf3 Nxe4 it is difficult for White to gain active play. In the 13th and 15th games of the Petrosyan-Spassky match (1969) there followed 5. Qe2 Qe7 6. d3 Nf6 7. Bg5 Qxe2+ 8. Bxe2 Be7 9. Nc3 c6 10. 0-0-0 Na6, and Black quickly achieved a draw in both games without any trouble.

3. ... exd4. (Black can also continue 3. ... Nxe4 4. Bd3; White draws Black's Pawn to d5, so that it shouldn't be able to chase his Knight away from the e5 square 4. ... d5 5. Nxe5 Bd6. In the symmetrical position that arises in this case it is not easy for White to prove his advantage.)

4. e5 Ne4 5. Qxd4 d5 6. exd6. (White is compelled to take the Pawn *en passant* since there threatens 6. ... Bc5.)

6. ... Nxd6 7. Nc3 Nc6 8. Qf4. (Here White's Queen occupies an invulnerable active position, but the absence of Pawns in the centre facilitates Black's defence.)

8. ... g6 9. Bd2 Bg7 10. 0-0-0 Be6. (After 11. Ng5! Qf6 12. Qxf6 Bxf6 13. Nxe6 fxe6 14. Re1 Kd7 15. Ne4 White has only a small advantage.)

Scotch Game

1. e4 e5 2. Nf3 Nc6 3. d4. (White makes an attempt to gain an advantage in the centre, but Black manages to establish equality by attacking the Pawn on e4.)

3. ... exd4 4. Nxd4 Nf6. (Another continuation here is 4. ... Bc5. To 5. Nxc6 Black replies 5. ... Qf6! and takes the Knight on c6 with the Queen without spoiling his own Pawn position.

If 4. ... Bc5, White can reply with either 5. Be3 or 5. Nb3.)

5. Nc3. (In the case of 5. Nxc6 bxc6 6. e5 Qe7 7. Qe2 Nd5 8. Nd2 Bb7 9. Nb3 0-0-0 10. c4 Nb6 White lags in development.)

5. ... Bb4 6. Nxc6 bxc6 7. Bd3 d5 8. exd5. (Weaker is 8. e5 because of 8. ... Ng4 9. 0-0 Bc5 with the threat 10. ... Qh4.)

8. ... cxd5 9. 0-0 0-0 10. Bg5 Be6. (It is necessary to protect the Pawn on d5. In the case of 10. ... Be7 there would follow 11. Bxf6 Bxf6 12. Qh5 g6 13. Qxd5 Qxd5 14. Nxd5 Bxb2 15. Rab1 Be5 16. Rfe1 to White's advantage. In the position that has arisen the chances of the two sides are even. Possibly the game would proceed 11. Nb5 c5 12. a3 Ba5 13. b4 cxb4 14. axb4 Bxb4 15. Rxa7 Rxa7 16. Nxa7 h6!=.

A. ALEKHINE *Em. LASKER*

Moscow, 1914

1. e4 e5 2. Nf3 Nc6 3. d4 exd4 4. Nxd4 Nf6 5. Nc3 Bb4 6. Nxc6 bxc6 7. Bd3 d5 8. exd5 cxd5 9. 0-0 0-0 10. Bg5 Be6. (Also possible is 10. ... c6 11. Qf3 Be7.)

11. Qf3. (It is bad for White to play 11. Bxf6 Qxf6 12. Nxd5? Bxd5 13. Qh5 Rfd8! or 12. Qh5 g6 13. Nxd5? Qd8!, winning a piece.)

11. ... Be7 12. Rfe1. (White prepares for the following combination.)

12. ... h6 13. Bxh6! (This sacrifice permits White to force a draw.)

13. ... gxh6.

14. Rxe6 fxe6 15. Qg3+ Kh8. (Cannot play 15. ... Nf7 due to 16. Qg6++.)

16. Qg6! (Now Black cannot avoid perpetual check 17. Qxh6+ and 18. Qgh+. If 16. ... Qe8 then 17. Qxh6+ Kg8 18. Qg5+, etc. Agreed to a draw.

Diagram 98

When this game was played Em. Lasker was world champion, whereas Alekhine had just started on his chess career.

Giuoco Piano

1. e4 e5 2. Nf3 Nc6 3. Bc4 Bc5 4. c3. (White prepares with this move to capture the centre, 4. d3 leads to calmer play.)

4. ... Nf6. (Black should attack the Pawn on e4 immediately. After the passive 4. ... d6 5. d4 exd4 6. cxd4 Bb6 7. Nc3 he gets a cramped position.)

5. d4 exd4 6. cxd4 Bb4+. (Black has to retreat with a check so as to deal a counterblow in the centre.)

7. Bd2. (More active is 7. Nc3. See below the Greco Analysis and the W. Steinitz versus Kurt von Bardeleben game.)

7. ... Bxd2+. (The line of play 7. ... Nxe4 8. Bxb4 Nxb4 9. Bxf7+Kxf7 10. Qb3+ d5 11. Ne5+ Ke6! 12. Qxb4 c5 leads to unnecessary complications with unclear play.)

8. Nxd2 d5 9. exd5 Nxd5 10. Qb3 Ne7 11. 0-0 0-0 12. Re1 c6. (Black has a strong Knight position on d5).

The Greco Analysis

Gioacchino Greco (Il Calabrese, 1600-1634), an Italian player of the 17th century, left a manuscript with an analysis of many topical opening variations of his times. Here is one of them, a well-known variation with a Rook sacrifice in the Giuoco Piano.

1. e4 e5 2. Nf3 Nc6 3. Bc4 Bc5 4. c3 Nf6 5. d4 exd4 6. cxd4 Bb4+ 7. Nc3 Nxe4 8. 0-0 Nxc3 9. bxc3 Bxc3 10. Qb3! Bxa1 11. Bxf7+ Kf8 12. Bg5 Ne7 13. Ne5! (An excellent attack move! There is now the threat of 14. Bg6! For instance, 13. ... d6 14. Bg6 and both in the case of 14. ... dxe5 and 14... hxg6 there follows 15. Qf7++. It is also important that now the f3 square become accessible to White's Queen.)

13. ... Bxd4 14. Bg6! d5 15. Qf3+ Bf5 16. Bxf5 Bxe5 17. Be6+! Bf6 18. Bxf6 gxf6 19. Qxf6+ Ke8 20. Qf7++. (We know that such swift and crushing defeats are only possible as a result of a bad blunder by one of the sides. However, it was only 300 years later that chess players discovered a way of strengthening Black's play in this Greco variation. It turned out that instead of 10. ... Bxa1? or 10. ... Bxd4?, which also loses, the continuation should be 10. ... d5 11. Bxd5 0-0 12. Bxf7+ Kh8 13. Qxc3 Rxf7 14. Qb3 with a somewhat better position for White. But the variation continued to interest chess players. Several decades ago the distinguished Soviet Grandmaster Paul Keres showed that in reply to 9. ... Bxc3 White should not continue 10. Qb3 but 10. Ba3!, which leads to a forced win.

Here are the main continuations (see Diagram 99): a) 10. ... Ne7 11. Qb3 d5 12. Qxc3 dxc4 13. Rfe1 Be6 14. Bxe7 Kxe7 15. d5! Qxd5 16. Rad1 Qc5 17. Re5 Qb6 18. Rxe6+!;

b) 10. ... d5 11. Bb5 Bxa1 12. Re1+ Be6 13. Qa4;

c) 10. ... d6 11. Rc1 Ba5 12. Qa4 a6 13. Bd5 Bb6 14. Rxc6! Bd7 15. Re1+ Kf8 16. Bxd6!

Diagram 99

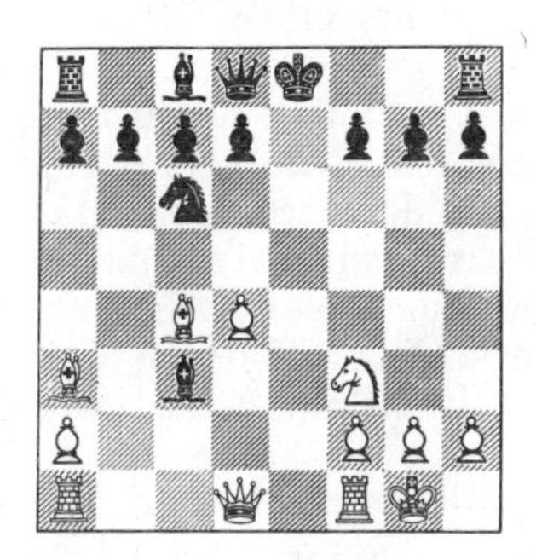

Modern theory recommends in reply to 9. bxc3 the continuation 9. ... d5! 10. cxb4 dxc4 11. Re1+, Ne7, leading to approximately even play. For instance, 12. Qe2 Be6 13. Bg5 Qd7 14. Bxe7 Kxe7 15. Qc2 f6!, parrying the threats Re5 and d5, and preparing the King's retreat to f7.

STEINITZ *BARDELEBEN*

Hastings, 1895

1. e4 e5 2. Nf3 Nc6 3. Bc4 Bc5 4. c3 Nf6 5. d4 exd4 6. cxd4 Bb4+ 7. Nc3 d5. (Though this continuation is condemned in some manuals on the opening it is better than it is reputed to be.)

8. exd5 Nxd5 9. 0-0 Be6. (With the open situation of the King in the centre an attempt to win a Pawn would be disastrous for Black, for instance: 9. ... Bxc3 10. bxc3 Nxc3? 11. Qe1+ and 12. Qxc3 or 9. ... Nxc3 10. bxc3 Bxc3 11. Qb3! Bxa1 12. Bxf7+ Kf8 13. Bg5 Ne7 11. Re1.)

10. Bg5 Be7. (Not, it goes without saying, 11. ... f6 because of 12. Re1, attacking the Bishop on e6. Now White undertakes a series of exchanges to prevent his opponent from castling.)

11. Bxd5 Bxd5 12. Nxd5 Qxd5 13. Bxe7 Nxe7 14. Re1! (After this move Black won't be able to castle. If, let us say, 14. ... Qd7, then White in his turn will include the Queen in the attack along the e-file, 15. Qe2. The attempt to include the Rook in the defence on a8 (Ra8-d8-d7) does not make it easier since in this interval White strengthens his position even more, for instance, 14. ... Rd8 15. Qe2 Rd7 16. Ne5 Rd6 17. Ng6! Re6 18. Nf4! Rxe2 19. Nxd5, winning the exchange.

14. ... f6! (Correct solution! Black plans an artificial castling manoeuvre: Kf7 and Re8.)

15. Qe2 Qd7 16. Rac1. (White's only spurious move in this game. Evidently stronger is 16. Qe4! c6 17. Re2 Kf7 18. Rae1 Nd5 19. Qh4.)

16. ... c6. (The correct move would have been 16. ... Kf7, with even play. Black hastens to neutralise White's pressure along the c-file and to cover up the Pawn on b7, evidently believing he will be able to move Kf7 later on.

17. d5! (The prelude to an excellent combination. White sacrifices a Pawn in order to bring the Knight into battle through the evacuated square.)

17. ... cxd5 18. Nd4 Kf7. (It is necessary to repulse the threat of Nf5.)

19. Ne6 Rhc8. (A natural striving on the part of the defending side to improve his situation through exchanges.)

20. Qg4 (Threatening mate in two moves: 21. Qxg7+ and 22. Qf8++.)

20. ... g6. (But not 20. ... Ng6? 21. Ng5+, winning the Queen.)

Diagram 100

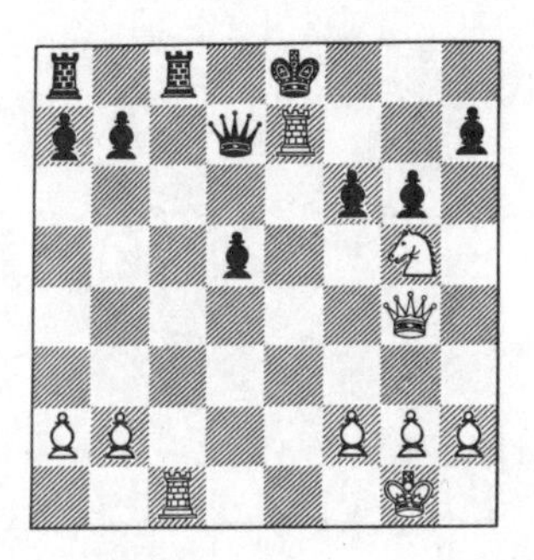

21. Ng5+ Ke8 22. Rxe7+! The combination starts! If 22. ... Qxe7, then 23. Rxc8+, winning. In the case of 22. ... Kxe7 there follows 23. Re1+ Kd6 (or 23. ... Kd8 24. Ne6+ Ke7 25. Nc5+) 24. Qb4+ Kc7 (if 24. ... Kc6, then 25. Rc1++, and if 24. ... Rc5, then 25. Re6+, winning) 25. Ne6+! Kb8 26. Qf4+ Rc7 27. Nxc7 Qxc7 28. Re8++.)

22. ... Kf8! (An excellent reply underscoring the weakness of White's last rank. All of his pieces are still under fire, and in addition there threatens mate on c1.)

Who then plays for a win?

23. Rf7+! Kg8. (The following line of play leads to the loss of a piece: 23. ... Qxf7 24. Rxc8+ Rxc8 25. Qxc8+ Qe8 26. Qxe8+.)

24. Rg7+!

The apex! This is precisely the position Steinitz foresaw when starting the combination. The defenceless Rook continues to harass the King.

24. ... Kh8. (If 24. ... Kf8?, then 25. Nxh7+ Kxg7 or Ke8 26. Qxd7+.)

25. Rxh7+!

At this point Bardeleben stood up and, without making another move on the board, left the

Diagram 101

tournament hall. He did not return that day. Here is the finale of the game as envisaged by Steinitz, who demonstrated it to the public: 26. ... Kg8 27. Rg7+ Kh8 28. Qh4+ Kxg7 29. Qh7+ Kf8 30. Qh8+ Ke7 31. Qg7+ Ke8 (in the case of 31. ... Kd6 Black is mated in two moves) 32. Qg8+! (but not 32. Re1+ Kd8 33. Ne6+ Qxe6!, and now it is Black who wins) 32. Ke7 33. Qf7+ Kd8 34. Qf8+ Qe8 35. Nf7+ Kd7 36. Qd6++. (Steinitz started his combination with the move 22. Rxe7+ and figured it out to this moment, i.e., 14 moves ahead!

Two Knights' Defence

1. e4 e5 2. Nf3 Nc6 3. Bc4 Nf6. (The Two Knights' Defence is the most energetic reply to White's move 3. Bc4. Black attacks the e4-Pawn with the Knight standing on f6 and prepares the counterblow d5. In the case of Nc3, an exchange combination is possible: 4. ... Nxe4 5. Nxe4 d5 6. Bd3 dxe4 7. Bxe4 Bd6, ridding Black of all kinds of difficulties. We present here the two main variations of the Two Knights' Defence.)

I

4. Ng5. (White attacks the Pawn on f7. Black has to play with great precision.)

4. ... d5 5. exd5 Na5! (The move 5. ... Nxd5? is bad. See the Polerio versus Domenico game on this page below.)

6. d3. (As regards 6. Bb5+ see the Ciocaltea versus Nezhmetdinov game on page 100.)

6. ... h6 7. Nf3 e4 8. Qe2. (An interesting sacrifice of a piece was employed by D. Bronstein against E. Rojahn at the 12th Chess Olympiad (1956): 8. dxe4 Nxc4 9. Qd4 Nb6 10. c4. In exchange for his piece White gets two Pawns and a powerful position in the centre.)

8. ... Nxc4 9. dxc4 Bc5 10. Nd2 0-0 11. Nb3 Bg4 12. Qf1 Bb4+ 13. c3 Be7. (In return for his Pawn Black gets the possibility of making some strong moves.)

II

4. d4 exd4 5. 0-0. (Also possible is the continuation 5. e5 d5 6. Bb5 Ne4 7. Nxd4 Bb7 8. Bxc6 bxc6 9. 0-0 Bc5 with mutually sharp play.)

5. ... Nxe4 6. Re1 d5 7. Bxd5! Qxd5 8. Nc3 Qa5 9. Nxe4 Be6 10. Ng5 0-0-0! 11. Nxe6 fxe6 12. Rxe6 Bd6. (Note Black's method of defence: after accepting the sacrificed Pawns in the opening Black proceeds to return them and, beating back the attack, has a good position.

POLERIO *DOMENICO*

Rome, 1602

1. e4 e5 2. Nf3 Nc6 3. Bc4 Nf6 4. Ng5 d5 5. exd5 Nxd5? 6. Nxf7! (Theory recommends here the less risky move 6. d4, but the sacrifice of a piece is evidently the strongest continuation of the attack.)

6. ... Kxf7 7. Qf3+ Ke6. (Otherwise White will regain the piece, preserving the extra Pawn and attack.)

8. Nc3 Ne7. (More persistent is 8. ... Nb4, but also in this case, after 9. Qe4 c6 10. a3 Na6 11. d4, Black is faced by a most difficult defence.)

9. d4! c6 10. Bg5 h6. No stronger is 10. ... Kd7 11. dxe5 Ke8 12. 0-0-0! Be6 13. Nxd5 Bxd5 14. Rxd5 Qxd5 (14. ... exd4 15. Bb5+!) 15. Bxd5 Nxd5 16. e6 and White wins.

11. Bxe7 Bxe7 12. 0-0-0 Rf8 13. Qe4 Rxf2 14. dxe5! (The strongest move in this position.)

14. ... Bg5+ 15. Kb1 Rd2 16. h4! Rxd1+ 17. Rxd1 Bxh4 18. Nxd5 cxd5 19. Rxd5. (With the fall of the d5 square, the chief citadel of Black's defence, the outcome of the game is settled. Also good is 19. Bxd5+ Ke7 20. Qxh4+.)

19. ... Qg5 20. Rd6+ Ke7 21. Rg6. Black resigns.

CIOCALTEA *NEZHMETDINOV*

Bucharest, 1954

1. e4 e5 2. Nf3 Nc6 3. Bc4 Nf6 4. Ng5 d5 5. exd5 Na5 6. Bb5+. (Thus White wins a Pawn but lags in development and hands over the initiative to the opponent.)

6. ... c6 7. dxc6 bxc6 8. Be2 h6 9. Nf3 e4 10. Ne5 Qc7 11. Ng4. (Better is 11. d4. Now White lags behind even more in developing his pieces.)

11. ... Bxg4! (Black parts with one of his Bishops but gains time. In the position here this is more important.)

12. Bxg4 Bc5 13. Be2 Rd8 14. c3? Tempted by the chance of winning a piece, White weakens his position. It would be preferable to castle.)

14. ... Nb7 15. 0-0 h5! (We call the readers' attention to the fact that Black himself refrains

from castling. The point is that, having a big advantage in development, he is preparing to launch a devastating attack against White's King, for which purpose he wants to keep the Rook on the h-file.)

16. d4 exd3 e.p. 17. Bxd3 Ng4 18. Qe2+ Kf8! (Loss of the opportunity to castle is of no significance here since Black completely holds the initiative.)

19. g3 Qd7! (Black attacks the Bishop on d3 while simultaneously defending the Knight on g4. This enables him to open up the h-file and obtain a decisive attack.)

20. Be4 h4 21. Bf4 Nxh2! (This Knight cannot be taken since after 22. Kxh2 hxg3+ White's King finds himself in a mating net.)

22. Re1 Ng4 23. Bf3 Nxf2. (It goes without saying that 23. ... Bxf2+ wins too, but Nezhmetdinov prefers to wind up the game with a direct attack.)

24. Be3 hxg3 25. Bxc5+ Nxc5 26. Bxc6. (White's last hope. The Bishop cannot be taken because of 27. Qe7+.)

26. ... Nh3+ 27. Kf1 Qf5+. White resigns. After 28. Bf3 g2+! 29. Qxg2 (29. Kxg2 Nf4+) 29. ... Nf4 30. Qg3 Rh3 31. Qf2 Ncd3, Black's threats cannot be repulsed.

Ruy Lopéz

1. e4 e5 2. Nf3 Nc6 3. Bb5.

This opening is met with in the writings of the outstanding Spanish chess players of the 15th and 16th centuries Luis Ramirez de Lucena and Ruy Lopéz. Old though it is, the opening enjoys great popularity in modern tournament chess thanks to the wealth of ideas it contains. Complicated and diversified positions that meet the tastes of players of different creative trends arise in it.

In the Ruy Lopéz, after c3 White usually strives to move the central Pawn to d4. In reply Black can choose different systems, many of which are bound up with the names of outstanding players of the past: the Steinitz Defence, Tchigorin systems, the Marshall Variation, etc. Soviet players have contributed many new features to Ruy Lopéz theory.

The numerous systems of the Lopéz are ordinarily divided into two groups. The first group consists of variations without the move 3. ... a6. Here old systems predominate. The second group includes branches of the Ruy Lopéz with the move 3. ... a6: the Exchange Variation, Strong Point (Tchigorin), Open Variation and other continuations more popular in our time. In this chapter we will examine only the main variations belonging to the second group.

I.

Exchange Variation

3. ... a6 4. Bxc6 dxc6 5. Nc3.

After 5. Nxe5 Black regains a Pawn by continuing 5. ... Qd4.

Nowadays 5. 0-0 is played more frequently, to which Black can reply 5. ... f6 or 5. Qd6.

5. ... f6 6. d4 exd4 7. Qxd4 Qxd4 8. Nxd4 Bd7 9. Be3 0-0-0 10. 0-0-0 Bd6.

In the Exchange Variation White has a better Pawn structure, but Black preserves the Bishops, which evens out the chances. Many of the games played with this variation ended in draws.

II.

Steinitz Defence Deferred

3. ... a6 4. Ba4 d6.

The move 4. ... b5 is premature. After 5. Bb3 it is bad for Black to play 5. ... Nf6 due to 6. Ng5. The advance of the a- and b-Pawns on the Q-side is not bound up with any definite plan and merely weakens Black's position.

5. c3.

It is possible to play 5. d4 b5 6. Bb3 Nxd4 7. Nxd4 exd4. If now comes 8. Qxd4?, there follows 8. ... c5 9. Qd5 Be6 10. Qc6+ Bd7 11. Qd5 c4 with the gain of a piece. Instead of 8. Qxd4? White should play 8. Bd5 Rb8 9. Qxd4 or, to continue in a gambit style, 8. c3 dxc3 9. Nxc3 with initiative for the Pawn.

Sometimes the play continues 5. Bxc6+ bxc6 6. d4, after which Black should reply 6. ... f6, propping the e5-Pawn in the centre.

5. ... Bd7 6. d4 Nf6.

Another plan here consists in the development of the Knight on g8 to e7 followed by its transfer to g6, i.e., 6. ... Nge7 7. Bb3! h6 (there threatens Ng5) 8. 0 0 Ng6 9. Be3 Be7 10. Nbd2 0-0. White has wide space, but Black occupies a stable position.

7. 0-0 Be7.

A possible continuation here is 7. ... Nxe4 8. Re1 Nf6 9. Bxc6 Bxc6 10. dxe5 dxe5 11. Qxd8+ Rxd8 12. Nxe5 Be4 13. Nd2 Bc7 14. Nxe4 Nxe4 15. Bh6 gxh6 16. Rxe4 0-0 17. Nc6 bxc6 18. Rxe7 Rd2 19. Rxc7 Rfd8! followed by 20. ... Rxb2 and an even position.

8. Nbd2 0-0 9. Re1 Be8.

Another continuation is 9. ... exd4 10. cxd4 Nb4. Games played in recent years showed that after 11. Bxd7 Qxd7 12. Nf1 c5 13. a3 Nc6 14. d5 Ne5 15. Ng3 White has superior play.

10. Nf1 Nd7 11. Ng3 f6.

A variation used at one time by Alekhine. Black's position is somewhat cramped.

III.

Open Variation

3. ... a6 4. Ba4 Nf6 5. 0-0 Nxe4.

A sharp variation. Taking advantage of the open position of Black's King, White easily regains a Pawn. Black can maintain equality only by very exact play.

6. d4.

After 6. Re1 Nc5 7. Nxe5 Be7 8. Nc3 0-0 9. Bxc6 dxc6 Black has a good position.

6. ... b5.

The continuation 6. ... exd4 (the so-called Riga Variation) 7. Re1 d5 8. Nxd4 is dangerous for Black. An attempt at perpetual check by means of 8. ... Bd6 9. Nxc6 Bxh2+ is refuted by 10. Kh1 (10. Kxh2 Qh4+ leads to perpetual check) 10. ... Qh4 11. Bg5! Qxg5 12. Qxd5! Qxd5 13. Nb4+, and White retains material advantage. But it was discovered recently that after 13. ... Kd8! 14. Nxd5 Be5! or 14. ... Nc5 Black has a clear advantage. Hence, the usual continuation in the Riga Variation remains in force: 11. Rxe4+ dxe4 12. Qd8+ Qxd8 13. Nxd8+ Kxd8 14. Kxh2 with a small advantage for White.

7. Bb3 d5 8. dxe5 Be6 9. c3.

Black can reply to Keres' continuation 9. Qe2 with 9. ... Bc5 10. Be3 Qe7 11. Rd1 Rd8.

9. ... Be7.

The move 9. ... Bc5 leads to mutually sharp positions.

10. Nd2 0-0

A complicated position with a slight advantage for White. The best moves here are considered to be 11. Bc2 or 11. Qe2 with the aim of compelling Black to exchange the Knight or to retreat to c5.

3. ... a6 4. Ba4 Nf6 5. 0-0.

Black attacks the Pawn on e4. White's simplest way to defend it would seem to be by playing either 5. Nc3 or 5. d3. However, those moves run counter to the main strategy of White's play in the centre through c3 and d4. White defends the Pawn with the Rook and then goes on to implement his plans.

5. ... Be7 6. Re1 b5 7. Bb3 0-0 8. c3 d6.

The gambit variation employed for the first time by Frank Marshall of the USA and developed in detail by Soviet players deserves attention: 8. ... d5 9. exd5 Nxd5 10. Nxe5 Nxe5 11. Rxe5 c6 (in a game against Capablanca Marshall played Nf6, but then this stronger continuation was discovered) 12. d4 Bd6 13. Re1 Qh4 14. g3 Qh3. In return for his sacrificed Pawn Black gets an opportunity to attack. It is best of all for White to continue 15. Qd3, transferring the Queen to f1 to defend the K-side.

9. h3.

If 9. d4 is played at once, then after 9. ... Bg4 (with the threat 10. ... Bxf3) 10. d5 Na5 11. Bc2 c6! 12. dxc6 Nxc6 13. Nbd2 b4! Black gets counterplay.

9. ... Na5.

Here the move 9. ... Nb8 is also employed (with the intention, after 10. d4, of continuing 10. ... Nbd7). This was developed by the Soviet players G. Borisenko and S. Furman (see the Ljubojević versus Karpov game on page 107).

10. Bc2 c5 11. d4

Sometimes the continuation here is 11. d3, in order, after completing development of the Q-side pieces, to advance the Pawn to d4.

11. ... Qc7 12. Nd2.

This is the main position of Tchigorin's Strong Point.

GELLER *PORTISCH*

International Tournament
Moscow, 1967

1. e4 e5 2. Nf3 Nc6 3. Bb5 a6 4. Ba4 Nf6 5. 0-0 Be7 6. Re1 b5 7. Bb3 d6 8. c3 0-0 9. h3 h6.

This is Smyslov's continuation in Tchigorin's Strong Point. Black deprives White's Knight of the g5-square and gets the chance of placing his Rook on e8.

10. d4 Re8 11. Nbd2 Bf8 12. Nf1 Bb7.

Black not only defends his Pawn on e5 but also puts pressure on White's Pawn on e4.

13. Ng3 Qd7

Usually 13. ... Na5 14. Bc2 c5 is played here, inviting White to determine the situation in the centre. Portisch makes a new move but it proves faulty.

14. dxe5 dxe5 15. Nh5!

White takes advantage of the Black Queen's suspended situation. Now, after 15. ... Qxd1 16. Nxf6+ gxf6 17. Bxd1, Black's position will be considerably worse since his Pawns on the King's flank are scattered and White's Knight threatens to occupy f5.

In the attempt to avoid this variation, Black gets into worse trouble.

15. ... Qe7 16. Nh4 Nxh5 17. Qxh5 Na5?

This loses at once. Black does not notice White's reply: 17. ... Nd8 in order to bolster the defence of the f7-square, Black could still hang on.

18. Bg5!!

This Bishop cannot be taken either by the Queen because of 19. Qxf7+Kh7 20. Qg8++ or by the Pawn because of 19. Ng6, with mate on the next move. Thus Black's Queen is compelled to retreat, but in doing so it has to protect the f7-square.

18. ... Qd7 19. Rd1 Bd6

Black's Bishop has to vacate the f8-square, and now White wins by sacrificing the Bishop on h6.

20. Bxh6 gxh6 21. Qg6+ Kf8 22. Qf6 Kg8

There threatened 23. Ng6+ followed by mate.

23. Re3. Black resigns.

In the case of 23. ... Kh7, White wins immediately through 24. Nf5.

Anatoly Karpov

"The Spanish Rack"*

The great Capablanca viewed the Ruy Lopéz as the touchstone for understanding a position. Tartakover christened it "The Spanish Rack", evidently bearing in mind the troubles that beset Black.

From the very start of my serious occupation with chess this opening served me faithfully in playing White and also Black. Here I should like to describe two encounters which I won playing Black and in which this opening became a "Spanish Rack" for those playing White.

LJUBOJEVIĆ — *KARPOV*

Manila, 1976

1. e4 e5 2. Nf3 Nc6 3. Bb5 a6 4. Ba4 Nf6 5. 0-0 Be7 6. Re1 b5 7. Bb3 d6 8. c3 0-0 9. h3 Nb8 10. d4 Nbd7 11. Nbd2 Bb7 12. Bc2 Re8 13. b4 Bf8 14. a4

---

* This is an excerpt from an article by world champion Anatoly Karpov carried in the Soviet chess weekly "64" (No. 47, 1976).

Diagram 102

I do not dwell on any of the moves so far quite intentionally because the first 10 to 15 moves of this variation of the Ruy Lopéz have no need of comment in general. This is one of the oldest openings which has been constantly employed up to now and which fully preserves its attractiveness. Many of the variations have been studied thoroughly, while some require more elaboration and a practical check. I must say that the players who believe the Ruy Lopéz does not deserve any more attention, that it has been covered in length and breadth by many generations of players and that it is now impossible to find anything new in it are mistaken. Even more mistaken are those, who, having read and learned by heart the variations given in books, think they can employ them successfully in tournaments...

In this game Ljubojević chooses a continuation that became fashionable after the Spassky versus Fischer match of 1972, where it appeared in the 10th game.

14. ... Nb6

That is the same move as in the above-mentioned 10th game. I used to think 14. ... a5 is stronger, but after the discovered strengthening of play for White—15. bxa6 Rxa5 16. Rb1 Ba6 17. axb5 followed by 18. Bb3—there was no longer any need to defend Black's position.

15. a5 Nbd7 16. Bb2 Rb8.

In that game of the match against Fischer Spassky played 16. ... Qb8. Soon after the match he used this stronger move, which he had discovered himself, in a game against A. Planinc in Amsterdam in 1973. Both continuations were directed against a breach of the centre by White, at c4, which would give him excellent operative possibilities.

17. Qb1

A new move bound up with the well-known idea of exerting pressure along the a2-g8 diagonal. The move met more often is 17. Rb1.

17. ... Nh5!?

The Queen departs, and with it the indirect attack on the h5-square. The idea is not only to get the Knight on the strategically important f4-square. Black also prepares for a counterblow in the centre with c5, but this isn't good right off: 17. ... c5 18. bxc5 dxc5 19. dxe5 Nxe5 20. Nxe5 Rxe5 21. c4, with a clear advantage for White.

18. c4

Ljubojević, striving for the initiative, gets into difficulties. What with the unpleasant opposition of the Queen and the Rook along the b-file, the active play is by no means in White's favour. A calmer move is 18. Nf1, though in this case Black is no longer in fear of 18. ... c5 19. bxc5 dxc5 20. dxe5 (or 20. Nxe5 Nxe5 21. dxe5 c4) because of 20. ... c4 followed by 21. ... Nxe5.

18. ... bxc4 19. Nxc4

After the exchange 19. dxe5 dxe5 the Pawn on b4 would have been under attack.

19. ... exd4

Just right! Black won't have a better moment for counterplay.

20. Bxd4

The move 20. Nxd4 that suggests itself meets with the thrust 20. ... Ne5! 21. Bb3 (the Knight on e5 is immune: 21. Nxe5 dxe5 and 22. ... Bxb4) 21. ... Nf4 with numerous threats. If in this variation the move 21. Nd2 is played, then comes 21. ... Bc8!, with the clear threat 22. Rxb4 and a camouflaged one: 22. ... Bxh3.

Diagram 103

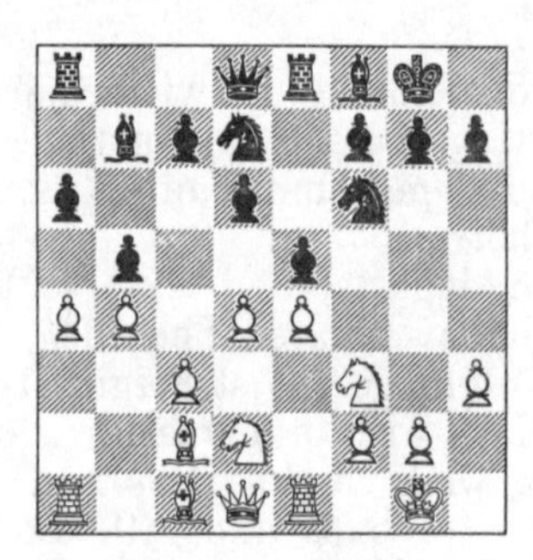

20. ... c5 21. Be3

Of course, 21. bxc5 is impossible due to 21. ... Bxe4, with the capture of White's Pawn, and in the case of 21. Bc3 the simple 21. ... Bc6 is unpleasant. But here Ljubojević conceives interesting play which, however, encounters a combinational refutation.

21. ... cxb4

In reply to the prosaic 21. ... Bc6, the Queen calmly leaves the b-file: 22. Qd1.

22. Nb6 Nhf6

It's time to go back... The move seems simple but it was quite difficult to discover. It took long pondering to bring me to the conclusion that the return was most expedient.

23. Qxb4

Risky? But what else can be done? After all, the extra Pawn might have remained Black's for good.

23. ... d5

23. ... Bxe4 would have ensured Black a minimal material advantage but ceded part of the positional advantage.

24. Qb3 dxe4 25. Ng5

It goes without saying that in choosing the continuation Ljubojević figured it out many moves ahead, but I managed to see a bit farther.

25. ... Bd5 26. Qa4 Nxb6

Otherwise the extra Pawn cannot be retained, for instance: 26. ... h6 27. Nxd5 Nxd5 28. Nxe4 Rb4 29. Qa2 (it is curious how White's Queen is trapped in the variation 29. Qc6 Nb8! 30. Qa8 Nc7 31. Qa7 Nc6!).

27. Bxb6

In the case of 27. axb6 White Knight is lost: 27. ... h6.

Diagram 104

27. ... Qe7!

This is possibly the first surprise for White. The Queen voluntarily gets on the same file as White's Rook. But everything has been taken into account: White cannot make use of this circumstance.

28. f3

Nor can White take advantage of the pin if 28. Bxe4 Bxe4 29. Nxe4 Nxe4 30. f3 Rxb6! 31. axb6 Qc5+ 32. Kh1 Nf2+ 33. Kh2 Rb8.

28. ... Rxb6!

Nonetheless there is a sacrifice! It would be absurd to think Ljubojević did not see this blow. But what he did not see was something farther on.

29. axb6 Qc5+ 30. Kh1 Bc6!

Not a complicated double blow but quite an effective one: the Queen is attacked while the Knight hangs in the air on g5.

31. Qa5 exf3

Here is a surprise White failed to take into account in the preliminary calculations. An exchange of Queens is out of the question and the reason is obvious. Nonetheless, I would like to show here a colourful mating finale: 32. Qxc5 Rxe1+ 33. Qg1 (33. Rxe1 fxg2+ 34. Kh2 Bxc5, with an easy win) 33. ... fxg2+ 34. Kh2 Bd6++.

32. Nxf3 Qxc2 33. Qxa6

The move 33. Rac1 (33. Rec1 Qe4) 33. ... Rxe1+ 34. Qxe1 Qa4 would merely drag out the battle.

33. ... Bxf3 34. gxf3 Rxe1+ 35. Rxe1 Nh5!

The threat is quite plain: 36. ... Ng3+ and 37. ... Bc5+. The Knight also prevents the Queen's return to the defence via the e2 and f1 squares. It would be a mistake to play 35. ... Qf2 36. Rf1 Qg3 37. Qc8! Nd5 38. b7 Ne3 39. Rg1 Qxf3+ 40. Kh2 Qf2+ 41. Kh1, with only a draw.

36. Re8

In the case of 36. Rg1 the move 36. ... Qc6 wins: simultaneously the Pawn on b6 is pinned and the Pawn on f3 is attacked.

36. ... Qf2

White's King is pressed to the wall but there is no perpetual check. The rest is forced.

37. Rxf8+ Kxf8 38. Qa3+ Ke8 39. Qa4+ Ke7 40. Qb4+ Kf6 41. Qd6+ Kg5 42. Qe5+

The final trap: 42. ... Kh4 43. Qe4+ Kxh3 44. Qg4++, but that is something for beginners.

42. ... Kh6. White resigns.

ARSENIEV — *ZHUKHOVITSKY*

Leningrad, 1967

1. e4 e5 2. Nf3 Nc6 3. Bb5 a6 4. Ba4 Nf6 5. 0-0 Nxe4 6. d4 b5 7. Bb3 d5 8. dxe5 Be6 9. c3 Be7 10. Nbd2 0-0 11. Bc2 f5

The following line, 11. ... Nxd2 12. Qxd2 f6 13. exf6 Bxf6 14. Ng5 Bxg5 15. Qxg5 Qxg5 16. Bxg5, leads to an unfavourable ending for Black.

12. exf6 e.p.,Nxf6 13. Nb3

If 13. Ng5, there follows 13. ... Bg4 14. f3 Bd7 15. Re1 Qc8, with a somewhat better position for Black.

13. ... Bg4 14. Qd3 Ne4

Diagram 105

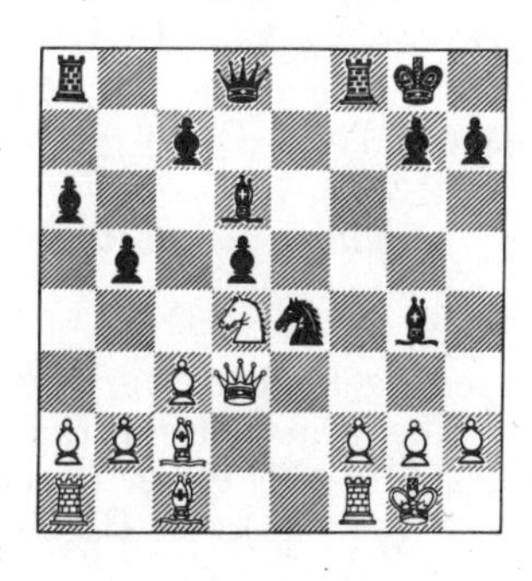

This sets White more difficult problems than 14. ... Bh5 15. Nbd4 Nxd4 16. Nxd4 Bg6, with even play.

15. Nbd4 Nxd4 16. Nxd4 Bd6!

17 Nxb5?

White undertakes a faulty combination to gain material (17. ... axb5 18. Qxd5+ Kh8 19. Qxe4). Actually the situation on the board obliges him to show much discretion. It is bad to play 17. Nc6 Qh4 18. Qxd5+ Kh8 19. h3 Rxf2, with an irresistible attack for Black. And if 17. Bb3, then comes 17. ... Kh8! 18. Bxd5 Bxh2+ 19. Kxh2 Qxd5, with an obvious advantage for Black. Necessary is 17. h3 Qh4 18. Nxb5 Nxf2 19. Bg5! Nxd3 20. Bxh4 axb5 21. Bxd3 Bd7, with even play (Ragozin vs. Ravinsky, Moscow, 1947).

17. ... Bxh2+! 18. Kxh2 Qh4+ 19. Kg1 Rf5! 20. Bb3.

20. f3 doesn't work because of 20. ... Rh5! 21. fxe4 Qh2+ 22. Kf2 Rf8+ 23. Ke1 Qh4+ 24. g3 Rxf1+ 25. Kxf1 Qh1+ 26. Kf2 Rh2 27. Ke3 Qg1+, winning.

20. ... Kh8! 21. f3

In the case of 21. Qxd5 there follows 21. ... Rxd5 22. Bxd5 Rf8! 23. Bxe4 Be2, winning.

21. ... Rh5! 22. fxe4 Qh2+ 23. Kf2 Rf8+ 24. Bf4. If 24. Ke1, there follows 24. ... Qh4+ 25. Kd2 Rf2+, winning.

24. ... Qxf4+ 25. Ke1 Rh1!!

White resigns. The move 27. Rxh1 is impossible because of 27. ... Qf2++.

King's Gambit

1. e4 e5 2. f4

This old opening leads to very keen and interesting play. The aim behind the Pawn sacrifice is to get rid of the Pawn on e5 and set up a Pawn centre (e4, d4). If Black puts up an incorrect defence White launches a powerful attack. Good defence lines bound up with the counterblow d5! in the centre have now been found, and the King's Gambit is comparatively rare today.

The King's Gambit is subdivided into the King's Gambit Accepted (if Black takes the Pawn sacrifice) and the Gambit Declined.

A distinction is made in the King's Gambit Accepted between the Knight's Gambit, if White plays 3. Nf3, and the Bishop's Gambit, if White plays 3. Bc4. The gambit may be declined by playing 2. ... Bc5 or offering, in turn, a Pawn sacrifice, 2. ... d5 (Counter-Gambit).

Knight's Gambit

2. ... exf4 3. Nf3 d5!

Formerly the gambit Pawn was defended through 3. ... g5. After 4. Bc4 g4 many difficulties arose. Another defence method is bound up with fast development of the pieces on the K-side: 3. ... Be7 4. Bc4 Nf6! (but not 4. ... Bh4+ because of the simple reply 5. Kf1! The Bishop is ineptly placed on h4 and hampers the development of Black's pieces) 5. e5 Ng4 6. 0-0 Nc6 7. d4 d5 8. exd5, e.p. Bxd6, and Black has good play.

4. exd5 Nf6

The move 4. ... Qxd5 is weak because of 5. Nc3 Qe6+ 6. Kf2! with the threat 7. Bb5+ and 8. Re1.

5. Bb5+

Black replies to 5. c4 with 5. ... c6 6. dxc6 Nxc6 7. d4 Bb4+ 8. Nc3 0-0. An even position.

5. ... c6 6. dxc6 bxc6 7. Bc4 Nd5

Black's position is quite satisfactory.

Bishop's Gambit

2. ... exf4 3. Bc4 d5

Weaker is 3. ... Qh4+. Although White is deprived of the chance to castle, after 4. Kf1! g5 5. Nc3 Nf6 6. Nf3 Black's Queen is pushed back, and White receives an advantage in the centre and in development of the pieces.

4. Bxd5 Nf6! 5. Nc3 Bb4 6. Nge2

After 6. Nf3 Bxc3 7. dxc3 c6 8. Bc4 Qxd1+ 9. Kxd1 0-0 10. Bxf4 Nxe4 11. Re1 the play is even.

6. ... Bxc3 7. bxc3 Nxd5 8. exd5 Qh4+ 9. Kf1 Bg4

The chances of the two sides are even. For instance, the following variation is possible: 10. Qe1 Qxe1+ 11. Kxe1 f3 12. gxf3 Bxf3 13. Rg1 Bxd5 14. Rxg7 Nc6 15. Nf4 0-0-0 16. Kf2.

King's Gambit Declined

2. ... Bc5 3. Nf3

It would be a mistake to play 3. fxe5? because of 3. ... Qh4+ 4. g3 Qxe4+, winning the Rook.

3. ... d6 4. Bc4 Nc6 5. d3 Nf6 6. Nc3 Bg4

White's position is a bit more active. It would be best of all for him to play 7. Na4, exchanging the unpleasant Bishop.

Falkbeer Counter Gambit

2. ... d5 3. exd5 e4

A fine move preventing the development of White's Knight on f3.

4. d3 Nf6 5. Nd2

Here Bronstein recommends 5. dxe4 Nxe4 6. Be3. True enough, in this case big complications arise after 6. ... Qh4+ 7. g3 Nxg3 8. Nf3.

5. ... exd3 6. Bxd3 Nxd5 7. Ne4 Be7, with even play.

TCHIGORIN *DAVYDOV*

St. Petersburg, 1874

1. e4 e5 2. f4 exf4 3. Nf3 g5 4.Bc4 g4 5.0-0 Tchigorin offers the sacrifice of the Knight, the so-called Muzio Cambit.

Despite the big material loss White's chances are at the least no worse than Black's. He has brilliant development and a powerful attack along the e- and f-files.

The following moves by both White and Black (from the 5th to 12th inclusive) are the best, as is demonstrated by detailed analyses.

5. ... gxf3 6. Qxf3 Qf6 7. e5 Qxe5 8. d3 Bh6 9.Nc3 Ne7 10. Bd2 Nc6 11. Rae1 Qf5 12. Nd5 Kd8 13. Bc3!

White could play 13. Qe2 Qe6! 14. Qf3 Qf5, forcing a draw.

13. ... Re8?

A mistake. Here the Rook is attacked by White's Knight. Preferable is 13. ... Rf8, after which White could continue the attack by playing 14. g4! Qg6 15.h4.

14. Bf6 Bg5 15. g4! Qg6 16. Bxg5 Qxg5 17. h4! Qxh4 18. Qxf4 d6 19. Nf6! Ne5?

Diagram 106

19. ... Rf8 is better. Now, sacrificing the Exchange, Tchigorin opens wide the position of Black's King and pushes ahead with the final attack.

20. Rxe5!! dxe5 21. Qxe5 Bxg4 22. Qd4+ Kc8 23. Be6+!! Kb8 24. Nd7+ Kc8 25. Nc5+ Kb8 26. Na6+! bxa6 27. Qb4++.

BRONSTEIN *BOTVINNIK*

Moscow, 1952

1. e4 e5 2. f4 exf4 3. Nf3 d5!

One of the best defence methods. Were White to play now 4. e5, a very strong reply would be 4. ... g5!

4. exd5 Nf6! 5. Bb5+ c6 6. dxc6 bxc6 7. Bc4 Nd5! 8. d4 Bd6 9.0-0 0-0 10. Nc3 Nxc3

More exact is 10. ... Be6.

11. bxc3 Bg4 12. Qd3 Nd7 13. g3?

An inept move weakening the K-side. 13. Bd2 is better.

13. ... Nb6

In the case of 13. ... fxg3? 14. Ng5! White obtains an irresistible attack.

14. Bb3 c5 15. c4?

A mistake that excludes the Bishop from play. Black should have proceeded 15. dxc5 Bxc5+ 16. Kh1 fxg3 17. Ng5 Qxd3 18. cxd3.

15. ... Qf6 16. Ne5

16. ... c3 is bad in view of Bf5! 17. Qd1 fxg3, etc.

16. ... Bxe5 17. dxe5 Qxe5 18. Bxf4 Qh5 19. Rfe1 Re8 20. a4 Be2!

The start of the final attack.

21. Qc3 Nd7 22. a5 Nf6 23. Ba4 Re6
24. Kg2 Ne4 25. Qa3 g5!

White resigns. After the retreat of the Bishop 26. ... Rh6 settles the issue.

SEMI-OPEN OPENINGS

French Defence

1. e4 e6 2. d4 d5.

A solid opening in which Black usually gets a somewhat cramped but firm position. The shortcoming of this opening is that in some variations the Bishop on c8 is locked up. On the other hand, the active counterplay in the centre bound up with the move c5 gives Black good counterchances. White's Pawn on e4 is attacked. But he can exchange it by playing 3. exd5, move it ahead, 3. e5, or protect it through 3. Nc3 or 3. Nd2. These are the four main variations of the French Defence.

I. Exchange Variation

3. exd5 exd5

In the Exchange Variation there arises a symmetrical position in which it is hard for either side to hope for an advantage.

4. Bd3 Nc6 5. c3 Bd6 6. Qf3 Be6 7. Ne2 Qd7 8. Bf4 Ne7 9. Bxd6 Qxd6 10. Qg3 Qxg3

Even play.

II. Variation With the Move e4-e5

3. e5 c5! 4. c3 Qb6!

This move deserves attention. Black preserves the pressure against the Pawn on d4 and sets the Pawn on b2 as its target. Thus the development of White's pieces on the Q-side—the Bishop on c1 and the Knight on b1—is held up. The emergence of the Queen in the early stage of the opening is fully justified in this case, the more so since White has nothing with which to attack the Queen on b6.

5. Nf3 Nc6 6. a3

The move 6. b3? is bad because of 6. ... cxd4 7. cxd4 Bb4+ 8. Bd2 Nxd4. White's aim in playing 6. a3 is to continue with 7. b4, freeing himself from pressure. However, Black hampers this.

6. ... a5 7. Bd3

While developing his pieces White sets a trap. If Black attempts to win a Pawn by 7. ... cxd4 8. cxd4 Nxd4? 9. Nxd4 Qxd4?, then after 10. Bd5+ he will lose his Queen.

7. ... Bd7 8. 0-0!

The sacrifice of a Pawn for initiative.

8. ... cxd4 9. cxd4 10. Nxd4 Qxd4 11. Nc3! Qb6

It is dangerous to take another Pawn, 11. ... Qxe5, due to 12. Re1 Qd6 13. Nb5, with a powerful attack.

12. Qe2

White has the initiative, which compensates for the sacrificed Pawn.

III. Nimzovitch's Variation

3. Nc3 Bb4

3. ... Nf6 is also possible.

4. e5 c5 5. a3 Bxc3+ 6. bxc3 Ne7
7. a4 Nc6 8. Nf3 Qa5

Diagram 107

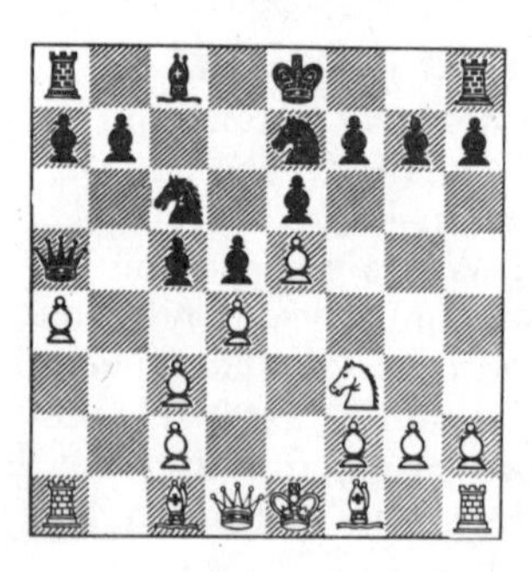

An intricate position. In case of 9. Bd2 Black can reply 9. ... c4, and if 9. Qd2 he can continue Bd7 and Rc8, with counterplay on the Q-side.

IV. Tarrasch Variation (3. Nb2)

3. Nd2 c5!

Though with this move Black receives an isolated Pawn, nonetheless this is the best because he simplifies the position and safely winds up the development of his pieces. Other continuations here—3. ... Nf6 4. e5 Nfd7 5. f4 or 3. ... Nc6 4. Ngf3 Nf6 5. e5 Nd7 6. Bd5—lead to more complicated play but give Black cramped position.

4. exd5 exd5

In regard to the capture of the Queen on d5 see the Stein-Uhlmann game.

5. Nf3 Nf6

Here also 5. ... Nc6 is played, but after 6. Bb5 it is more difficult for Black to defend himself. For instance, 6. ... Bd6 7. 0-0 Nge7 8. dxc5 Bxc5 9. Nb3 Bb6 10. Be3! Bxe3 11. Bxc6+ bxc6 (11. ... Nxc6 12. Re1) 12. fxe3 and White exerts strong pressure along the black squares.

6. Bb5+ Bd7 7. Bxd7+ Nbxd7 8. 0-0 Be7 9. dxc5 Nxc5

The chances of the two sides are approximately even. The Pawn on d5 gives Black control over the central points c4 and e4.

STEIN *UHLMANN*

International Tournament,
Moscow, 1967

1. e4 e6 2. d4 d5 3. Nd2 c5 4. exd5 Qxd5

Capture with the Pawn is more reliable. By using the Queen Black lags behind in development and has to play further with great precision.

5. Ngf3

This temporary Pawn sacrifice is the best continuation. White manages to develop his forces fast.

5. ... cxd4 6. Bc4 Qd6 7. 0-0 Nf6

Black cannot retain his Pawn on d4. In the case of 7. ... e5? there would follow, of course, 8. Nxe5 Qxe5 9. Re1.

8. Nb3 Nc6 9. Nbxd4 Nxd4 10. Nxd4 Be7 11. b3

White brings his Bishop out on the long diagonal to join in the attack on Black's K-side.

11. ... a6

A needless move. Better is 11. ... 0-0 12. Bd2 Bd7, winding up development of the pieces.

12. Bb2 0-0 13. Qf3 Qc7 14. Rfe1 b5

A faulty plan. True enough, it is now unprofitable for White to play 15. Qxa8 because of 15. ... Bb7 16. Qa7 Ra8 with the capture of the Queen since 17. Nxe6 will be followed by 17. ... Qc6. But Black is chasing White's Bishop where it wants to go itself. 14. ... Bd7 would be better and Black's Bishop would protect the important point e6.

15. Bd3 Bb7 16. Qh3 g6

Compelled to weaken the K-side because of the threat 17. ... Nxb5 axb5 18. Bxf6

17. a4! bxa4

This exchange is not, of course, favourable for Black, but he cannot play 17. ... b4 because of 18. Kxe6 fxe6 19. Qxe6+ Rf7 20. Bc4, and White has two extra Pawns since in the case of 20. ... Rf8 there may follow either 21. Bxf6 or 21. Qxe7!

18. Rxa4 Nh5

18. ... Qb6 is better, but Black underestimates the impact of the ensuing sacrifice.

19. Nxe6 fxe6 20. Qxe6+ Rf7 21. Bc4 Qf4

This loses at once. More persistent would be 21. ... Bd6, after which White could continue 22. Qh3 (threatening 23. Qc3) Bf8 23. Ra5. White threatens 24. Rxh5 with an irresistible attack, and if 23. ... Qxa5 there follows 24. Bxf7+ Kxf7 25. Qxe6++.

22. Qxf7+ Qxf7 23. Rxe7!

Black resigns since after 23. ... Bd5 24. Rxf7 Bxf7 25. Rxa6 he remains three Pawns short in the endgame.

Sicilian Defence

1. e4 c5

One of the more popular modern openings leading to a keen, substantial battle. Quite a number of books have been written about the Sicilian Defence, but to this very day chess theoreticians do not concur on many complicated variations.

The Sicilian Defence is employed by almost all the world's leading players.

White usually develops his initiative on the K-side, and Black on the Q-side.

I. Closed System

2. Nc3

White declines to prepare for an advance in the centre to d4, striving to build up a Pawn attack on the K-side. Black's plans include capture of the central square d4 and development of the initiative on the Q-side.

2. ... Nc6 3. g3 g6 4. Bg2 Bg7 5. d3 d6 6. Be3 e6 7. f4

Here 7. Nge2 with the subsequent 8. Qd2 were usually played, but now preference is given to 7. f4 since this makes it possible to move the Knight to f3, a much more active position than on e2.

7. ... Nge7 8. Nf3 0-0 9. 0-0 Nd4

White gets ready to launch an attack on the K-side, while Black, after Rb8, will move b5 with counterplay on the Q-side.

II. Scheveningen Variation

This system owes its name to the Dutch city of Scheveningen, where it was first employed at an international tournament in 1923.

2. Nf3 e6 3. d4 cxd4 4. Nxd4 Nf6 5. Nc3 d6 6. Be2

This Bishop development is characteristic of the Scheveningen Variation. Subsequently the Bishop may be transferred to d3 if White starts to attack Black's K-side, or to f3 if Black limits himself to exerting pressure in the centre.

6. ... Nc6 7. Be3 Be7 8. 0-0 0-0 9. f4 Bd7

Without losing time on the moves a6 or Qc7 Black strives to transfer the Bishop to c6 to attack White's central Pawn.

10. Qe1 Nxd4 11. Bxd4 Bc6 12. Qg3 g6!

Black has no fear of weakening the K-side since he has already managed to obtain counterplay. If 13. Bd3 or 13. Bf3 there will follow 13. ... b5. White has to think again about defence of the Pawn on e4.

III. Rauzer Variation

The system developed by the noted Soviet theoretician Vsevolod Rauzer is one of the sharpest and most involved continuations of the Sicilian Defence. Castling long, White combines pressure along the d-file with an attack on the K-side.

2. Nf3 Nc6 3. d4 cxd4 4. Nxd4 Nf6 5. Nc3 d6 6. Bg5 e6 7. Qd2 Be7

In reply to 7. ... h6 White goes 8. Bxf6, and Black is compelled to play 8. ... gxf6 since 8. ... Qxf6 is bad because of 9. Ndb5 Qd8 10. 0-0-0 without any chances for Black to save his Pawn on d6.

Another continuation here is 7. ... a6 8. 0-0-0 Bd7. In this case Black also frequently castles long.

8. 0-0-0 0-0

A touch-and-go position with mutual chances. The most frequent continuation here is 9. f4 Nxd4 10. Qxd4 h6 11. Bh4 (after 11. Bxf6 Bxf6 12. Qxd6 Qa5 Black has strong counterplay for his Pawn) 11. ... Qa5 12. Bc4 e5 13. fxe5 dxe5 14. Qd3.

IV. Dragon Variation

2. Nf3 d6 3. d4 cxd4 4.Nxd4 Nf6 5.Nc3 g6 6. Be3 Bg7

6. ... Ng4? is erroneous because of 7. Bb5+ Bd7 8. Qxg4. 7. Be2

This is the so-called classic continuation of the Dragon. Currently 7. f3 is employed more often.

7. ... 0-0 8. 0-0 Nc6 9. Nb3

Black replies to 9. f4 with 9. ... Qb6!, pinning the Knight on d4, attacking the Pawn on b2 and threatening 9. ... Nxe4.

9. ... Be6 10. f4

The main position of this variation, so named because the pattern of Black Pawns (d6, e7, f7, g6 and h7) resembles a lizard, i.e., Dragon.

White expects to develop an attack against the King, while Black can continue 10. ... Qc8, preventing the advance f5 or start counterplay on the Q-side through 10. ... a5.

BOLESLAVSKY *BÖÖK*

International Tournament
Stockholm, 1948

1. e4 c5 2.Nf3 d6 3. d4 cxd4 4. Nxd4 Nf6 5. Nc3 e6 6. Be2 a6

As noted above, nowadays Black tries to get along without this and the next move.

7. 0-0 Qc7 8. f4 Nc6 9. Be3 Be7 10. Qe1 Nxd4 11. Bxd4 e5?

This counterblow in the centre proves premature and leads to a poor position. Black should have castled and then transferred the Bishop to c6 via d7.

12. fxe5 dxe5 13. Qg3

With this move White attacks two Pawns. Black avoids material loss but his position is unsatisfactory.

13. ... Bc5 14. Bxc5 Qxc5+ 15. Kh1 Kf8

Of course, it is unpleasant for Black to lose the chance to castle but otherwise he cannot protect the Pawn on g7. 15. ... 0-0 cannot be played because of 16. Rxf6.

16. Nd5!

White has to play energetically to take advantage of the Black King's deplorable situation.

16. ... Nxe4

If Black plays 16. ... Nxd5, then comes 17. Qxe5, and at the best Black remains a Pawn down with a worse position.

17. Qxe5 Nf6

17. ... Nf2+ 18. Rxf2 Qxf2 19. Qe7+ leads to mate.

18. Rad1 Be6

In the case of 18. ... Nxd5 the move 19. Bh5 wins; if 18. ... Ng4, then comes 19. Bxg4 Bxg4 20. Rxf7+ Kxf7 21. Rf1+ and White wins.

19. b4 Qc6

If 19. ... Qxc2 mate follows in five moves: 20. Qd6+ Kg8 21. Ne7+ Kf8 22. Ng6+ Kg8 23. Qf8+ Rxf8 24. Ne7++.

20. Nxf6 gxf6 21. Rxf6 Rg8 22. Bf3 Qb6

This leads to the loss of a piece but even after 22. Qc4 there follows 23. Rf4 Qxa2 24. Bd5 Bxd5 25. Qd6+ Ke8 26. Rxd5. Black should resign.

23. Rd6 Qf2 24. Bxb7 Qxc2 25. Rxe6

Black resigns.

SPASSKY *PETROSYAN*

World Championship, 1969

1. e4 c5 2. Nf3 d6 3. d4 cxd4 4. Nxd4 Nf6 5. Nc3 a6

This is also one of the sharpest variations of play in the Sicilian Defence.

6. Bg5 Nbd7

The usual continuation here is 6. ... e6 but the move made by Petrosyan is quite often too.

7. Bc4 Qa5

In the case of 7. .... e6 Black has to take into account the Bishop sacrifice 8. Bxe6.

8. Qd2 h6

A new continuation. Black wants to determine the White Bishop's position. Usually 8. ... e6 was played here.

9. Bxf6

White has no intention of losing time on the Bishop's retreat and counts on receiving chances for an attack by developing his pieces quicker than his opponent.

9. ... Nxf6 10. 0-0-0 e6 11. Rhe1 Be7

Black prepares to castle short but the King's position there would be dangerous. Worthy of attention is 11. ... Bd7, followed by castling long. Since White's King is also on the Q-side it is not simple at all for White to develop an offensive on this sector.

12. f4 0-0 13. Bd3

White improves the King's position before going over to the offensive. Meanwhile Black tries to prop up the e6-point.

13. ... Re8 14. Kb1 Bf8 15. g4!

White cedes a Pawn in order to open up a line against Black's King. Since the Pawn threatens to go ahead, Black decides to accept the sacrifice.

15. ... Nxg4 16. Qg2 Nf6 17. Rg1 Bd7 18. f5 Kh8

Black does not take any steps against further opening up of the lines. 18. ... e5 is somewhat better.

19. Rf1 Qd8

Black makes haste to bring up the Queen for defence but this now proves to be insufficient.

20. fxe6 fxe6 21. e5!

The start of a beautiful final combination.

21 ... dxe5 22. Ne4 Nh5

Clearly, 22. ... Nxe4 cannot be played because of 23. Rxf8+Rxf8 24. Qxg7++. After 22. ... exd4 23. Nxf6 Black has no defence against 24. Qg6.

23. Qg6! exd4

This loses immediately. But white also wins after 23. ... Nf4 24. Rxf4 exf4 25. Nf3 Qb6 26. Rg5!! with the irresistible threat 27. Nf6.

24. Ng5!

Black resigns since after 24. ... hxg5 there follows 25. Qxh5+ Kg8 26. Qf7+ Kh8 27. Rf3, with inevitable mate.

SHAGALÓVICH *GUFELD*

Fourth USSR Games, 1967

1. e4 c5 2. Nf3 d6 3. d4 cxd4 4. Nxd4 Nf6 5. Nc3 g6 6. Be3 Bg7 7. f3

The Rauzer Attack in the Dragon Variation. This continuation with castling in opposite directions leads to very sharp play.

7. ... 0-0 8. Qd2 Nc6 9. Bc4

An important move with which White forestalls a Black advance—9. ... d5—in the centre.

9. ... Bd7 10. h4

The usual continuation here is 10. 0-0-0, but White wants to attack the K-side without wasting time.

10. ... Qa5 11. Bd3 Rfc8

Black has played all this in keeping with the latest advances in theory. He vacates the f8-square for the King and seeks counterplay on the c-file.

12. h5

White sacrifices a Pawn to bolster the attack. Black accepts the sacrifice since he cannot in any case forestall the opening of the h-file.

12. ... Nxh5 13. g4 Nxd4?

Black exchanges two minor pieces in order to transfer the Knight from h5 to a stronger position. In doing so he fails to take into account the fact that his King proves defenceless.

After 13. ... Nf6 the whole battle is still ahead. White would have to castle long to draw up reserves for an attack.

14. Bxd4 Bxd4 15. Qxd4 Nf4 16. Bxf7+!

Evidently Black did not take this sacrifice into account in his preliminary calculations.

16. ... Kxf7 17. Rh7+ Ke6 18. Qg7 Re8 19. Qf7+

Now Black's King is forced to start on the way to the middle of the board, where inevitable doom awaits him.

19. ... Ke5 20. 0-0-0!

White winds up the development of his pieces, simultaneously creating new threats.

20. ... Rac8 21. Nd5 Rxc2+

Black has no satisfactory defence. After 21. ... Ne6 22. f4+ Kxe4 23. Qxg6+ Kf3 24. Qd3+ he is mated within several moves.

22. Kb1!

After 22. Kxc2 Qa4+! Black could count on salvation since White's King would not have a satisfactory retreat. For instance, 23. Kc1 Rc8+ 24. Nc3 Ne2+ 25. Kd2 Qd4+, and White is compelled to agree to a repetition of moves by 26. Ke1 Qg1+ 27. Kd2 since in case of capture of the Knight 26. Kxe2 there follows 26. ... Bb5+ 27. Nxb5 Rc2++.

22. ... Nd3

Nor is 22. ... Rxb2+ of any help since after 23. Kxb2 Qb5+ 24. Ka1 Black has no continuation of the attack.

23. Qg7+

Black resigns since he receives a forced mate: 23. ... Ke6 24. Qxe7+Rxe7 25. Rxe7++.

Caro-Kann Defence

1. e4 c6

As in the French Defence, Black paves the way for the move d5. But as distinct from the French Defence, in some Caro-Kann variations Black can bring out the Bishop from c8 without shutting it off by the move e6. The Pawn advance to c5, which Black quite frequently has to carry out, is achieved here in two moves.

I. Variation with the Advance 3. e5

2. d4 d5 3. e5 Bf5! 4. Bd3 Bxd3 5. Qxd3 e6 6. Ne2

In the case of 6. Nf3 Black can carry out a manoeuvre recommended by Nimzovitch: 6. ... Qa5+ 7. c3 Qa6, leading to an exchange of Queens since the Queen's retreat holds up White's castling.

6. ... Qb6 7. Nc3 c5

Black has excellent counterplay in the centre.

II. Panov's Attack

2. d4 d5 3. exd5 cxd5 4. c4 Nf6

In the case of 4. ... dxc4 5. Bxc4 play goes over to the Queen's Gambit Accepted.

5. Nc3 e6

Weaker is 5. ... Nc6. 6. Bg5, and if 6.... dxc4, then comes 7. d5 Ne5 8. Qd4 Nd3+ 9. Bxd3 cxd3 10. 0-0-0 and White has a big advantage in development (Botvinnik-Flohr match, 1934).

6. Nf3 Be7 7. c5 0-0 8. b4

White has some advantage on the Q-side. In the Botvinnik-Golombek game (Alekhine Memorial Tournament, 1956) there followed: 8. ... b6 9. Bd3 Bd7 (it would be preferable to play 9. ... a5 10. Na4 Nfd7) 10. Be3 Ng4 11. 0-0 a5 12. Na4! with a clear advantage for White.

III. Main Variation

2. d4 d5 3. Nc3 dxe4 4. Nxe4 Bf5

Also possible is 4. ... Nd7, preparing for 5. ... Nf6 (see the Tahl versus Füster game below).

5. Ng3 Bg6 6. Nf3 Nd7 7. h4 h6 8. h5

A modern interpretation of this variation: White clamps the opponent's K-side.

8. ... Bh7 9. Bd3 Bxd3 10. Qxd3 Qc7!

Black is preparing to castle long and simultaneously does not allow White to move the Bishop out to f4.

11. Bd2 0-0-0 12. 0-0-0 Nf6 13. Qe2!

White strengthens his position by setting up the Knight on e5.

13. ... e6 14. Ne5 Nxe5

After 14. ... Nb6 15. Ba5 White's play is also considerably freer.

15. dxe5 Nd7 16. f4 Be7 17. Ne4 Nc5

That is how the 13th game in the Spassky-Petrosyan world title match in 1966 continued. White's play is freer.

IY. Variation
With the Move 2. Nf3

2. Nf3 d5 3. Nc3

With this sequence of moves White does not allow the opponent any defence bound up with Bf5. Thus, the line 3. ... dxe4 4. Nxe4 Bf5? will be followed by 5. Ng3 Bg6 6. h4 h6 7. Ne5 Bh7 8. Qh5! (see the E. Lasker versus H. Müller game on page 163).

3. ... Bg4

The line 3. ... d4 4. Ne2 c5 is weak because of 5. c3!, and if 5. ... Nc6, there follows 6. cxd4 cxd4 7. Qa4!, winning a Pawn.

4. h3 Bxf3 5. Qxf3 e6 6. d4! Nf6 7. Bd3 dxe4 8. Nxe4 Nxe4

It is dangerous to accept the sacrifice of the Pawn since Black lags in development.

9. Qxe4 Nd7

White has a slight advantage in the centre.

TAHL *FÜSTER*

Portorož, 1958

1. e4 c6 2. d4 d5 3. Nc3 dxe4 4. Nxe4 Nd7 5. Nf3 Ngf6 6. Nxf6+ Nxf6 7. Bc4 Bf5.

7. ... Bg4? would be a crude mistake because of 8. Bxf7+ Kxf7 9. Ne5+.

8. Qe2

White is preparing to castle long.

8. ... e6 9. Bg5 Be7

The move 9. ... Bg4! is stronger. This subtle play by Petrosyan in a game with Fischer (Bled, 1961) forestalls many latent hazards.

10. 0-0-0 h6 11. Bh4 Ne4

A questionable move. Black retains the King in the centre in order to simplify the situation by an exchange of Bishops.

12. g4!

An unexpected reply. 12. ... Bxg4 is no good because of 13. Bxe7 Bxf3 14. Qxf3, nor 12. ... Bxh4 because of 13. gxf5 exf5 14. Nxh4 Qxh4 15. f3. In both cases white gains a piece.

12. ... Bh7 13. Bg3 Nxg3 14. fxg3!

According to the rules White should play 14. hxg3, but every rule has its exceptions. This move permits White to use the f-file for his major pieces.

14. ... Qc7 15. Ne5 Bd6 16. h4!

Hampering both long and short castling.

In the case of 16 ... 0-0-0 the move 17. Nxf7! wins, and if 16. ... 0-0, then, 17. g5 immediately destroys the Black King's Pawn cover.

16. ... f6

Black counts on castling long after the Knight's retreat.

17. Bxe6!

Familiar tactics: if the opposing King is in the centre it is necessary to open the files immediately.

17. ... fxe5 18. dxe5 Be7

No better is 18. ... Bxe5 19. Rhe1!

19. Rhf1

With the threat of 20. Bf7+ Kf8 21. Bg6+ Kg8 22. Qc4++.

19. ... Rhf8. 20. R1xf8+ Bxf8 21. Qf3!

Forbidding Black to put into play the Rook: 21. ... Rd8? 22. Rxd8+, winning.

21. ... Qe7 22. Qb3

With a new threat: 23. Bd7+ Qxd7 24. Rxd7 Kxd7 25. Qxb7+.

22. ... Rb8 23. Bd7+! Qxd7 24. Rxd7 Kxd7 25. Qf7+ Be7 26. e6+ Kd8

Or 26. ... Kd6 27. Qf4+, winning the Rook.

27. Qxg7. Black resigns. Black's Bishop on h7 is doomed.

Alekhine Defence

1. e4 Nf6

The idea behind this clever defence is to draw out White's central Pawns and then exchange them or attack them with the pieces. However, Black has to take into account the fact that his opponent receives an advantage in space.

2. e5 Nd5 3. d4 d6 4. Nf3

By means of 4. c4 Nb6 5. f4 dxe5 6. fxe5 White can gain what is called the "big centre", consisting of three Pawns. This gives him pretty good chances for an attack but Pawns could prove to be weak (see the Jokšić versus Hazai game below).

If White has no wish to complicate the struggle he can continue 4. c4 Nb6 5. exd6 exd6 6. Nc3.

4. ... Bg4 5. Be2 e6 6. 0-0 Nc6

Attacking the Pawn on e5, Black forces an exchange on d6.

7. exd6 cxd6 8. c4 Nb6. 9. b3 Be7 10. Nc3 0-0 11. Be3

The main position of the Alekhine Defence. White's play is freer but Black has a firm position.

JOKŠIĆ *HAZAI*

Hungary, 1975

1. e4 Nf6 2. e5 Nd5 3. d4 d6 4. c4 Nb6 5. f4

A variation leading to an intricate and keen struggle. Connoisseurs of the Alekhine Defence believe that if a refutation of the opening does exist it should be sought in this variation.

5. ... Bf5 6. Nc3 dxe5 7. fxe5 e6 8. Nf3

More exact than 8. Be3 Bb4 9. Nf3 c5, with unclear play.

8. ... Bb4

Black refrains from 8. ... Nc6 in order to put himself in a favourable situation for the move c5 and to prevent White's typical retaliatory blow d5.

9. Bd3 c5

After 9. ... Bg4 10. 0-0 Nc6 11. c5 Bxc3 12. bxc3 Nd5 13. Qe1 White's position is better. The move 9. ... Bxd3 in the Ivkov versus Timman game (Amsterdam, 1974) was followed by 10. Qxd3 c5 11. 0-0 cxd4 12. Ne4, with excellent play for White (there threatens 13. c5 or 13. Nfg5).

10. d5!

This is better than 10. Bxf5 exf5 11. d5 Nxc4, with intricate play. Now White has a somewhat better position.

10. ... Bxd3

Not, of course, 10. ... 0-0? 11. Bxf5 exf5 12. Qe2, with an overwhelming advantage for White.

11. Qxd3 exd5

The one and only move.

12. Ng5!

A new move in this position.

12. ... Nc6

In the case of 12. ... d4 White expected to continue 13. 0-0! dxe4 14. Qxd8+ Kxd8 15. Nxf7+, winning. Also bad is 12. ... h6 13. Nxf7! with a decisive attack.

13. Nxf7! Kxf7 14. Qf5+ Ke8

14. ... Kg8 15. Qe6+ Kf8 16. 0-0+ is entirely bad.

15. 0-0 Qe7

Diagram 108

Black's situation is difficult. It is bad to play either 15. ... Qd7? 16. e6 or 15. ... Qc7 16. Nb5, with an irresistible attack.

16. Nb5!

White threatens 17. Nd6+ or 17. Bg5.

16. ... g6

The moves 16. ... Rf8 17. Nc7+ or 16. ... h6? 17. Nd6+ lose. No better is the line 16. ... Nd4 17. Nxd4 cxd4 18. Bg5 Qd7 19. e6 Qc7 20. c5! Bxc5 21. Rac1 Nc4 22. Qxd5, with a powerful attack for White.

17. Qh3 Nxe5

The lines of play 17. ... Kd8? 18. Rf6! or 17. ... Rd8 18. Bg5! are bad and White wins (18. ... Qxg5? 19. Qe6+ Qe7 [Ne7] 20. Nc7++).

Nor is salvation provided by 17. ... Rf8 18. Bg5! Qxg5 (18. ... Rxf1+ 19. Rxf1 Qxg5 20. Nc7+ Ke7 21. Qe6+ Kd8 22. Qd6+ Kc8 23. Ne6 Qe3+ 24. Kh1 Qxe5 25. Rf8+) 19. Nc7+ Ke7 20. Qe6+ Kd8 21. Qd6+ Kc8 22. Rxf8+ Nd8 23. Ne6.

18. Bg5! Qxg5

If 18. ... Qd7, there follows 19. Nc7+! Qxc7 20. Qe6+ and mate on the next move.

19. Nc7+ Ke7

Not 19. ... Kd8, of course, because of 20. Ne6+.

20. Qe6+ Kd8 21. Qd6+ Kc8 22. Ne6! Qd8.

The only defence against mate on c7.

23. Nxd8, and White wins.

This game is of considerable value for the theory of the Alekhine Defence.

Ufimtsev Defence

1. e4 d6

A modest preparatory move. Black is striving for an Old Indian structure, employing the flank development of the King's Bishop (*fianchetto*).

2. d4 Nf6 3. Nc3 g6 4. Nf3.

Currently the move 4. f4 is very often played here (see the Boleslavsky versus Mosionzhik game below).

4. ... Bg7 5. Bg5 0-0

A more flexible move is 5. ... c6. Black can be in no hurry about castling until his opponent reveals his plans.

6. Qd2 c6

White's play is freer. He has good attacking chances.

BOLESLAVSKY *MOSIONZHIK*

Fourth USSR Games, 1967

1. e4 d6 2. d4 Nf6 3. Nc3 g6 4. f4

A more energetic continuation aiming at preparing the advance of the central e-Pawn.

4. ... Bg7 5. Nf3 c6 6. Bd3 0-0 7. 0-0 b5 8. e5! Ne8 9. Ne4 a5 10. Qe1!

Preparing an attack, White transfers the Queen to the K-side.

10. ... Nc7 11. Qh4 Nba6 12. c3 f5 13. Neg5 h6 14. Nh3 Bd7 15. Nf2 c5 16. dxc5 dxc5 17. Qg3 Qe8 18. Re1 Be6 19. h4 Rd8 20. h5! gxh5

21. Nh4 Kh7 22. Qh3 Qf7 23. Bc2 Bc8 24. Nh1 e6 25. Ng3 Rg8.

Diagram 109

Black's position is a difficult one already, and his last move with the Rook is a mistake that brings defeat nearer. Boleslavsky shatters Black's defence by a spectacular combination.

26. Ngxf5! exf5 27. e6! Qf6

In the case of 27. ... Bxe6 White will reply 28. Rxe6! Nxe6 29. Bxf5+ Kh8 30. Ng6+ Kh7 31. Ne5+, and Black cannot avoid mate.

28. Qxf5+!

Black resigns. The capture of the Queen would be followed by mate in four.

CLOSED OPENINGS

Queen's Gambit

1. d4 d5 2. c4

In the Queen's Gambit the struggle for possession of the centre starts with the very first moves. The aim behind the Pawn sacrifice is to eliminate the central Pawn on d5. After 2. ... dxc4 White easily regains the Pawn by continuing 3. Nf3 (not immediately 3. e4 or 3. e3 because of the reply 3. ... e5 freeing Black's play) 3. ... Nf6 (it is unprofitable for Black to retain the Pawn by means of 3. ... b5 because after 4. a4 c6 5. e3 a6 6. b3! cxb3 7. axb5 cxb5 8. Bxb5+ White regains the Pawn anyway and receives a clear advantage) 4. e3 e6 5. Bxc4.

After 1. d4 d5 2. c4 e6 3. Nc3 Nf6 4. Bg5 Nbd7 it seems to the beginner that he can win a Pawn: 5. cxd5 exd5 6. Nxd5 since Black's Knight is pinned. A disappointment is in store for him, because after 6. ... Nxd5 7. Bxd8 Bb4+ 8. Qd2 Bxd2+ 9. Kxd2 Kxd8 White is minus a piece. A variety of such mistakes happens sometimes in the games of strong chess players too.

The line 2. ... Nf6 3. cxd5 e4 leads to the ceding of the centre.

It is best of all for Black to defend the Pawn on d5 by a Pawn, playing 2. ... e6 or 2. ... c6. These are the two main defences in the Queen's Gambit.

I.

Orthodox Defence

2. ... e6 3. Nc3 Nf6 4. cxd5 exd5

Besides the exchange on d5 the following continuation is frequently met: 4. Bg5 Be7 5. e3 0-0 6. Nf3 Nbd7 7. Rc1 c6. White's play is a bit freer. After 8. Bd3 Black usually continues 8. ... dxc4 9. Bxc4 Nd5 10. Bxe7 Qxe7 11. 0-0 Nxc3 12. Rxc3 e5, simplifying the play and restoring equilibrium in the centre.

5. Bg5 Be7 6. e3 c6

This move protecting the Pawn on d5 is usually made in the Queen's Gambit, and the Knight on b8 is moved to d7.

7. Bd3 0-0 8. Qc2 Nd7 9. Nf3 Re8 10. 0-0 Nf8 11. Rb1

Subsequently White continues b4 and Rc1, making play on the Q-side, while Black places the Knight on e4 and attempts to cause complications on the K-side.

II.

Slav Defence

2. ... c6 3. Nf3 Nf6 4. Nc3 dxc4

In this defence Black cedes the centre but exerts pressure with his pieces on the central squares. White's simplest reply to 4. ... e6 is 5. cxd5 exd5 6. Bg5, boiling down the play to the first variation. 4. ... Bf5? is bad because of 5. cxd5 cxd5 6. Qb3, and Black's Bishop will have to return to c8 since 6. ... b6 weakens the position too much.

5. a4 Bf5 6. e3 e6 7. Bxc4 Bb4 8. 0-0 0-0 9. Qe2

White feels freer but Black has a firm position.

NERONSKY *ZHUK*

Postal Chess Game, 1966

1. d4 d5 2. c4 dxc4 3. Nf3 Nf6 4. e3 e6 5. Bxc4 c5 6. 0-0

White should not waste his time developing the K-Rook because then Black might get counterplay.

6. ... a6

The start of the modern defence by Black in the Queen's Gambit Accepted envisaging development of the white-square Bishop to b7. Steinitz solved this problem differently: he gave White an isolated Pawn on d4, employed the manoeuvre Nc6 b4-d5 to gain firm possession of the d5 point, and led the Bishop through the d7 square to c6 or e8 (after the preliminary Rfd8), attaining a cramped but firm position.

7. Nc3 b5

White could prevent this move by playing 7. a4, but it would seriously weaken the b4-square.

8. Bb3 Bb7 9. Qe2 Nbd7 10. Rd1 Qb8 11. d5

Following the well-known rule: if your opponent is slow in castling open the lines!

11. ... exd5 12. Nxd5 Nxd5 13. Bxd5 Bxd5 14. Rxd5 Qb7 15. e4 Be7 16. Bg5 Nb6 17. Rad1! Nxd5

In one of his games Boleslavsky replied to 17. ... h6? with 18. Bxe7 Nxd5 19. Bxc5 Ne7, and carried White's attack to a successful end. Here Black decides to accept immediately the offered sacrifice of advantage.

18. exd5 f6 19. d6!

White continues the attack without pausing before the Bishop sacrifice.

19. ... fxg5 20. Re1 Rd8

Also possible is 20. ... 0-0 21. dxe Rfe8 22. Qe6+ Kh8 23. Nxg5, with decisive threats.

21. Qe6 Rd7 22. Nxg5 Rf8 23. Nxh7 Rf7 24. Qg6!

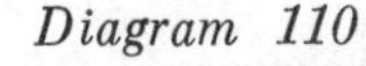
Diagram 110

Although he has an extra Rook Black is completely helpless. The variation 24. ... Qd5 25. Nf6+!! gxf6 26. Qg8+ Rf8 27. Qxd5, with the win of the Queen, is spectacular.

24. ... Qc6 25. Ng5 Qd5 26. Nxf7 Qxf7 27. Qxf7+ Kxf7 28. Rxe7+ Rxe7 29. dxe7 Kxe7 30. h4. White resigns.

This game is a valuable contribution to theory.

PETROSYAN *BYKHOVSKY*

Moscow Championship, 1968

1. c4 e6 2. d4 d5 3. Nc3 Be7 4. Bf4 Nf6 5. e3 0-0 6. Rc1 c5

More reliable is 6. ... c6. The opening of the lines is favourable for White.

7. dxc5! Nc6 8. Nf3 Bxc5 9. a3 d4

Bykhovsky discovers a clever possibilility for counterplay. Now 10. Na4 is no good because of 10. ... Qa5+ 11. b4 Nxb4! The play sharpens.

10. exd4 Nxd4 11. Ne5! b6 12. Bd3 Bb7 13. 0-0 h6 14. Re1 Nc6

The Knight's retreat is illogical. Better is 14. ... a5, forestalling the movement of the b-Pawn and preserving the Knight's powerful position in the centre.

15. Rc2

Not 15. b4? because of 15. ... Bxf2+ 16. Kxf2 Qd4+ 17. Kg3 g5!, regaining a piece.

15. ... Qc8 16. Ng4! Be7 17. Nxf6+ Bxf6 18. Ne4 Be7 19. Qh5

White goes over to the offensive, and Black has to defend himself with precision. Instead of 19. ... Nd4. Black makes a mistake by shifting the Rook away from defence of the K-side.

19. ... Rd8 20. Rc3 f5 21. Ng3 Bf6

Black attacks the Rook but Petrosyan ignores this threat and sacrifices the Knight. He has set his sights on Black's King!

22. Nxf5!! Bxc3

Entirely bad is 22. ... exf5 23. Bxf5 Rd7 24. Be6+ Kh8 25. Bxh6!, and Black is defenceless.

23. Nxh6+! gxh6 24. Qg6+ Bg7

Not 24. ... Kf8 because of 25. Bxh6+ Ke7 26. bxc3, with the threat 27. Bg5+. Now, how-

Diagram 111

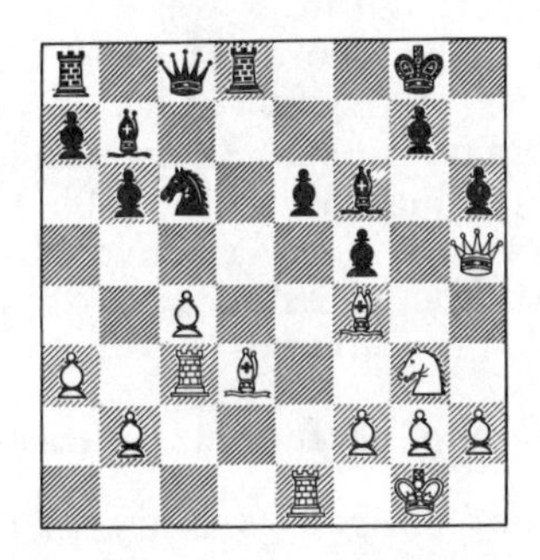

ever, new troubles are in store for Black.

25. Bxh6 Rd7 26. Qh7+ Kf8 27. Rxe6! Re7 28. Rf6+ Ke8 29. Qg8+. Black resigns.

Veresov's Opening

1. d4 Nf6 2. Nc3 d5 3. Bg5

The initial position of Veresov's Opening. This opening rarely appears in tournaments. The variations of this opening were developed in detail by the Byelorussian chess master, Veresov, who successfully employed it for more than 20 years.

After 3. Bg5 the move 3. ... Ne4 is hardly good because of 4. Nxe4 dxe4 5. e3. For instance: 5. ... Qd5 6. Bf4 c5 7. Ne2 cxd4 8. Nc3!, with advantage for White. The main continuations are 3. ... Bf5, 3. ... c5, 3. ... Nbd7 and 3. ... c6.

3. ... Nbd7 4. Nf3 g6

In the Veresov versus Shagalovich game (Byelorussian Championship, 1954) the play continued 4. ... h6 5. Bh4 e6 6. e4!? g5 7. Bg3 Nxe4 8. Nxe4 dxe4 9. Ne5 Bg7 10. h4, with keen play.

5. e3 Bg7 6. Bd3 c5

More precise than 6. ... c6, which was followed in the Spassky versus Geller game (17th USSR Championship, 1960) by 7. h4 h5 8. Ne2 Qb6 9. 0-0 0-0 10. b3 Re8 11. Nf4 Ne4 12. c4, with better play for White.

7. 0-0 0-0 8. Re1 b6 9. e4 dxe4 10. Nxe4 Bb7

The chances of the two sides are about even. In the Veresov versus Shagalovich encounter (Byelorussian Championship, 1957) there followed: 11. c3 cxd4 12. Nxd4 Nc5 13. Bxf6 exf6 14. Nxc5 bxc5, and after a short struggle the game ended in a draw.

Group of Indian Defences

Black is not obliged to reply to the move 1. d4 with 1. ... d5. He can decline the symmetry and continue 1. ... Nf6. This move, which develops the Knight, simultaneously prevents White from playing e4. After 1. d4 Nf6, different opening structures arise, depending on the further development of play. These are known as the group of Indian openings. Let us examine some of them.

Nimzovitch Defence

1. d4 Nf6 2. c4 e6 3. Nc3 Bb4

The idea of this opening is to gain control over the e4-square and pin the Knight on c3. What is known as the main variation of the Nimzovitch Defence is most often met in tournament practice.

4. e3 0-0 5. Bd3 d5

Black doesn't give White a chance to play e4.

6. Nf3 c5 7. 0-0 Nc6

Another branch is 7. ... Nbd7, with the approximate continuation 8. a3 dxc4 9. Bxc4 cxd4

10. exd4 Bxc3 11. bxc3 Qc7 12. Qe2 b6, in which Black winds up his development satisfactorily.

8. a3 Bxc3 9. bxc3 dxc4 10. Bxc4 Qc7

Black plans e5, opening the road for his Bishop on c8. White usually plays 11. Bd3 or 11. Bd2, and the chances of the two sides are approximately even.

Gruenfeld Defence

1. d4 Nf6 2. c4 g6 3. Nc3 d5

Black lets his opponent set up an extensive Pawn centre and then attacks it with pieces and Pawns. Usually a tense situation arises. Black has to be very careful since by inexact play he can easily succumb to an attack. The main variation of the defence follows:

4. cxd5 Nxd5 5. e4 Nxc3

If 5. ... Nb6 White continues 6. h3! (to prevent pinning of the Knight on f3 by Black's white-square Bishop) 6. ... Bg7 7. Nf3 0-0 8. Be2 Nc6 9. Be3 firmly retains the position in the centre.

6. bxc3 c5

Transposing the moves, Black can also play 6. ... Bg7 and then 7. ... c5.

7. Bc4 Bg7 8. Ne2

A better place for the Knight than f3 since after 9. Nf3 Bg4 10. Be3 Qa5 Black, attacking the Pawns on c3 and d4, develops strong pressure.

8. ... cxd4 9. cxd4 Nc6 10. Be3 0-0

In the case of 10. ... Qa5+ there follows 11. Bd2 Qh5 12. d5!. However, if 12. ... Bxa1? 13. Qxa1 Ne5 14. f4, White wins.

11. 0-0

White fortifies the Pawn centre and feels more free. Best of all for Black is to continue 11. ... Na5 12. Bd3 b6, developing the Knight on b7.

As soon as White's Rook leaves the a1 square Black should play e6 in order to prevent White's Pawn from reaching d5.

Old Indian Defence

This is the most popular of all the Indian openings and leads to a keen and difficult battle. We present here its two main systems.

I.

Sämisch Variation

1. d4 Nf6 2. c4 g6 3. Nc3 Bg7 4. e4 d6 5. f3

White occupies the centre with Pawns and tries to strengthen it. Black is preparing counterplay in the centre by means of e5 or c5.

5. ... 0-0 6. Be3 e5 7. d5

White may not close up the centre but continue 7. Nge2. In this case Black plays 7. ... c6, then at a convenient moment makes an exchange on d4 and with the move d5 liquidates the centre.

7. ... Nh5 8. Qd2 f5 9. 0-0-0

Castling on the other sides. A strenuous double-edged struggle is coming.

White is preparing the move g4 (after the exchange on f5) while Black strives, in his turn, to open a line on the Q-side.

II.

System With Development of the Bishop on g2

1. d4 Nf6 2. c4 g6 3. Nf3 Bg7 4. g3 d6 5. Bg2

In this variation both sides castle short.

5. ... 0-0 6. 0-0 Nbd7

The moves 6. ... c5 and 6. ... Nc6 are also met.

7. Nc3

Sometimes White plays 7. Qc2 e5 8. Rd1 in an effort to build pressure along the d-file.

7. ... e5 8. e4

White's play is freer but Black's pieces can put pressure on the c4, d4 and e4 points, obtaining significant counterplay.

The game below illustrates Black's possibilities for initiative.

BRANTS *VERESOV*

Byelorussian Championship, 1956

The first eight moves are the same as in the second of the above variations.

8. ... c6

More precise here is 8. ... Re8 9. h3 exd4 10. Nxd4 Nc5, striving to put pressure on the Pawn on e4.

9. h3 exd4 10. Nxd4 a5 11. Be3 Re8 12. Qc2 Nc5 13. Rad1 Nfd7

It would be a mistake to play 13. ... a4? because of 14. Nxc6! bxc6 15. Bxc5, winning a Pawn.

14. Rfel

Better is 14. Nb3! Qe7 15. Nxc5 16. f4, as was played in one of the games of Botvinnik-Smyslov match.

14. ... a4 15. Ne2 Qa5

Black sacrifices a Pawn, counting on an interesting combination.

16. Rxd6 Ne5 17. b3?

White should play 17. Rdd1, returning the Pawn.

17. ... axb3 18. axb3 Bxh3!

The start of an involved combination calculated far ahead. In the case of 19. Bxh3 there will follow Nf3+ 20. Kf1 Nxe1 21. Kxe1 Nxe4

22. Rd3 Nxc3 23. Nxc3 Qa1+ 24. Nd1 Ra2! and White loses his Queen.

19. b4 Bxg2!

Diagram 112

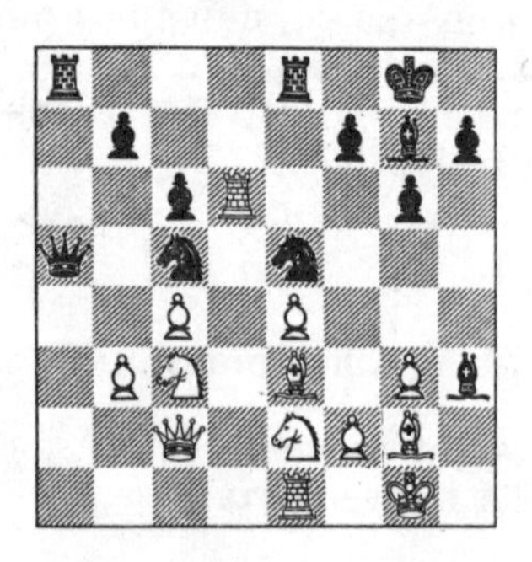

A clever reply! If now White plays 20. bxa5, there follows 20. ... Nf3+ 21. Kxg2 Nxe1+ 22. Kf1 Nxc2 and Black wins. In this combination the double blow theme is spectacular.

20. Rb1 Bxe4! 21. Nxe4 Qa4! 22. Qxa4 Nxa4

As a result of the combination Black wins a Pawn. White faces further inevitable losses.

23. Nf6+

White cedes another Pawn. The line of play 23. Rc1 Nb2! 24. c5 is bad because of 24. ... Nec4! 25. Nf6+ Bxf6 26. Rxf6 Nxe3, etc.

23. ... Bxf6 24. Rxf6 Nxc4.

Possessing two extra Pawns, Black wins easily.

LETELIER *FISCHER*

Leipzig, 1960

1. d4 Nf6 2. c4 g6 3. Nc3 Bg7 4. e4 0-0 5. e5

A premature advance that merely weakens White's centre. He should have continued to develop his pieces.

5. ... Ne8 6. f4 d6 7. Be3

More exact is 7. Nf3, although White cannot count on any advantage here either.

7. ... c5!

Black starts to undermine White's centre.

8. dxc5 Nc6

Black develops purposefully, not balking at sacrifices.

9. cxd6

A typical case of gobbling up Pawns. White should have thought about development and avoided opening the lines: 9. Nf3 Bg4 10. Be2.

9. ... exd6 10. Ne4

After this move White will never castle. 10. Nf3 is better.

10. ... Bf5! 11. Ng3

The lesser evil is 11. Nxd6 Nxd6 12. Qxd6 Qxd6 13. exd6 Bxb2 14. Rd1 Nb4! (threatening 15. ... Bc2) 15. Kf2 Nxa2 16. Ne2 a5, with advantage for Black, although White retains some chances of a draw.

11. ... Be6 12. Nf3 Qc7 13. Qb1 dxe5 14. f5

This thrust encounters an unexpected refutation.

14. ... e4! 15. fxe6

15. Nxe4 is bad because of 15. ... Bxf5, and if 15. Qxe4 there follows 15. ... gxf5! 16. Qh4 (16. Nxf5? Qa5+) Bxb2.

15. .. exf3 16. gxf3 f5! 17. f4 Nf6 18. Be2 Rfe8 19. Kf2 Rxe6

Black regains a Pawn while preserving the initiative.

20. Re1 Rae8 21. Bf3

White's King is barely covered, while his Queen and Rook stand far from the scene of the battle. Black is in possession of almost the entire board. No wonder he can launch a decisive combinational blow.

21. ... Rxe3! 22. Rxe3 Rxe3 23. Kxe3 Qxf4+!!

Diagram 113

An excellent combination for a decoy. If White takes the Queen, Black mates: 24. ... Bh6++. If 24. Kf2 there could follow 24. ... Ng4+ 25. Kg2 Ne3+ 26. Kf2 Nd4 27. Qh1 Ng4+ 28. Kf1 Nxf3 and Black wins. White resigns.

Nimzoindian Defence

1. d4 Nf6 2. c4 e6 3. Nf3 b6

This opening usually leads to calm play. In the main variation White develops the Bishop on g2.

4. g3 Bb7 5. Bg2 Be7

In reply to 5. ... Bb4+ it is best of all to play 6. Bd2 Bxd2+ 7. Qxd2 0-0 8. Nc3. The line 8. ... Ne4 9. Qc2 Nxc3 is bad due to 10. Ng5!

6. 0-0 0-0 7. Nc3 Ne4

7. ... d5 is weaker because of the unpleasant pin and the pressure on the Q-side, and if 7. ... d6 there will follow 8. Qc2! Nbd7 9. e4, with advantage for White in the centre.

8. Qc2 Nxc3 9. Qxc3

Here the combination with 9. Ng5 is refuted by 9. ... Nxe2+! 10. Qxe2 (or 10. Kh1 Bxg2+) 10. ... Bxg2 11. Kxg2 Bxg5, and Black wins.

9. ... f5

Black retains control over the e4-square, and the chances of the sides are approximately even.

Dutch Defence

1. d4 e6 2. c4 f5

In this opening, just as in the Queen's Gambit (1. d4 d5 2. c4 e6) or in the Nimzovitch's Defence (1. d4 Nf6 2. c4 e6 3. Nc3 Bb4) Black takes under his control the e4-square. Much more infrequently Black replies to 1. d4 with 1. ... f5 since White can successfully sacrifice a Pawn through 2. e4!

If after 1. d4 e6 White plays 2. e4 and Black replies 2. ... d5 the game boils down to the French Defence.

3. g3!

The best move, aiming at impeding development of the Bishop on c8. If Black replies 3. ... b6?, then after 4. Bg2 Nc6 5. d5! he will land in difficulties.

3. ... Nf6 4. Bg2 Be7 5. Nf3 0-0 6. 0-0

Now Black can play 6. ... d5 7. b3 c6, getting a firm but somewhat cramped position (it is difficult to put into play the Bishop on c8).

This is called the "Stonewall Variation." Another line after 6. ... d6 7. Nc3 Qe8 prepares for the advance e5.

In both variations Black encounters certain difficulties in developing his forces, and so the Dutch Defence is less popular than the Queen's Gambit or Indian openings.

English Opening

1. c4

This move is frequently used by strong players. In this flexible opening the play often boils down to already familiar variations of other openings (for instance, after 1. c4 e6 2. Nc3 d5 3. d4 the Queen's Gambit arises). Quite often after 1. c4 we see an Old Indian Defence or the Gruenfeld Defence. But if Black replies to 1. c4 with 1. ... c5 or 1. ... e5, the play assumes a specific character and it is called the English Opening.

We present here one of the possible development patterns.

1. ... e5 2. Nc3 d6 3. g3

After 3. Nf3 Nf6 4. d4 Nd7 5. g3 g6 the play boils down to the main variation of the Old Indian Defence.

3. ... Nc6 4. Bg2 g6 5. d3 Bg7 6. Nf3 Ne7 7. 0-0 0-0 8. Rb1

White plans the movement of the b-Pawn in order to gain an advantage on the Q-side. Black should prepare counterplay on the King's flank. (For instance, by moving the f-Pawn or playing Bd7, Qc8 and Bh3.)

Whereas in this variation White starts play on the Q-side, the next game is characteristic of White's initiative on the King's flank.

BOTVINNIK *PORTISCH*

International Tournament

Monte Carlo, 1968

1. c4 e5 2. Nc3 Nf6 3. g3 d5 4. cxd5 Nxd5 5. Bg2 Be6 6. Nf3 Nc6 7. 0-0 Nb6 8. d3 Be7

The variation played here reminds one of the position in the Sicilian Defence with the colours changed. Hence, White has sort of an extra tempo, as it were.

9. a3 a5

Black's move weakens the Q-side. It would be better to castle.

10. Be3 0-0 11. Na4 Nxa4 12. Qxa4 Bd5 13. Rfc1 Re8 14. Rc2 Bf8

The Bishop should have been placed on d6 to protect the Pawn on c7.

15. Rac1 Nb8

Portisch thought Botvinnik couldn't capture the Pawn on c7 and was preparing to strengthen the position with the move c6.

16. Rxc7! Bc6

Diagram 114

The impression here is that Black gets an advantage. White's Rook finds itself in a trap. Botvinnik, however, foresaw this turn of events. There follows a cascade of beautiful sacrifices!

17. R1xc6 bxc6 18. Rxf7!! h6

The Rook cannot be taken. In the case of 18. ... Kxf7 there will follow 19. Qc4+ Kg6 20. Qg4+ Kf7 21. Ng5 + Kg8 22. Qc4+ Kh8 23. Nf7+ Kg8 24. Nh6+ Kh8 25. Qg8++.

19. Rb7 Qc8 20. Qc4+ Kh8 21. Nh4!! Qxb7 22. Ng6+ Kh7 23. Be4!

There threatens 24. Ne7+ and 25. Qg8 mate. Black removes the Bishop to defend the g8 square.

23. ... Bd6 24. Nxe5+ g6

A comparatively better defence. If 24. ... Kh8 25. Nf7+ Kg8 26. Nxd6+, Black loses the Queen.

25. Bxg6+ Kg7 26. Bxh6+!

The final sacrifice that forces the victory.

Black resigns. In reply to 26. ... Kxh6 White will play 27. Qh4+ Kg7 28. Qh7+ Kf6 29. Ng4+! Ke6 30. Qxb7, and Black not only loses the Queen but suffers further losses. A beautiful game!

Réti Opening

1. Nf3

In the Réti Opening, just as in the English, the advance of the central Pawns is postponed until a suitable moment. First, the pieces developed and focussed on the central squares. Usually the Bishops are fianchettoed. All this is characteristic of relatively new openings that won popularity in recent years. Soviet chess players have made a big contribution to the theory of the opening.

1. ... d5 2. c4 c6

If 2. ... d4 it is best of all for White to play 3. b4 followed by 4. Bb2, attacking the presumptive Pawn. Besides 2. ... c6, frequently 2. ... e6 is played. 2. ... dxc4 is weaker because of 3. Na3.

3. b3 Nf6 4. Bb2 Bf5 5. g3 e6 6. Bg2 Nbd7 7. 0-0 h6

This is necessary in order, after 8. Nh4, to shift the Bishop to h7 to prevent an exchange.

8. d3 Be7 9. Nbd2 0-0

The main position of the Réti Opening. White can employ 10. Rc1 or 10. Re1, preparing for the move e4. Black's position, however, is so firm that it is not easy for White to develop initiative.

Sokolsky Opening

1. b4

Though we claim that White usually begins play with the central Pawns c, d and e, the move 1. b4 is by no means a violation of any opening principles. From the very first move White maps a plan for play on the Q-side and subordinates to it the entire further distribution of pieces and Pawns. Tournament practice has confirmed the vitality of this opening.

1. ... d5

Another continuation here is 1. ... e5, which, after 2. Bb2 f6 3. b5 d5 4. e3 Be6 5. d4 e4 6. Nd2 c6 7. a4 Bd6 8. c4, leads to a complicated struggle, with mutual chances.

2. Bb2 Nf6 3. e3

3. g3 with the subsequent development of the Bishop to g2 would be incorrect in this case because it would make it difficult for White to prepare the important move c4.

3. ... Bf5 4. Nf3 e6

The move 4. ... Nbd7 is weak because of 5. c4 dxc4 (in the case of 5. ... e6 White can reply 6. c5!) 6. Bxc4 e6 7. b5, gaining superior play.

5. c4 Nc6

It is bad to play 5. ... Bxb4 due to 6. Qa4+ Nc6 7. Nd4 Qd6 8. Nxc6 bxc6 9. a3 Bc5 10. d4. In reply to 5. ... Nbd7 or 5. ... Be7 White can continue 6. c5!

6. a3 dxc4

Otherwise there will follow 7. b5.

7. Bxc4 Bd3

If Black moves 7. ... Bd6 8. d4 he gives White an advantage in the centre.

8. Bxd3 Qxd3 9. Qe2

Black cannot hold the d3-square. Both an exchange of Queens and the retreat of Black's Queen give White a slight advantage.

SOKOLSKY — *STRUGACH*

Byelorussian Championship, 1958

1. b4 e5 2. Bb2 f6 3. e4

A gambit variation. In sacrificing the Pawn on b4 White strives to take advantage of the weakened position of Black's K-side after the move f6.

3. ... Bxb4

The acceptance of the sacrifice gives White an opportunity to develop a powerful attack. But he can also develop his initiative if Black refuses to take the Pawn on b4.

4. Bc4 Nc6

4. ... Ne7 is weaker due to 5. Qh5+ g6 (in the case of 5. ... Ng6, there can follow 6. f4 exf4 7. Nh3 Qe7 8. e5 fxe5 9. Ng5 with dangerous threats) 6. Qh4 Nec6 7. f4 Be7 8. f5! with an attack.

5. f4 exf4

Black has more chances for defence after 5. ... d6, followed by White's choice of moves between 6. f5 and c3.

6. Nh3 Nge7 7. Nxf4 Nxa5

A mistake in a difficult situation. However, it is not clear how Black could defend himself against the threat of 8. Qh5+ .

8. Bxf6! Rf8

If 8. ... gxf6 there would follow 9. Qh5+ Ng6 10. Nxg6 with an easy win. And if 8. ... Nxc4, then either 9. Bxg7 or 9. Qh5+ is possible.

9. Nh5! Nxc4

9. ... gxf6? is no good because of 10. Ng7++. As for 9. ... Rxf6, it could be followed by 10. Nxf6+ gxf6 11. Qh5+ Ng6 12. Rg8! Qe7 13. a3 Bc5 14. Bxh7 Qxe4+ 15. Kh1, and White wins.

10. Nxg7+ Kf7 11. 0-0 Ng8 12. Qh5

The most exact. 12. Qg4 is weaker due to 12. ... Rxf6 13. Rxf6 Ne5 14. Qg3 N7g6. In reply to 12. Nh5 Black will play 12. ... Qe8! Now there already threatens 13. Qg5.

12. ... Rxf6 13. Rxf6 Ng6 14. Rxg6! hxg6 15. Qxg6 Kh8

In the case of 15. ... Ne5 White, continuing 16. Qg3 Qf6 17. Nh5+ Qg6 18. Qxe5 d6 19. Qg3!, remains with two extra Pawns.

16. Ne8!

This is stronger than 16. Nh5, for Black will reply 16. ... Qg8!

If 16. Nf5 Black, continuing 16. ... Qf8, could also put up resistance.

16. ... Qe7

After 16. ... Bc5+ 17. Kh1 Bd4 18. Qh5+ (18. c3 is also good) 18. ... Kg8 19. Qd5+ Black loses.

17. Nf6. Black resigns.

VI. SHORT GAMES AND TRAPS

The following short games will help the beginner to gain a better mastery of the main principles of the opening by acquainting him with typical mistakes, elementary traps and combinations. But first a few words about the names of *openings*.

The word "opening" is used to designate both the first stage of the game and also opening systems, of which there are many. Some of their names are geographical, such as the Vienna Game, English Opening, the Sicilian Defence, etc. Some are named after players who did much to develop them, for instance, Alekhine Defence and the Réti Opening. And some are purely of a chess nature: Bishop's Opening, Two Knights' Defence, Queen Pawn Game, etc.

THE PERFIDIOUS PIN

Caro-Kann Defence

KERES *ARLAMOVSKY*

Szczawno Zdroj, 1950

1. e4 c6

Black is paving the way for d5. This opening was invented in the 19th century by two German players, Caro and Kann.

2. Nc3 d5 3. Nf3 dxe4 4. Nxe4 Nf6 5. Qe2 Nbd7?? 6. Nd6++

It goes without saying that Black cannot take the Knight because of the pin on the e-file, Black's own pieces deprive the King of all squares for retreat. This situation is called *smothered mate.*

Diagram 115

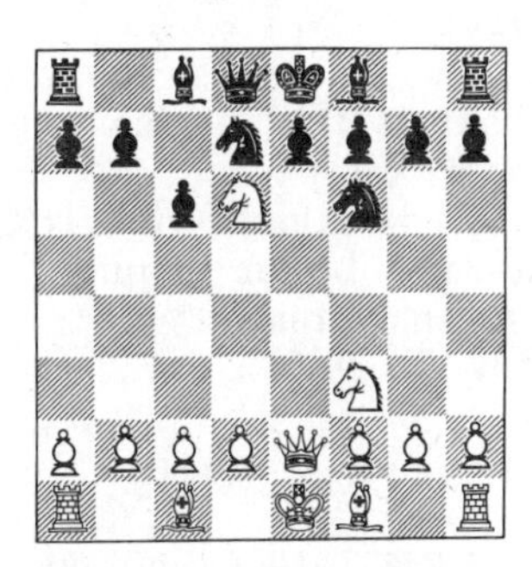

ATTENTION: SQUARE f7!

Ufimtsev (Pirc-Robatsch) Defence

HAMLISH *AMATEUR*

Vienna, 1899

1. e4 d6
2. d4 Nd7

An inexactitude. Black usually plays here 2. ... g6, without hurrying to develop the Q-Knight.

3. Bc4 g6 4. Nf3 Bg7?

Black has no suspicion of the danger in store.

5. Bxf7+!! Kxf7

Better 5. ... Nf8, though in this case, too, after 6. Ng5 Black's outlook is poor.

6. Ng5+ Kf6

Black did not want to retreat with the King to f8 because of the fork 7. Ne6+, and after 6. ... Ke8 decisive is 7. Ne6, catching the Queen. But there follows 7. Qf3++.

AN ILL-STARRED QUEEN

Scandinavian Defence

1. e4 d5

The early move of the d-Pawn is the characteristic feature of the Scandinavian Defence.

2. exd5 Qxd5 3. Nc3

Black now has to lose a tempo to remove the Queen. That is the shortcoming of the defence.

3. ... Qa5 4. d4 Nf6 5. Bd2 Nc6?

A mistake. It is better to play 5. ... c6, ensuring the Queen retreat.

6. Bb5 Bd7 7. Nd5!

Diagram 116

Now Black is compelled to cede the Queen, after which, of course, the game is lost.

7. ... Qxb5 8. Nxc7+

Such a double blow is called a *fork*.

8. ... Kd8 9. Nxb5. Black resigns.

A SUDDEN ENCIRCLEMENT

Scotch Game

FRASER *TAUBENHAUS*

Paris, 1888

1. e4 e5 2. Nf3 Nc6 3. d4

This old opening was named Scotch Game after Scotch players used it with success in a correspondence match between Edinburgh and London in 1824.

3. ... exd4 4. Nxd4 Qh4 5. Nc3

The sacrifice of the Pawn 5. Nb5!, which gives White a strong attack, is considered the best reply to the Queen's thrust.

5. ... Nf6?

A mistake. 5. ... Bb4 should be played.

6. Nf5! Qh5 7. Be2 Qg6 8. Nh4. Black resigns.

A MISTAKEN RAID

Caro-Kann Defence

BOTVINNIK *SPIELMANN*

Moscow, 1935

1. e4 c6 2. d4 d5 3. exd5 cxd5 4. c4 Nf6 5. Nc3 Nc6 6. Bg5 Qb6

At that time a new move in this situation. The venerable Austrian player, Grandmaster R. Spielmann, prepared it especially for his encounter with the young Soviet champion. However, 6. ... Qb6 is unsatisfactory mainly because Black tries to attack with the Queen alone instead of developing his pieces.

7. cxd5 Qxb2?

A losing move. It was discovered later that it is better to take a different Pawn: 7. ... Nxd4, but even in this case after 8. Nge2! Nf5! 9. Qd2 Nd6 10. Be3 Qa5 11. Ng3 White's position is superior. Of course Spielmann knew very well that such deep raids by the Queen into the opponent's position were very dangerous in the opening, but what ruined him was a mistake made during home analysis. Evidently, he thought White had to play 8. Na4 and hoped to obtain attack after 8. ... Qb4+ 9. Bd2 Qxd4 10. dxc4 Ne4 11. Be3 Qb4+ 12. Ke2 bxc4!

8. Rc1!

Diagram 117

A move which Black did not expect but is logical: instead of a dubious chase after material advantage White strengthens his position decisively. No matter how the Knight now retreats from the c6-square Black loses:

1) 8. ... Nb8 9. Na4 Qb4+ 10. Bd2, winning the Bishop on c8.

2) 8. ... Na5 9. Qa4+, and the Knight on a5 perishes.

3) 8. ... Nd8 9. Bxf6 exf6 10. Bb5+ Bd7 11. Rc2 Qb4 12. Qe2+! Be7 13. Bxd7+ Kxd7 14. Qg4+, with a winning attack.

8. ... Nb4 9. Na4 Qxa2 10. Bc4 Bg4 11. Nf3 Bxf3 12. gxf3. Black resigns.

The Queen is trapped, and in order to free it a piece has to be given away (12. ... Qa3 13. Rc3 Kc2+).

THE EXULTANT KNIGHT

Giuoco Piano

MÖLOCK *KOSTIĆ*

Cologne, 1912

1. e4 e5 2. Nf3 Nc6 3. Bc4 Nd4

A pure decoy move. Of course, Grandmaster Kostić knows his move is by no means the best. Playing 4. c3 Nxf3+ 5. Qxf3, White outstrips Black in development. Also good are both 4. Nxd4, doubling Black's central Pawns, and the simple 4. d3. However, the Grandmaster counts on his opponent being tempted by a Pawn.

4. Nxe5? Qg5! 5. Nxf7?

This capture is a mistake too. 5. Ng4 is also bad because of 5. ... d5!, with a Pawn attack against the Bishop on c4 and Knight on g4. It is better to play 5. Bxf7+ Kd8 6. 0-0 Qxe5 7. c3 and then 8. d4. White gets some compensation for the lost piece.

5. ... Qxg2 6. Rf1

Or 6. Nxh8 Qxh1+ 7. Bf1 Qxe4+ 8. Be2 Nxc2+, and Black wins (in the case of 9. Kf1?? mate follows: 9. ... Qh1++).

6. ... Qxe4+ 7. Be2? Nf3++

Smothered mate.

OPENING FINESSE

Caro-Kann Defence

LASKER *MÜLLER*

1934

1. e4 c6 2. Nc3 d5 3. Nf3 dxe4 4. Nxe4 Bf5?

White refrains from d4 and thanks to the saved tempo develops his K-Knight. In the circumstances Black's last move is a mistake. The correct move is 4. ... Bg4. Also 4. ... Nd7 or 4. ... Nf6 is possible.

5. Ng3 Bg6?

Better to play 5. ... Bg4 6. h3 Bxf3 7. Qxf3 e6.

6. h4! h6

Otherwise there would follow h5, winning the Bishop.

7. Ne5! Bh7 8. Qh5!

Diagram 118

Threatens mate on f7. White repeats this four times in a row.

8. ... g6 9. Qf3

Also very powerful is 9. Bc4 e6 10. Qe2 (threatoning 11. Nxf7 Kxf7 12. Qxe6++) 10. ... Qe7 with an overwhelming position for White.

9. ... Nf6

9. ... Qd5 is out because of 10. Qxd5 cxd5 11. Bd5+.

10. Qb3! Qd5 11. Qxb7 Qxe5+ 12. Be2 Qd6

There threatens 13. Qc8++.

13. Qxa8 Qc7

Black hopes to catch White's Queen.

14. a4!

To bring the Rook on a1 so as to come to the Queen's aid by the shortest route.

14. ... Bg7 15. Ra3 0-0 16. Rb3. White wins.

A player naturally wants to accept, and keep, the offered sacrifice of a Pawn. The cunning trap in the Queen's Gambit is based on that.

A POISONED PAWN

1. d4 d5 2. c4 dxc4

This opening is called the Queen's Gambit Accepted.

3. e3 b5?

It would be better not to try to hold on to the Pawn and continue 3. ... e6 4. Bxc4 c5! Also good is 3. ... e5.

4. a4! c6?

Not, of course, 4. ... a6 because of axb5, Black cannot take the Pawn on b5 since the Rook on a8 is not protected. Relatively better is 4. ... bxa4 5. Bxc4 e6, agreeing to return the captured Pawns.

5. axb5 cxb5? 6. Qf3!

Diagram 119

What is to be done? The Rook is under attack while there is nothing to defend it with. The lesser evil is to give up the Knight (6. ... Nc6

7. Qxc6+ Bd7). By chasing after a Pawn Black thus loses a piece.

Another trap in the Queen's Gambit leads to an unexpected defeat. The main hero here is a black Pawn.

A KNIGHT BETTER THAN A QUEEN

1. d4 d5 2. c4 e5 3. dxe5 d4

This opening with a Pawn sacrifice is called the Albin Counter-Gambit.

4. e3?

The line of play recommended by Tchigorin, 4. Nf3 Nc6 5. g3, is better.

4. ... Bb4+ 5. Bd2 dxe3!

Black evidently made a blunder. We'll take the Bishop.

6. Bxb4?

The gift shouldn't be accepted, as Black's reply shows. The best move is 6. fxe3, even though the Pawns are doubled.

6. ... exf2+ 7. Ke2

The Pawn on f2 should not be taken since White's Queen will be defenceless. Now comes a surprise!

7. ... fxg1N+!

Diagram 120

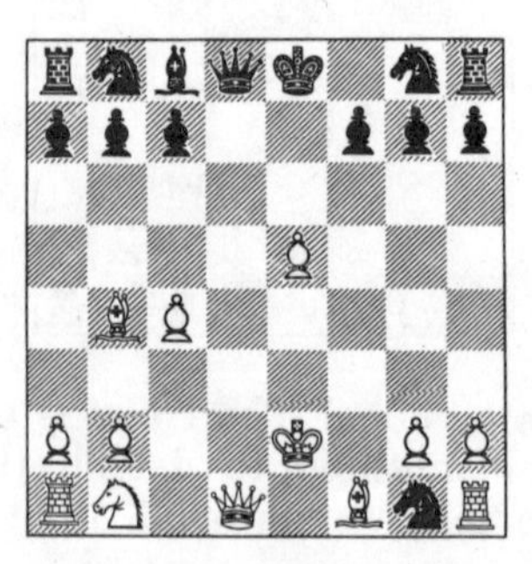

A rare case! Though there is a full set of chessmen on the board, a Black Pawn reaches the first rank and, promoted to a Knight, inflicts a deathly blow by checking the King. Queening of the Pawn is considerably weaker. In the case of 7. ... fxgQ White can exchange Queens by playing Qxd8+, and after 8. ... Kxd8 can gobble up the newly appointed Queen.

8. Rxg1 Bg4+. Black wins.

"MODERNISED LÉGAL MATE"

Philidor's Defence

CHÉRON — *AMATEUR*

1929

1. e4 e5 2. Nf3 Nc6 3. Bc4 d6 4. Nc3 Bg4 5. h3!

This game was played in a simultaneous exhibition. A. Chéron, a many-time champion of France and well-known theoretician, sets his opponent a clever trap.

5. ... Bh5?

After 5. ... Bxf3 6. Qxf3 Nf6 (defending himself against mate on f7) 7. d3 White stands better but the battle is still in the offing.

6. Nxe5!

Now this Queen sacrifice à la Légal is entirely correct.

6. ... Bxd1??

Black should reconcile himself to the loss of the Pawn after 6. ... Nxe5 7. Qxh5 Nxc4 8. Qb5+ and 9. Qxc4.

7. Bxf7+ Ke7 8. Nd5++.

PSEUDOSACRIFICE

Three Knights' Game

CAPABLANCA *AMATEUR*

USA, 1914

1. e4 e5 2. Nf3 Nc6 3. Nc3 Bc5

This move allows White to put through favourable opening combination that is well known in theory under the name of *pseudosacrifice.* It is carried out in different openings.

4. Nxe5 Nxe5

Black could deprive White of the chance to castle by replying 4. ... Bxf2+, but after 5. Kxf2 Nxe5 6. d4! White captures the centre and gets an even better position than in this game.

5. d4

A double blow by a Pawn is also called a *fork.*

5. ... Bxd4

After 5. ... Bd6 6. dxe5 Bxe5 White has good play too.

6. Qxd4 Qf6

Threatening to win the Queen by the move 7. ... Nf3+.

7. Nb5!

A very powerful move: the Knight defends the Queen and attacks the c7 point.

7. ... Kd8?

A crucial mistake in a poor situation. Black should continue 7. ... c6, to which White replies 8. Nd6+ with a big positional advantage (but not 8. Nc7+? Kd8, with the threats 9. ... Kxc7 and 9. ... Nf3+, winning the Queen!).

8. Qc5!

A double attack against the points c7 and f8.

8. ... Nc6??

Saving the Pawn but mate follows : 9. Qf8++.

Diagram 121

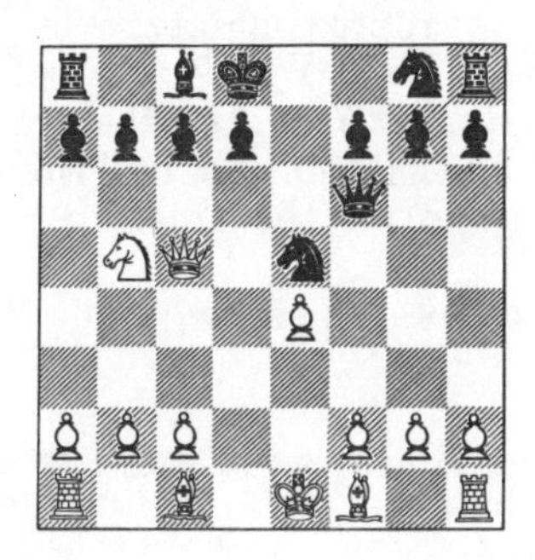

Exercise.

Demonstrate that Black has no satisfactory defence in the position in Diagram 121.

THE QUEEN AS A SPECTATOR

Dutch Defence

RÉTI — *EUWE*

Rotterdam, 1920

1. d4 f5

Black takes the e4-square under control, preventing White from creating a Pawn centre. This opening was named the Dutch Defence.

2. e4

The Staunton Gambit, invented by the outstanding 19th-century English player Howard Staunton.

2. ... fxe4 3. Nc3 Nf6 4. Bg5

The sharper 4. f3 is also used. White does not strive to regain the Pawn but opens lines for attack.

4. ... g6

Better 4. ... Nc6.

5. f3!

After 5. Bxf6 exf6 6. Nxe4 d5 7. Ng3 Bd6 the position is approximately even.

5. ... exf3 6. Nxf3 Bg7 7. Bd3 c5

Fearing that after 7. ... 0-0 there would follow 8. Qd2, and then 0-0-0 and h4, Black launches active operations on the Queen in the centre.

8. d5 Qb6

Continuation of the same plan. 8. ... d6 is better.

9. Qd2!

Encouraging Black, as it were, to attack with the Queen alone.

9. ... Qxb2?

This loses. It isn't too late to play 9. ... d6.

10. Rb1! Nxd5

If 10. ... Qa3, there follows 11. Nb5 Qxa2 12. 0-0 with an irresistible attack. After the next move the impression is that Black's precocious attack is successful: he has three extra Pawns and powerful threats.

Diagram 122

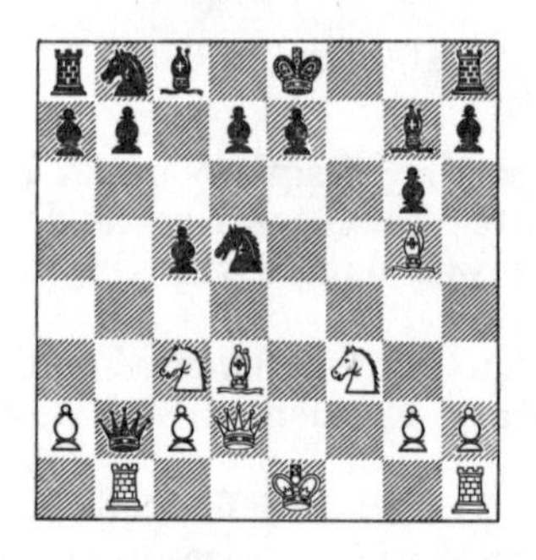

11. Nxd5!!.

Vengeance!

11. ... Qxb1+ 12. Kf2 Qxh1

Black's Queen is safe and sound but is stuck in the farthest corner of the board and is fated to look on helplessly as White's excellently developed pieces make short shrift of Black's King within several moves.

13. Bxe7 d6 14. Bxd6 Nc6 15. Bb5 Bd7 16. Bxc6 bxc6 17. Qe2+.

Black resigns.

After 17. ... Kd8 18. Bc7+ or 17. ... Kf7 18. Ng5+ Kg8 19. Ne7+ Kf8 20. Nxg6+, mate is inevitable.

Here the outstanding Czech Grandmaster Richard Réti (1889-1929) gave the young Max Euwe, a future world champion, an instructive lesson in opening strategy.

ROAMING KING

Two Knights' Defence

MORPHY *AMATEUR*

New Orleans, 1858

1. e4 e5 2. Nf3 Nc6 3. Bc4 Nf6 4. d4 exd4 5. Ng5

The correct move is 5. 0-0

5. ... d5

More powerful here is 5. ... Ne5, with equal play for Black.

6. exd5 Nxd5?

It is not too late to move 6. ... Ne5.

7. 0-0 Be7

If 7. ... Be6, then 8. Re1 Qd7 (8. ... Be7 9. Rxe6 fxe6 10. Nxe6 followed by 11. Qh5+ and 12. Qxd5) 9. Nxf7 Kxf7 (9. ... Qxf7 10 Bxd5) 10. Qf3+ Kg8 11. Rxe6, winning.

8. Nxf7! Kxf7 9. Qf3+ Ke6 10. Nc3!

Another sacrifice to open the d-file.

10. ... dxc3

Forced move.

11. Rel+ Ne5 12. Bf4! Bf6 13. Bxe5 Bxe5

Diagram 123

14. Rxe5+!

The third and decisive sacrifice!

14. ... Kxe5 15. Re1+ Kd4

If 15. ... Kd6, then comes 16. Qxd5++.

16. Bxd5 Re8

In case of 16. ... Qd5 there follows 17. Qxc3++ If 16. ... cxb2, then 17. Re4+ Kc5 (17. ... Kxd5 18. Qd3+, etc.) 18. Qa3+ Kxd5 (If 18. ... Kb5 or 18. Kb6, then 19. Qb4+ Ka6 20. Bc4+ b5 21. Qxb5++.) 19. Qd3+ Ke5 20. Rc4+.

17. Qd3+ Kc5 18. b4+!

The shortest road.

18. ... Kxb4

If 18. ... Kb6, then 19. Qd4+ Ka6 20. Qc4+.

19. Qd4+ Ka5 20. Qc3+ Ka4 21. Qb3+ Ka5 22. Qa3+ Kb5 23. Rb1++

This game was played during a blindfold simultaneous exhibition on six boards.

UNPLEASANT SURPRISE

Ruy Lopéz

TARRASCH *MARCO*

Dresden, 1892

1. e4 e5 2. Nf3 Nc6 3. Bb5

Way back in the 15th and 16th centuries the

outstanding Spanish players Lucena and Lopéz were interested in this opening.

3. ... d6

A system of play for Black that was introduced by the first world champion Wilhelm Steinitz. The Steinitz Defence gives Black a somewhat cramped but firm position.

4. d4 Bd7 5. 0-0 Nf6 6. Nc3 Be7 7. Re1

Up to this point Black does not have to worry about his Pawn on e5. White's attempt to win it would lead simultaneously to loss of the Pawn on e4. However, White's last move changes matters: real danger threatens the Pawn on e5.

7. ... 0-0?

The correct move is 7. exd4. Now Marco falls victim to the novelty prepared by his famous opponent, one of the leading grandmasters at the end of the last century.

8. Bxc6 Bxc6 9. dxe5 dxe5 10. Qxd8 Rxd8

There is no salvation in 10. ... Rfxd8 11. Nxe5 Bxe4 12. Nxe4 Nxe4 13. Nd3 f5 14. f3 Bc5+ 15. Kf1!, and White wins.

11. Nxe5 Bxe4 12. Nxe4 Nxe4

Everything seems to be in order, for 13. Rxe4 is impossible because of Rd1+. But—

13. Nd3 f5

The only move left.

14. f3 Bc5+

Hoping for 15. Kf1 Bb6 16. fxe4 fxe4+, regaining a piece.

15. Nxc5! Nxc5 16. Bg5! (see Diagram 124).

The crux!

16. ... Rd5

Defending the Knight against the double blow 17. Be7

17. Be7. Black resigns.

If 17. ... Rfe8 (f7), then 18. c4, winning the exchange.

Diagram 124

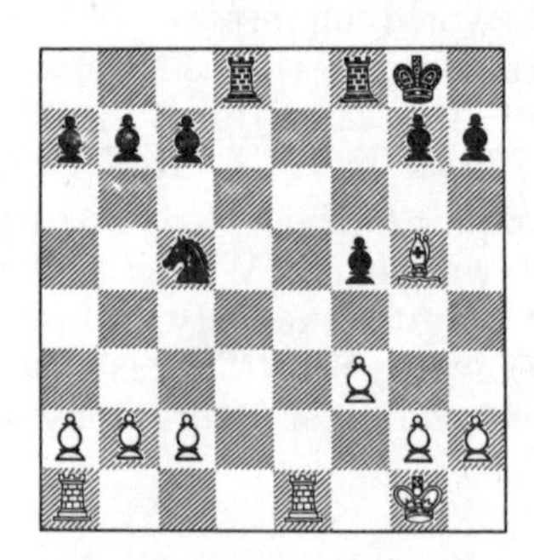

VII. MIDDLE GAME

TYPICAL COMBINATIONS

Combinations hold a special place in creative chess. It is in the field of combinations that such qualities as originality of thought, fantasy and capability for deep calculation manifest themselves.

The definition cited earlier correctly conveys the substance of combinations but bypasses some important features. A combination is always something unexpected that changes the habitual course of the game. Em. Lasker, the second world champion, stressed that it evokes an unexpected reassessment of values. Amplifying this idea, Mikhail Botvinnik says: "From the very first steps the chess player adapts himself to the habitual material correlation between chessmen. However, there are positions in which these correlations cease to function, in which the Queen, for instance, proves to be weaker than a Pawn. The path to such positions leads through sacrifices."

Another feature of combinations is their high aesthetic value. The beauty of chess manifests itself in many different ways, but most frequently in its combinations. At the same time, as we have seen, the shortest road to victory lies through a combination. Combinational vision, that is, the ability to discover a combination, is therefore an important quality which the player must work steadily to develop and improve.

Despite the inexhaustible variety of fine combinations that have been carried out, scholars noted long ago that there is a more or less limited number of typical ideas. This chapter introduces you to these ideas as embodied in relatively simple combinations. To master typical combinations you must develop combinational vision.

Bear in mind that there is no generally recognised classification of typical combinations, and that usually one combination includes several (if not many) typical ideas.

MATE ON THE FIRST TWO AND LAST TWO RANKS

Frequently, mate is carried out by a Rook or Queen on the last rank.

Diagram 125

The Pawns on the second and seventh ranks block White's King and Black's King. White will play 1. Qxe5 Rxe5 2. Rd8+ Re8 3. Rxe8++ If Black has the move, he mates thus: 1. ... Qe1+! 2. Rxe1 Rxe1++.

This is elementary, of course. An experienced chess player would not allow such a finale. Nonetheless, this kind of mate on the first or eighth rank occurs, and at times quite unexpectedly.

At the 33rd USSR Championship (1965) the following position arose in the Mikenas versus Bronstein game.

Diagram 126

It is Black's move. What struck him was the possibility of declaring check: 24. ... Qe1+? If White hastily takes the Queen 25. Rxe1? then after 25. ... Rxe1+ he is mated. If, however, White is not tempted by the offered gift and replies 25. Qf1! Black won't achieve anything. What a surprise it was for the spectators watching the game when Bronstein delivered a brilliant combinational blow: 24. ... Rxa3!!, after which White resigned at once. Indeed, just as in the case of 25. bxa3 Qxa1+ 26. Qd1 Qxd1+ 27. Bxd1 Re1++, White is mated on the first rank after 25. Qxa3 Qe1+! or 25. Qd1 Rxa1 26. Qxa1 Qe1+.

A beautiful ending was in the Cherepkov versus Sazonov game in 1967 (see Diagram 127).

Here too Black puts through a combination with mate on the first rank: 29. ... Bxe4! 30. Rxe4 Rxd4!! 31. Nf3 (in case of the capture of Black's Rook there will follow 31. ... Qc1+) 31. ... Rexe4! White resigns.

Diagram 127

Diagram 128

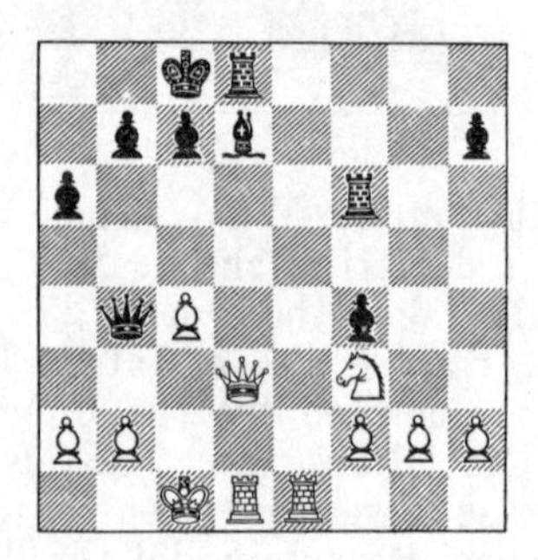

Exercise.

Find a decisive combination for White.

It is highly important for White to dominate the seventh rank with his major pieces. He often strives to build up mating threats on the seventh and eighth ranks.

The instructive example below comes from a game between Boleslavsky and Gottes in Hamburg in 1960 (see Diagram 129).

White's Rook gets on the seventh rank. How is this circumstance to be exploited? Boleslavsky plays 26. Bxe8 Rxe8 (not 26. ... Kxe8 because of 27. Rxg7).

Diagram 129

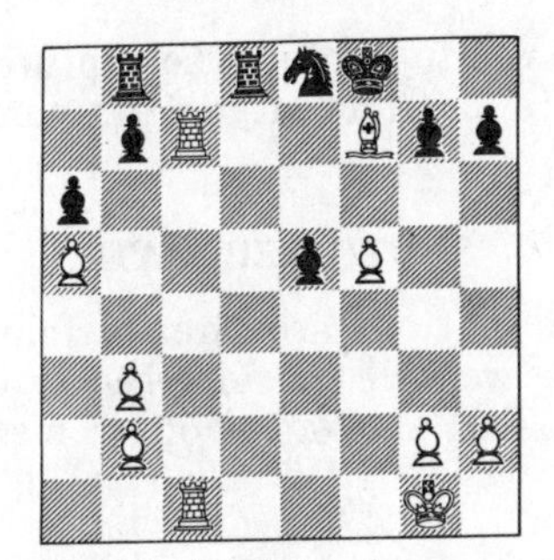

27. f6! gxf6 28. Rxh7 e4

Black cannot prevent the second Rook from penetrating to the seventh rank. Both after 28. ... Re7? 29. Rh8+, and after 28. ... Rec8? 29. Rxc8+ Rxc8 30. Rh8+, he loses a Rook.

29. Rcc7 Kg8

Otherwise 30. Rh8++.

30. Kf2 b6 31. h4!

If Black doesn't do anything about it White will push the Pawn up to h6 and declare mate in two moves: Rcg7+ and Rh8++.

31. ... Rbd8 32. Rcg7+ Kf8 33. Ke1 e3 34. axb6 e2 35. Rgd7!, preventing the Rook's check on d1.

35. ... Rdc8? 36. Rh8++.

Diagram 130

Exercise.

How can White exploit the capture of the seventh rank to conduct a mating combination?

SMOTHERED MATE

Such combinations are already familiar to the reader. Here we will consider the type of smothered mate that is most often met in actual play.

Diagram 131

What initial move should be picked? It is a mistake to play 1. Qf7+? Black's King will go to h8. With a correct continuation White mates within five moves.

1. Qc4+ Kh8

Not 1. ... Kf8? 2. Qf7++.

2. Nf7+ Kg8 3. Nh6+

Double check.

3. ... Kh8 4. Qg8+ Rxg8 5. Nf7++.

An impressive combination with a Queen sacrifice and a final position in which the lone Knight mates the King blocked by his own pieces.

Diagram 132

Exercise.

White to play and to produce a smothered mate.

THE "WHEEL"

The "Wheel" based on alternating checks and discovered checks declared by the attacking side, is a spectacular combination. The ending of the C. Torre versus E. Lasker game in Moscow in 1925, in Diagram 133, provides a classic example.

Diagram 133

In this position Torre, sacrificing the Queen, played:

1. Bf6!! Qxh5 2. Rxg7+ Kh8 3. Rxf7+

Discovered check. White could have regained the Queen right off through 3. Rg5+, but he prefers to capture the Bishop and Pawn first.

3. ... Kg8 4. Rg7+! Kh8 5. Rxb7+ Kg8 6. Rg7+ Kh8 7. Rg5+! Kh7 8. Rxh5 Kg6 9. Rh3 White resigns.

After 9. ... Kxf6 10. Rxh6+ White has three extra Pawns.

Diagram 134

Exercise.

How can the "Wheel" Combination be carried out in this position?

TRAPPING COMBINATIONS

In this situation (see Diagram 135) from the Vidmar-Euwe game (Karlsbad, 1929) Black threatens to mate with 1. ... Qh2++, but it is White's move. After 1. Qf8+!! Black resigns in view of inevitable mate: 1. ... Kh7 2. Qg7++ or 1. ... Kxf8 2. Rd8++. In the last variation White *lures* Black's King to the f8-square, where he is mated.

Diagram 135

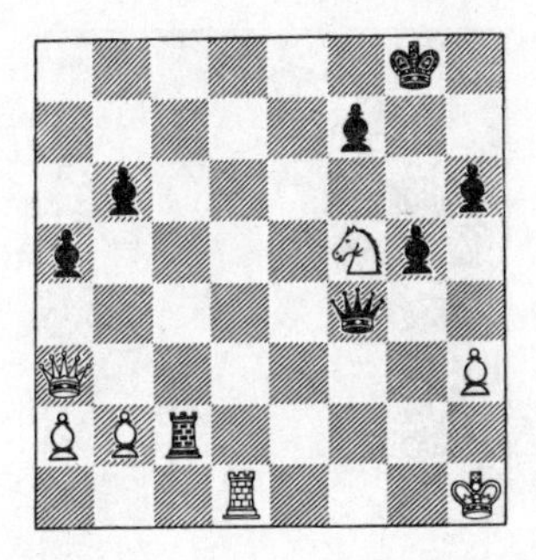

These combinations attract opposing pieces to disadvantageous squares.

Here, in Diagram 136, is the finale of one of L. Kubbel's endgame studies:

Diagram 136

1. Qa3+ !!, and White wins. Through a Queen sacrifice he draws the Black King a square that means death for him, the a3 square (1. ... Kxa3 2. Nc2++). Any retreat by the King leads to loss of the Queen.

Exercise (see Diagram 137).

Find a win for White by a trapping combination.

Diagram 137

DIVERSION

These combinations aim at drawing an opposing piece (or Pawn) away from protecting an important point or line.

A brilliant example is the ending, in Diagram 138, of a game played by Vera Menchik (White), the first woman champion of the world, against Sonya Graf-Stevenson.

Diagram 138

It is tempting to play 1. Qxh5? and in case of 1. ... gxh5, 2. Bh7++. But Black can reply 1. ... Qxh2+! and, exchanging Queens, beat back the attack. White moves 1. Rd7!! (diversion)

1. ... Qxd7 2. Qxh5!!, and Black resigns in view of inevitable mate.

In the Adams versus Torre game in New Orleans in 1920 white repeatedly and effectively exploits the blocked situation of Black's King on the last rank.

Diagram 139

1. Qg4!

To divert Black's Queen from defending the e8 square.

1. ... Qb5

The one and only move. After 1. ... Qxg4 Black is mated in two moves. 2. Rxe8+ Rxe8 3. Rxe8++. Now Black threatens 2. ... Qxe2! 3. Rxe2 Rc1+ 4. Ne1 Rxe1+ Rxe1 Rxe1++.

2. Qc4!

Another Queen sacrifice with the aim of *diverting* Black's Queen or Rook on c8 from defending the e8-square.

2. ... Qd7

Again the one and only move.

3. Qc7!

A third diversion! The Queen is still invulnerable.

3. ... Qb5 4. a4!

But not 4. Qxb7? Qxe2, and Black wins.

4. ... Qxa4 5. Re4 Qb5

Black lacks time to open an outlet 5. ... h6 (g6)? in order, after 6. Rxa4 to reply with 6. ... Rxe1+ and 7. ... Rxc7 because of 6. Qxc8! Qxe4 7. Qxe8+, winning the Rook .

6. Qxb7! Black resigns.

Black's Queen has no square for retreat along the a4-e8 diagonal, and the Rook on e8 is left defenceless.

Diagram 140

Exercise.

Find a combination for White resembling the preceding one.

BLOCKING COMBINATIONS

These restrict the mobility of opposing pieces, usually the King, by closing off their road to important squares or lines. The smothered mate is a variety of this type.

The position in Diagram 141 comes from the Kotov versus Bondarevsky game in Leningrad in 1936.

1. ... f4+!

Diverting the Knight from the f2-square and blocking the f4-square.

Diagram 141

2. Nxf4 Qf2+ 3. Kd3 Qxd4+!! 4. Kxd4 Bxc5+ 5. Kd3 Nxe5++.

Despite White's big material advantage, three minor pieces of Black prove to be stronger than White's whole army!

Diagram 142

In this endgame study by A. Troitsky White employs a block to press and win Black's Bishop.

1. f6! gxf6 2. Kb7 Bd8 3. Kc8 Be7 4. Kd7 Bf8 5. Be3+

To deprive Black's Bishop of the h6-square.

5. ... Kc2 6. Ke8 Bg7 7. Kxf7 Bh8 8. Kg8 White wins, queening the g-Pawn.

Diagram 143

Exercise.

Find a blocking combination for Black.

OBSTRUCTION

In an obstruction a player usually cuts off through the sacrifice of a piece or a Pawn, an important section of the board from the opposing forces protecting it.

Diagram 144

The position in Diagram 144 arose in the L. Polugayevsky versus L. Maslov game in the Third USSR Games in 1963.

1. Rd5!!

An excellent move on the obstruction theme! An important diagonal that was guarded by the Bishop on c4 is cut. Now there arise two threats: 2. Ne6+ or 2. Bxf6!

1. ... Nxd5 2. Be6! Rxe6

Or 2. fxe5 fxe5+ 3. Bxf1 4. Qg8+ Ke7 5. Qf7++.

3. Nxe6+ Ke7 4. Nd4! Qc5 5. Qxg7+ Ke8 6. Qxg6+ Ke7 7. Rf2 fxe5 8. Qe6+ Kf8 9. fxe5+. Black resigns.

Diagram 145

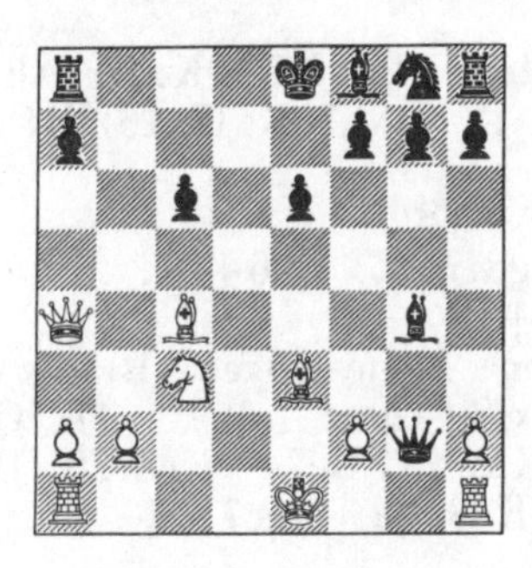

Exercise.

Find an obstruction combination enabling White to gain material advantage while preserving a powerful attack.

COMBINATIONS TO DESTROY DEFENCE FORCES

In these combinations an opponent's pieces or Pawns important for his defence are destroyed with the aid of sacrifices.

Diagram 146 shows a position from the Sokolsky versus Kofman game in Kiev in 1948.

Diagram 146

There follows 14. Nf7! Kxf7. Also losing is 14. ... Rg8 15. Qxh7 Kxf7 16. Rf1+ Ke8 17. Qxg8.

15. Rf1+ Ke8

15. ... Kg8?? 16. Qe6++.

16. Rxf8+!

The defence is destroyed! Black resigns.

If 16. Kxf8, there follows 17. Qxe7+ Kg8 18. Qe6+ Kf8 19. Be7+ Ke8 20. Bxd6+ Kd8 21. Qe7+ Kc8 22. Qxc7++.

Diagram 147

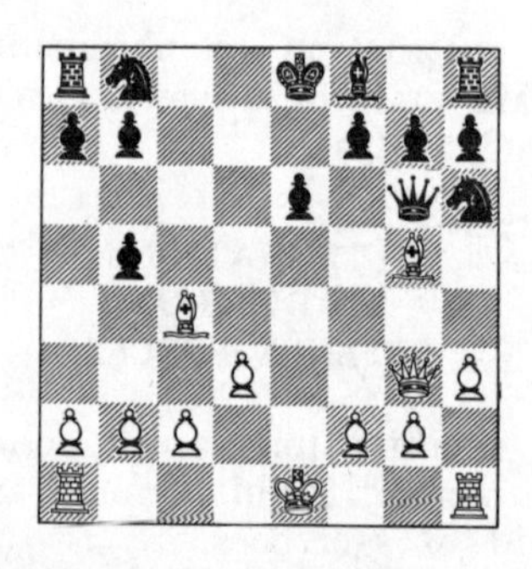

Exercise.

White mates in two moves.

SQUARE CLEARANCE COMBINATIONS

The player's aim is to free a square he needs for another of his pieces.

The example in Diagram 148 comes from a game played by Alekhine.

Diagram 148

Can Black's Queen be taken? At first glance this capture seems to be a loss because Black's Pawn will be queened. Alekhine, however, played 1. Rxf2! gxf2 2. Rxf5!! Kxf5 3. g4+! The solution of the riddle. The Pawn moved ahead with a check, freeing the g2 square for White's King. 3. ... Kxg4 4. Kg2 and White won by holding up the Pawn on f2.

Diagram 149

Exercise

White to play and mate in two by freeing an important square for himself.

LINE CLEARANCE COMBINATIONS

Here a player sacrifices a piece (or Pawn) standing in the path of another piece to enable the latter to deliver a decisive blow.

Diagram 150

The situation in Diagram 150 arose in the Romanovsky versus Rabinovich game in Moscow in 1935. There follows:

1. Bb5!!

White frees the d1-h5 diagonal, gaining a tempo and creating the double threat 2. Bxd7 and 2. Rxh7+! Kxh7 3. Qh5+ Bh6 4. Qxh6++.

1. ... Bh6

There is no other defence.

2. Bxd7 Bxg5 3. exd5 Rd8 4. Rxh7+ Kxh7 5. Qh5+ Bh6 6. Rh4 Ng4 7. Rxg4 Rxg4 8. Qxg4 Rxd7 9. f6! Black resigns.

If 9. ... Rc7?, then comes 10. Qe4+! K∽ 11. fxe7, winning. If 9. ... e6, there follows 10. dxe6 fxe6, 11. Qxe6, since after 11. ... Rc7 the issue is settled by 12. Qe7+!, and Pawn queens.

Diagram 151

Exercise.

White carries out a line clearance combination.

PAWN PROMOTION COMBINATIONS

A far advanced Pawn is dangerous, and it often settles the outcome of a game.

Here, in Diagram 152, is the finale of the Kapengut versus Shereshevsky game in the Byelorussian Championship of 1969.

Diagram 152

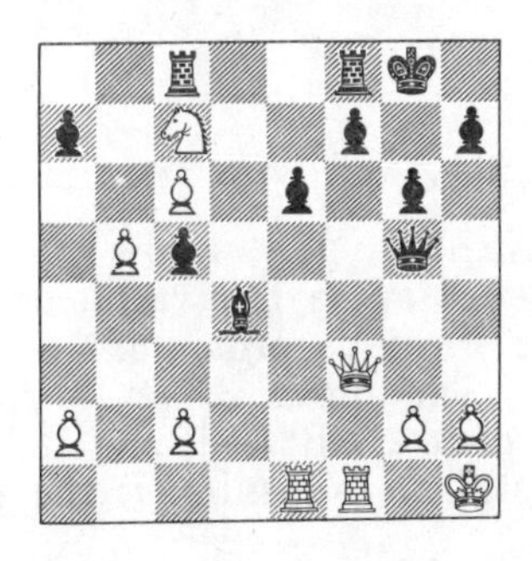

The presence of White's Pawn on c6 leads to the idea of carrying out an exchange combination:

25. Nxe6!! fxe6 26. Qxf8+ Rxf8 27. Rxf8+ Kg7

Or 27. Kxf8 28. c7! and promotion of the Pawn is inevitable.

28. c7 Qh4

The last hope. If 29. Ref1? Black will play 29. ... Be5!, threatening mate on h2 and attacking the Pawn on c7.

29. Rff1! Black resigns.

White's Pawn cannot be stopped from queening.

But a Pawn isn't always promoted to a Queen. Sometimes it is more profitable to turn it into a different piece, as the following beautiful endgame study by A. Troitsky shows.

Diagram 153

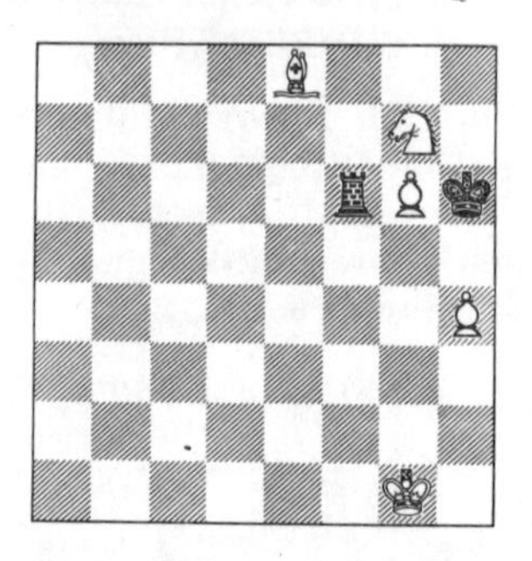

White to play and win. Here is the solution:

1. Nh5! Kxh5 2. g7+ Rg6+!

Quite interesting is the variation 2. ... Kh6 3. g8R!, the Pawn is promoted to a Rook and White wins. The move 3. g8Q? doesn't work out because of 3. ... Rf1+!, and if White takes the Rook a stalemate results. If the White King retreats to g2 Black replies 4. ... Rg1+!, achieving a draw.

3. Bxg6+ Kh6! 4. g8K+!

But not 4. g8Q? Or 4. g8R?, since it results in a stalemate.

4. ... Kxg6 5. Kg2, and White wins.

Thus Pawns are promoted to different pieces depending on the situation.

Diagram 154

White to play and win in two moves.

COMBINATIONS FOR A DRAW

When a player's position is worse or his opponent has a big material advantage he seeks every possible way of avoiding defeat.

One way out is perpetual check. That is what Black does in the situation in Diagram 155.

Black finds salvation through sacrificing his Bishop and Rook:

1. ... Bd4+! 2. R8xd4

It is necessary to take the Bishop. 2. Khl? is bad because of 2. ... Qe4+!

2. ... Rxb3+! 3. axb3

Not, of course, 3. Kxb3?? Qc3++.

3. ... Qc3+ 4. Kb1

Or 4. Ka2 Qc2+ 5. Ka1 Qc3+.

Diagram 155

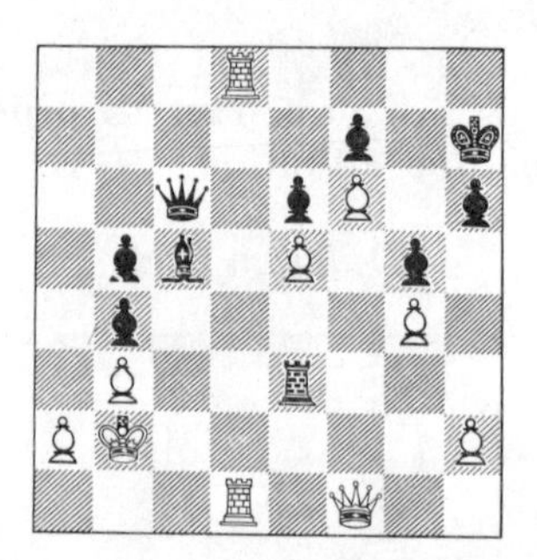

4. ... Qxb3+ 5. Ka1 Qa3+

Black forces a triple repetition of the position with the help of perpetual check. A draw.

Another way to get a draw is by forcing a stalemate.

Let us examine two endgame studies.

Diagram 156

In this study by H. Mattison White carries out a combination that winds up in a stalemate.

1. a4+! Kb6

Not, of course, 1. ... Kxa4? because of 2. Rxc5, and White wins. If 1. ... Kb4?, there follows 2. Be1+, and 3. Rxc5.

2. Bf2 c1Q 3. Rxc5! Qxc5 4. Kh1!!

That is precisely the point of the endgame. The trite 4. Bxc5+ Kxc5 leads to White's defeat.

4. ... Qxf2. Stalemate.

Of course, there are also other ways and means of achieving a draw. For instance, by causing a repetition of moves through an attack against an opposing piece in a position where the opponent cannot avoid repeating forced moves.

Diagram 157

In this endgame study by Troitsky White forces a draw by a continuous attack on Black's Bishop.

1. c3 Bf8

If 1. ... Ba5, then comes 2. b4! and the Bishop is caught.

2. Ke8 Bg7 3. Kf7 Bh8 4. Kg8 Bf6 5. Kf7 Bd8 6. Ke8! Ba5

The moves 6. ... Bc7 Kd7!, etc., make no difference.

7. b4 Bc7 8. Kd7 Bb8 9. Kc8. A draw.

* * *

More than 300 years ago chess players knew a drawn combination that was named "Furious Rook".

Diagram 158

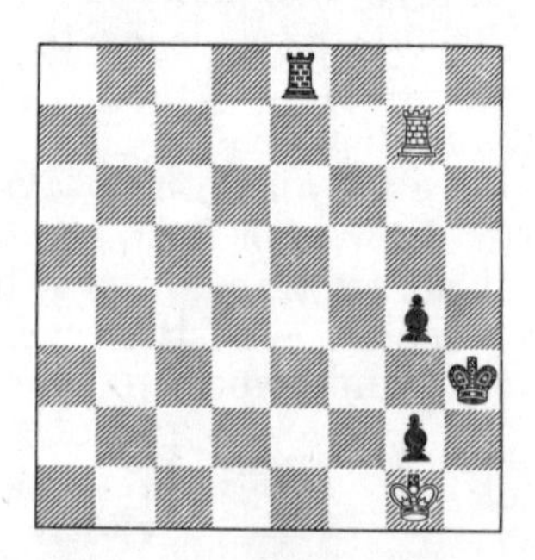

1. Rh7+! Kg3

Now that White's King is stalemated, the "infuriated" White Rook attacks the opponent's Rook, persistently striving for his own destruction.

2. Re7! Rd8 3. Rd7!, etc.

A draw.

Diagram 159

Exercise.

Black to play and draw.

SEVERAL IDEAS COMBINED

As noted above, combinations that include several ideas often occur. A striking example is furnished by a game between Andreyev and Dolukhanov in Leningrad in 1935 (see Diagram 160).

Diagram 160

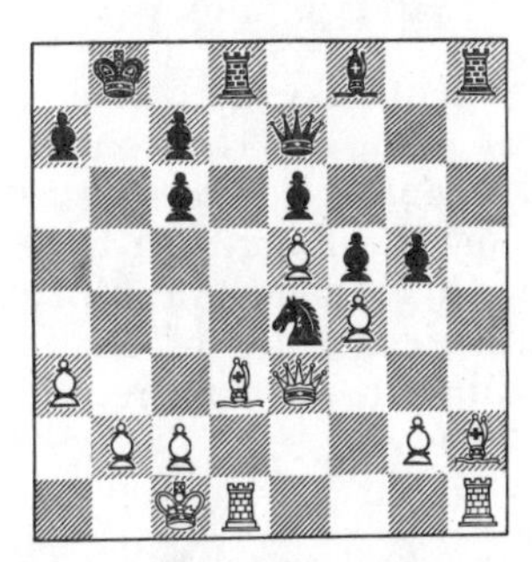

White has in readiness the threat 2. Bgl with a simultaneous attack against the King (there threatens 3. Qxa7+ and 4. Ba6++) and the Rook on h8.

1. ... Rxh2! (an unexpected diversion)

2. Rxh2 Qxa3!!

(an even more unexpected blow on the opposite flank!)

3. bxa3 Bxa3+ 4. Kb1 Nc3+ 5. Ka1 Bb2+! (decoy) 6. Kxb2 Nxd1+ (the fork is a result of the diversion of the Rook on hl on the first move) 7. K∾Nxe3 and as a result Black achieves material advantage.

Let us see whether it would have been better for White to decline the Queen sacrifice by playing 3. Kb1 or 3. c3 (preventing 3. ... Qa1++):

a) 3. Kb1? Nc3+! 4. bxc3 Ka8! and 5. ... Rb8++;

b) 3. c3 Qa1+! 4. Kc2 Qa4+! 5. Kc1 (5. b3? Qa2+ and 6. ... Ba3++) 5. ... Bc5 (winding up his development and preparing the f2 square for his Knight) 6. Qf3 (if 6. Qe2 or Qe1, then follows 6. ... Nf2!) 6. ... g4! 7. Qf1 Nf2! (with the threats 8. ... Nxd1 and 8... Qxf4+). Thus, the brilliant combination was correct from start to finish.

ATTACKING THE KING IN THE CENTRE

If your opponent takes his time about castling and leaves his King in the centre, you should seek ways of opening up the central lines for a direct attack on the King. We have seen classic examples on this theme in Morphy's games. Let us examine examples of an attack against a King standing in the centre.

Diagram 161

Diagram 161 shows a position from a game between Ravinsky and Panov in Moscow in 1943.

Believing that his King is sufficiently covered by his central Pawns, Black, without completing his development (Be7, 0-0) launches active operations on the Q-side and has just played Nxa3, counting on winning a Pawn after the natural 1. bxa3 Rxa3.

1. e5! dxe5

A single Pawn move brings important changes on the board: a central file and the long diagonal h1-a8 opened up, and White's timely developed pieces (Rd1, Bg2) are already on these lines. The opening of lines is advantageous for the player whose pieces are better developed.

2. Nc6

The first result of the opening of the lines.

2. ... Qc7 3. Nxe5 Nc4 4. Nxd7 Nxd7 5. Nd5! Qa7

No better is 5. ... Qe5 6. Qg4 with the threat 7. Rfe1.

6. Nf4!

Threatening to liquidate the Black King's Pawn cover by sacrificing the Knight on e6.

6. ... Ne5 7. Rxd7!

A bold sacrifice to expose the King.

7. ... Nxd7 8. Nxe6!

Another sacrifice, the logical consequence of the preceding one.

8. ... fxe6 9. Qxe6+ Be7

A line of play leads to mate: 9. ... Kd8 10. Bg5+ Kc7 11. Qc6+ Kb8 12. Bf4+ Rc7 13. Bxc7+ Qxc7 14. Qa8++.

10. Re1 Qc5

If 10. ... Nb6, there follows 11. Bg5 Rc7 12. Bc6+ Kf8 (12. ... Kd8 13. Rd1+ Nd7 14. Bxe7+ Kc8 15. Bxd7+ Rxd7 16. Rd6, winning). 13. Re3 and 14. Rf3+.

11. b4!

To divert the Queen from the g5 square, after which Bg5 is decisive. The move 11. Bf4 does not achieve its aim because of 11. ... Nf8.

11. ... Nf8

If 11. ... Qxb4, there follows 12. Bg5 Qxe1+ 13. Qxe1 Nf6 14. Qe6 Rxc2 15. Bb7!, winning.

12. Qg4! Qc3

Or 12. ... Qc7 13. Rxe7+ Qxe7 14. Qxc8+

Kf7 15. Bd5+ Kf6 16. Qc3+!, with an irresistible attack.

13. Rxe7+! Kxe7

Now the harmonious interaction of White's Bishops and Queen decides the issue.

14. Bg5+ Kd6

The state of affairs doesn't change in the case of 14. ... Ke8 15. Qe2+ Kf7 16. Bd5+ Kg6 17. Qe4+ Kxg5 18. Qf4+ Kh5 19. Bf7+ g6 and 20. Qh4++.

15. Qd1+! Kc7 16. Bf4+ Kb6 17. Qd6+ Ka7 18. Qe7+. White wins.

Sicilian Defence

BOLESLAVSKY *YANES*

USSR Team Championship, 1968

1. e4 c5 2. Nf3 Nc6 3. d4 cxd4 4. Nxd4 g6 5. Nc3 Bg7 6. Be3 Nf6 7. Bc4 d6 8. f3 Bd7 9. Qd2

At this point Black usually castles short and White on the Q-side, followed by keen play with mutual attacks. In this game Black neglects the castling move and tries to seize the initiative at once.

9. ... Rc8 10. Bb3 Ne5

A premature manoeuvre. Black should have castled.

11. Bh6! Bxh6 12. Qxh6 Nc4 13. 0-0-0! Qa5

Black is attacking, threatening to sacrifice the Knight on b2. However, Boleslavsky finds serious objections that delineate the shortcomings of Black's risky plan.

14. Nd5!! Nxd5 15. exd5 Qxd5 16. Rhe1!

Now the purpose behind the Pawn sacrifice becomes clear. The central lines are opened up and Black's King falls prey to an attack by White's pieces.

Diagram 162

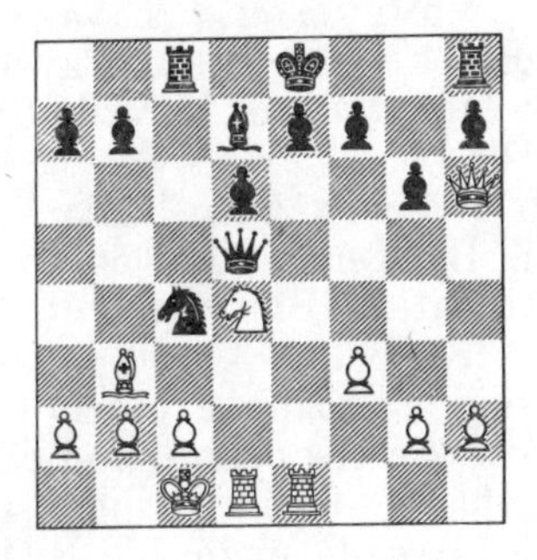

Usually the defending side seeks salvation from attack in exchanges.

17. Qg7! Qg5+ 18. Kb1 Rf8 19. Bxc4 Rxc4 20. g3 e6 21. f4! Qe7 22. f5! e5

22. ... gxf5? is bad because of 23. Nxf5? Qd8 24. Nxd6+, winning the Rook.

23. f6! Qd8 24. Nf3 Bf5

The strength of White's attack is illustrated by the variation 24. ... Qb6 25. Nxe5! dxe5 26. Rxd7! Kxd7 27. Qxf8, and White wins.

25. Rxe5+! Kd7

The King's move is forced. In the case of 25. ... dxe5 there follows 26. Qxf8+! Kxf8 27. Rxd8++.

26. Rxf5!. Black resigns.

If 26. ... gxf5 White replies 27. Ne5+, winning the Rook. In the following game White is the side that fails to castle on time.

PEEBO — *KUPREICHIK*

USSR Team Championship, 1968

1. e4 c5 2. Nf3 Nc6 3. d4 cxd4 4. Nxd4 g6 5. Be3 Nf6 6. Nc3 Bg7 7. f3

The same opening moves as in the preceding game. Here White should have played Bc4, preventing Black's important Pawn thrust d5.

7. ... 0-0 8. Qd2 d5! 9. exd5 Nxd5 10. Nxc6 bxc6 11. Nxd5 cxd5

As a result of the exchanges Black has a superior position. His central Pawns are dangerous. Now there threatens Bxb2 and d4.

12. c3 e5 13. Be2

Castling long is no good since Black would get an attack along the open b and c files. White wants to prepare to castle short.

13. ... d4! 14. cxd4 exd4 15. Rd1?

A decisive mistake. White wins a Pawn but loses the game. Better is 15. Bg5.

15. ... Re8! 16. Bxd4 Ba6! 17. Bxg7

No better is 17. Be3 in view of 17. ... Qxd2+ 18. Kxd2 Rad8+.

17. ... Qh4+! 18. g3 Qh3!

White resigns. If 19. Bc3, 19. ... Qg2! settles the issue.

ATTACKS AGAINST THE CASTLING SIDE

Mate by a Major Piece Supported by a Pawn or Piece

Attacks against the castling side often wind up in a combination on the theme of a mate carried out by a Queen or Rook on the g7, h7 and h8 squares (g2, h2 and h1) with the support of a Pawn or piece. Let us get acquainted with the main patterns (see Dias. 163-170).

Here are some examples of such combinational attacks (see Dias. 171-174).

Diagram 163

Diagram 164

Diagram 165

Diagram 166

Diagram 167

Diagram 168

Diagram 169

Diagram 170

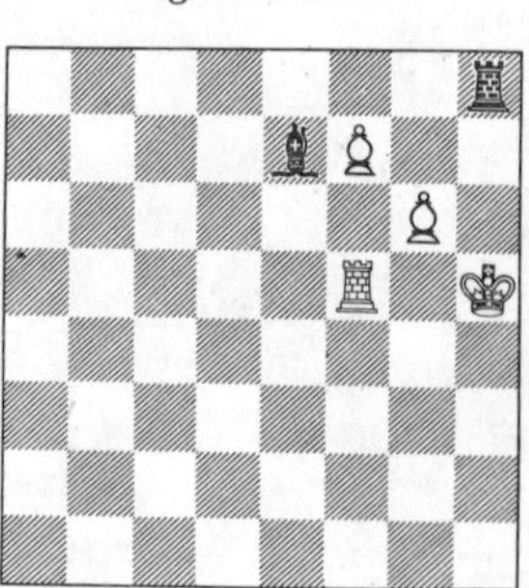

Diagram 171

ALEKHINE *LASKER*

Zurich, 1934

Diagram 172

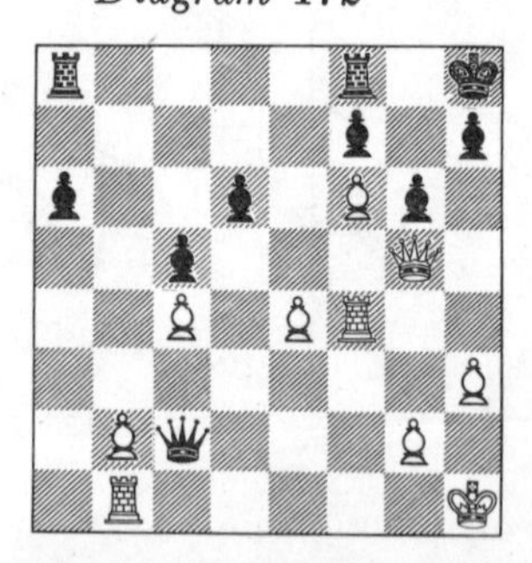

1. Nf5+ Kh8 2. Qxg6!! Black resigns.

If 2. ... hxg6, there follows 3. Rh3+ and 4. Rxh6++.

BRONSTEIN *KERES*

Budapest, 1950

1. Qh6! Black resigns.

The mating threat on g7 compels Black to block the g8-square: 1. ... Qxb1+ 2. Kh2 Rg8, and then White mates along the h-file: 3. Qxh7+! Kxh7 4. Rh4++.

Diagram 173

ROSSOLIMO *REISSMAN*

San Juan, 1967

1. Qg6!!

There threatens 2. Qxh7++. If 1. ... fxg6, then follows 2. Nxg6+ and 3. Rh3++.

1. ... Qc2 2. Rh3! Black resigns.

If 2. ... h6 there follows 3. Rxh6+ gxh6 4. Qxh6+, and if 2. Qxg6, then 3. Nxg6+ and 4. Rxh7++.

Diagram 174

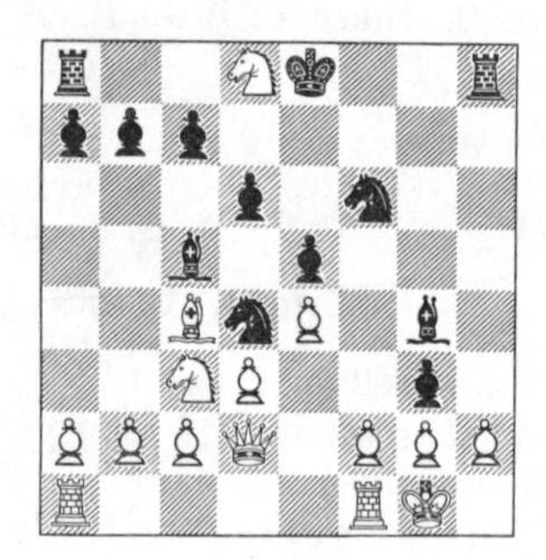

KNORRE *TCHIGORIN*

St. Petersburg, 1874

1. ... Nf3+! 2. gxf3 Bxf3. White resigns. Mate is inevitable. There threatens 3. ... gxh2++. There is no salvation in 3. hxg3 Rh1++ nor in 3. h3 Rxh3 followed by Rh1++.

Exercise. Find combinations in the following positions (see Diagrams 175-182).

COMBINATIONS FOR DESTRUCTION

The King can easily fall prey to an attack on the central files. Castling does not always safeguard the King, however. Frequently an attack on the castling position employs sacrifices of pieces on h7, g7, f7, h6, g6 (h2, g2, f2, h3, g3).

Sacrifice on h7 (h2) (Dia. 183)

Let us consider a game in which White carried out an impetuous attack on the K-side, taking advantage of the fact that Black castled without attending to the security of the King's flank.

Diagram 175

White to play

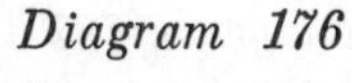

Diagram 176

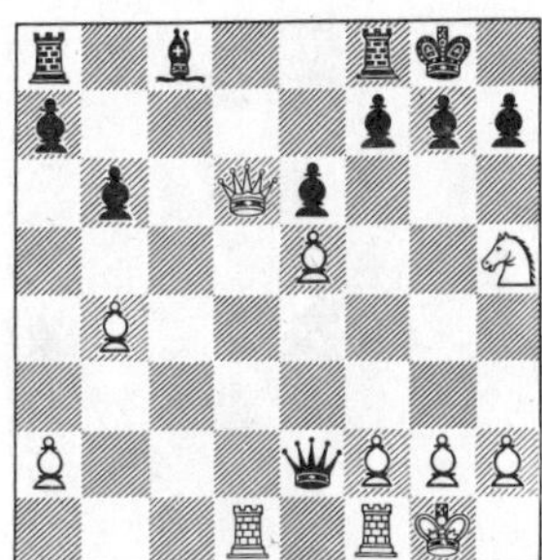

White to play

Diagram 177

White to play

Diagram 178

White to play

Diagram 179

Black to play

Diagram 180

White to play

Diagram 181

White to play

Diagram 182

Black to play

French Defence

1. e4 e6 2. d4 d5 3. e5 c5 4. Nf3 cxd4 5. Bd3 Nc6 6. 0-0 Bc5

White sacrifices a Pawn but places his pieces in active positions in the centre.

7. Bf4 Nge7 8. Re1 Bd7 9. Nbd2 0-0?

The move 9. ... Ng6 would be more correct. The castling in this position gives White an opportunity to carry out the following typical combination.

Diagram 183

10. Bxh7+! Kxh7 11. Ng5+ Kg8

In the case of 11. ... Kg6 there follows 12. Qg4 f5 13. Qg3, with the threat of 14. Nxe6+.

12. Qh5 Re8 13. Qh7+ Kf8 14. Qh8+ Ng8 15. Nh7+ Ke7 16. Bg5+. Black resigns.

An elegant combination with sacrifices on f7 and g7 was carried out by Y. Averbakh during a simultaneous exhibition in 1955.

Diagram 184

1. Rxf7! b5

Or 1. ... Kxf7 2. Qxh7, with the threat 3. Rf1+.

2. Rf1! bxc4 3. Rxg7+! Kxg7 4. Rf7+! Kxf7 5. Qxh7++.

White sacrifices three pieces to achieve mate!

In the Geller versus Papavlou game at the Eleventh Olympiad in Amsterdam in 1954 a sacrifice was carried out on h6 (see Dia. 185).

Sacrificing a Bishop for two Pawns, White destroys the Pawn cover of Black's King and mounts an irresistible attack against the King.

1. Bxh6! gxh6 2. Qxh6 Qa5 3. Ng5 e5 4. Bh7+ Kh8 5. Be4+ Kg8 6. Rae1

Transferring the Rook to the K-side to set up decisive threats.

6. ... Bg4 7. Re3 Rad8 8. Rg3 Rd4 Ne6! Black resigns.

Diagram 185

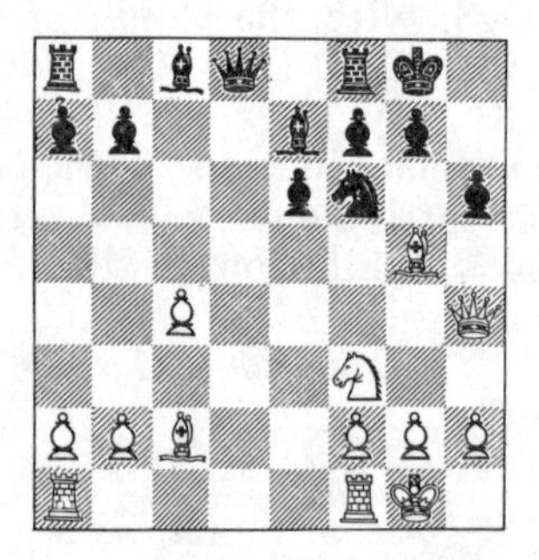

Threatening mate on g7 with the Knight-protected Queen. If Black takes the Knight with the Pawn 9. ... fxe6, there follows 10. Rxg4+! Nxg4 11. Qh7++ (mate by the Queen under protection of the Bishop). Finally, with the continuation 9. ... fxe6 10. Rxg4+ Kf7 11. Qg6++, White declares mate with the Queen protected by the Rook. An instructive example!

Exercise.

Find combinations in the following diagrams.

Diagram 186

Black to play

Diagram 187

White to play

Diagram 188

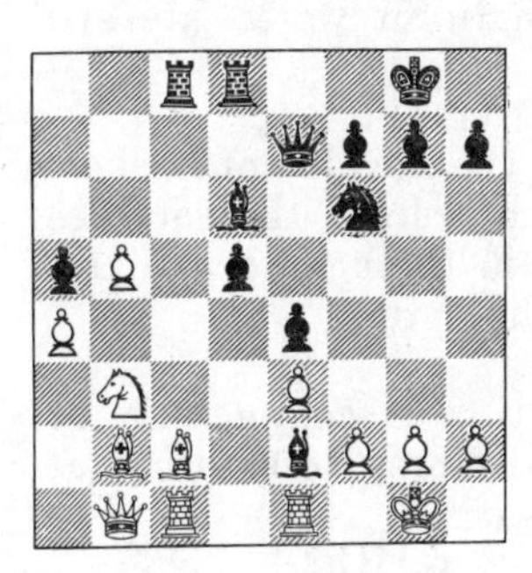

Black to play

Diagram 189

White to play

Sacrifice of Two Bishops

The sacrifice of two Bishops in order to break down the opposing King's Pawn cover was carried out by 21-year-old Emanuel Lasker, the future world champion, in a game against Johann Bauer in Amsterdam in 1889 (see Diagram 190).

Diagram 190

Black figures that after 1. Qxh5 f5 he will have quite a reliable position.

1. Bxh7+!

Only the start. The main fireworks are still to come.

1. ... Kxh7 2. Qxh5+ Kg8 3. Bxg7!

This second sacrifice is the novelty of Lasker's combination. Black cannot refuse the sacrifice. For instance, after 3. ... f6 there follows 4. Rf3 Qe8 5. Qh8+ Kf7 6. Qh7, etc.

3. ... Kxg7

Now the castling position is completely destroyed. Black's King falls prey to a lethal attack by the major pieces.

4. Qg4+ Kh7 5. Rf3 e5 6. Rh3+ Qh6 7. Rxh6+ Kxh6 8. Qd7

A decisive double blow: one of Black's Bishops perishes.

8. ... Bf6

9. Qxb7. White wins.

Ever since the sacrifice of two Bishops has come up time and again in tournaments.

Exercise.

Find a correct way of sacrificing two Bishops in the position below.

Diagram 191

White to play

The Attack After Castling on Opposite Sides

When the opponents castle on opposite sides the play is keener. Frequently both White and Black launch a Pawn attack to open up the files for an attack against the opposing King. The first to open up files and to transfer his pieces for an offensive has better chances of success.

Here is a characteristic example from a game between Tolush and Chiocaltea in Bucharest in 1953.

Black castles short. White prepared to castle long and, losing no time, starts moving the Pawns g and h forward.

Diagram 192

1. g4 e6 2. Be2 exd5 3. exd5 a6

Planning a Pawn advance to b5 after White castles.

4. h4! Nbd7 5. h5 Ne5 6. hxg6 hxg6

Complications arising after 6. ... Nxc4 7. gxf7+ Kxf7 8. Qf4 Nxb2 9. Kd2! are in White's favour.

7. 0-0-0 b5!

Black attacks, correctly sacrificing a Pawn to open the files.

8. cxb5 c4?

Better is 8. ... axb5 9. Bxb5 Bd7 10. Bxd7 Nfxd7, with the threat 11. ... Nc4. Now White, replying with a Pawn sacrifice, holds up Black's counterplay.

9. b6!

If 9. bxa6 Bxa6 both the a and b files open up but now the a-file remains closed.

9. ... Qxb6 10. Nh3 Rb8 11. Rh2!

Doubling the Rooks along the h-file permits White to create decisive threats, and in addition the Rook on h2 defends the second rank.

11. ... Nfd7 12. Rdh1 Nc5 13. Nf2 Rg7 14. Bh6!

To eliminate the King's chief protector, the Bishop on g7.

14 ... Bf6 15. Nfe4! Nxe4 16. Nxe4 Nxg4

If 16. ... Bh8, the move 17. Bf8! settles the issue.

17. Nxf6+ Nxf6 18. Bg7!!...

A beautiful finale! Black cannot take the Bishop due to mate in two moves.

18. ... Nh5 19. Rxh5! gxh5 20. Bd4 Qb4 21. Qh6 Re5! 22. Rxh5! Black resigns.

ELEMENTS OF POSITIONAL PLAY

The diverse combinations described above are usually carried out by the side that already gained a definite positional advantage, i.e., a better distribution of pieces and Pawns. In the opponent's position there are vulnerable spots of the kind or another: unprotected or pinned pieces, a poorly situated King, etc.

The beginner naturally would like to know how one of the sides gets a positional advantage. Well, he does this in the process of *positional play*, which is the preparatory phase for a combination.

As distinct from combinational play, positional play is not of a forced nature. Whereas combinations do not occur very often, positional play has to be conducted in every game. As a rule each player strives from the very start to gain small, and then on their basis more weighty, positional advantages. The main idea behind positional play is to gradually build up these advantages into positional superiority.

Positional play is an important and complex chess concept. Mastery of its methods is no less important than combinational insight. Now let us consider the main elements of positional play.

The Battle for an Open File and the Seventh Rank

In the middle game it is important to utilise the strength of the major pieces, the Queen and Rooks. To do this task a player needs a clear idea of the significance of an open file and of how to gain control over it.

As is known, an *open file* is one free of Pawns. A *semi-open* file has only Pawns of the opponent. Major pieces penetrate into the opponent's camp along open and semi-open files to attack his Pawns and pieces.

Penetration into the seventh and eighth (or second and first) ranks, where the main forces of the defending side are usually located, is especially effective.

The ending presented in Diagram 193 is an instructive example of opening up the a-file, followed by invasion of the second rank.

1. ... a5 2. a3

Black threatens to take the Pawn on b4, after which the powerful passed Pawn on c4, and

Diagram 193

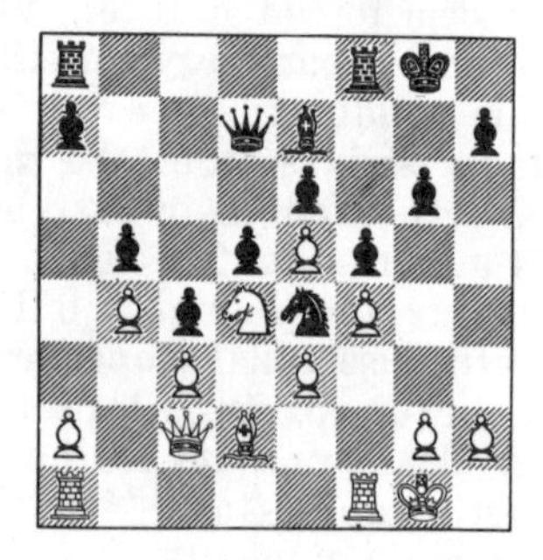

the pressure against the weak a2-Pawn on the semi-open file give him a clear advantage.

2. ... Ra6!

Immediate opening of the a-file doesn't yield Black anything. He lacks the prerequisites for taking possession of it. And so he first doubles the Rooks.

3. Ne2 Rfa8 4. Rab1

A forced move in view of the threat 4. ... axb4. The move Rab1 aims at defending the second rank by means of Rb2.

4. ... axb4 5. axb4 Ra3 6. Ng3 R8a4!

Black intends Qa7, and after that Ra2, penetrating to the second rank.

7. Nxe4 dxe4

Now the d-file is also at Black's disposal.

8. Rf2 Qd3! 9. Qc1 Ra2 10. Qe1

The move 10. Rb2 is wrong due to the reply 10. ... Ra1, winning the Queen.

10. ... Rc2! 11. Rd1 Raa2

After doubling his Rooks along the second rank Black has already won the game strategically.

12. g3 Bd8

Threatening Bb6. Black readily allows White's

following move because an exchange of the Queen for two Rooks merely hastens the issue.

13. Bc1 Rxf2 14. Rxd3 Rg2+ 15. Kf1 exd3. White resigns.

Black carried out all his plans:

1) to double his Rooks along the a-file;
2) to open up the a-file;
3) to break through to the second rank;
4) to double the Rooks along this rank.

The final position clearly demonstrates the strength of Rooks that penetrate into the opponent's camp.

Pressure Along a Semi-Open File

The position in Diagram 194 arose in the Smyslov versus Denker game in the USSR-USA match in Moscow 1946.

Diagram 194

Black has a weak Pawn, d6, on the semi-open d-file. Doubling the Rooks on this file, White exerts pressure on this Pawn and finally wins it.

1. Rd3 Rc7 2. Rd1 Rf7 3. Ne4 Bf8 4. Rd5 Strategically, White's position is won. The

weak Pawn on d6 is doomed. Black attempts to complicate the play fails.

4. ... Qg4 5. R1d3

White is preparing the move Qd2 in order to place all three major pieces along the d-file. Note that it is necessary to position the Queen behind the Rooks. The moves 5. Nxd6? Bxd6 6. Rxd6 are weaker because of Qxd1+, and Black receives two Rooks for the Queen. In this case it is difficult for White to realise his advantage.

5. ... Be7

5. ... Qe6 is hopeless due to 6. Qd2 Rfd7 7. c5! bxc5 8. Nxc5!, and White wins.

6. Nxd6 Bxd6 7. Rxd6 Rdxf8 8. Qxe5

The simplest. Besides the extra Pawn White now has a powerful attack at his disposal.

8. ... Rxf2 9. Rd7+ R2f7 10. Rxf7+ Rxf7 11. Rd8 Rg7 12. Qe8! g5 13. Qh8+ Kg6 14. Rd6+ Kf7 15. Qxh6

Having two extra Pawns, White easily wins.

15. ... Qf5 16. Rd1! Qc5+ 17. Kg2 Qe7 18. Rf1+ Kg8 19. Qf6 Qe8 20. Qf5 g4 21. Rf2 Qe7 22. Qd3 Rg5 23. Re2 Qf8 24. Qe4 Rg7 25. Qd5+ Qf7 26. Re6! Black resigns.

DISTRIBUTION OF PAWNS

Pawn distribution is highly important. There are three types of Pawns: *connected*, *isolated* and *doubled*.

Connected Pawns occupy a more advantageous position at the start, for instance, on a7 and b7, when they control all the squares in front of them and are capable of supporting each other. When the Pawns advance these advantages decrease. For instance, ahead of the Black Pawns a6 and b5 there arise uncontrolled squares (a5 and b4); the b-Pawn is now unable to support the a6-Pawn in case of an attack. In short, the advance of Pawns is bound up with their definite *weakening*.

During the advance of Pawns some of them may lag behind. A *backward* Pawn is one that cannot take its place beside another on the neighbouring file.

Diagram 195

In the position in Diagram 195 the Pawn on b2 lags behind, so that Black, having the equivalent of an extra Pawn, wins irrespective of who moves first.

1. Kc4 f4 2. h3 h5 3. Kb4 g4, followed by f3, etc.

Neither is 4. Kd4 of any help because of 4. ... Kf5, and Black forms a distant passed Pawn.

Doubled Pawns and the squares in front of them are weak.

Diagram 196 shows a won position for White. When Black has used up all his Pawn moves he will have to move his King, losing the c6 Pawn. For instance,

1. b4 a6 2. a4 g6 3. a5 h6 4. h4 h5 5. g3 K∽6. Kxc6, and White wins.

Diagram 196

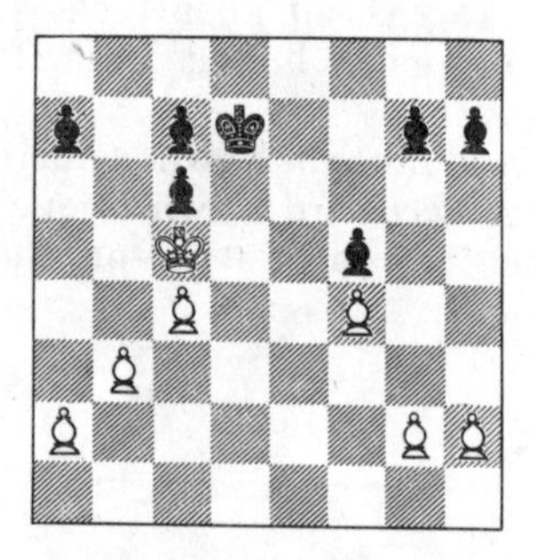

White has another course to victory: 4. b5! cxb5 5. cxb5 axb5 6. Kxb5, etc.

Diagram 197

In the position in Diagram 197 from a game between Erich Cohn and Akiba Rubinstein in St. Petersburg in 1909 White has a weak, isolated Pawn on h2, doubled Pawns on the f-file and Q-side Pawns weakened by their advance. It is instructive to see how Rubinstein takes advantage of these weaknesses.

1. ... Kf6

Black's King sets off for the h3 square.

2. Kd1 Kg5 3. Ke2 Kh4 4. Kf1 Kh3 5. Kg1

Now that White's King has been diverted to the edge of the board and riveted to the Pawn on h2, Black advances the Q-side Pawns in order fully to exchange them and attack White's remaining weak Pawns with his King.

5. ... e5! 6. Kh1

After 6. f4 there follows 6. ... exf4 7. exf4 Kg4. If 6. e4, then ... comes 6. ... g5 7. Kh1 h5 8. Kg1 h4 9. Kh1 g4 10. fxg4 Kxg4 11. Kg2 h3+ and 12. ... Kf3.

6. ... b5

Depriving the Q-side Pawns of mobility.

7. Kg1 f5 8. Kh1 g5 9. Kg1 h5 10. Kh1 g4

If now 11. fxg4 there comes 11. ... hxg4 12. Kg1 f4 13. exf4 exf4 14. Kh1 g3 15. fxg3 fxg3 16. hxg3 Kxg3, and White is incapable of hampering the march of Black's King to the Q-side Pawns.

11. e4 fxe4 12. fxe4 h4 13. Kg1 g3 14. hxg3 hxg3.

White resigns. The loss of his Pawns is inevitable.

However, one shouldn't exaggerate the danger of Pawn weaknesses and avoid at any cost the doubling of Pawns, the formation of isolated Pawns, etc. An isolated Pawn is not necessarily weak, while the possession of an open file or advantage in development may prove to be more than sufficient compensation for a doubled Pawn.

WEAK SQUARE

In the initial position the Pawns form a barrier on the third (or sixth) rank that is insurmountable for the opponent's pieces. As the Pawns advance this barrier weakens, weak squares appear in it. A *weak square* is one that cannot be attacked by a Pawn.

In Diagram 198 we see a position from a game between Tchigorin and Tinsley in London in 1899.

Diagram 198

The d6 and g5 squares in Black's camp on which White pieces have conveniently settled themselves are weak. Along the d-file the lagging d7-Pawn, whose defence ties Black's pieces, is weak. All of White's pieces hold excellent attack positions whereas Black's pieces play a passive, defensive role. Taking advantage of the distribution of the pieces, Tchigorin finds a beautiful path to victory.

1. a4!

A decisive thrust!

1. ... Kd8

Or 1. ... bxa4 2 Rb4 Rb7 3. Rxb7 Bxb7 4. Qxa7, etc.

2. axb5! Bxg2 3. Qa3! Bd5 4. Ra4! Rb7 5. Rxa7 Rxb5 6. Rdxd7+!, and mate in three more moves.

Thus a weak square in the camp of one side becomes a strongpoint for an opponent's piece if it can firmly establish itself there. A weak square that threatens to become a convenient point for an opposing piece is a serious danger.

Here is another classical example of a player

taking advantage of the weakness of an important point in his opponent's camp.

Diagram 199

Diagram 199 shows a position from a game between Teichmann and Bernstein in St. Petersburg in 1909.

1. Nd5!

Seemingly aiming at the c7-Pawn. Actually, however, this move launches a decisive attack against the weak f6-square.

1. ... Ra7 2. Bh4

White threatens, through Nf6+ or Bf6, to compel the exchange of the Bishop on g7, the chief defender of the weak f6-square.

2. ... Bd4+ 3. Kh1 Kg7 4. Bf2!

Compels the exchange of the Bishop since after 4. ... Be5 there would follow 5. f4 Bf6 6. Nxf6 Kxf6 7. Bh4+, etc.

4. ... Bxf2 5. Rxf2

White has put through the first stage of his plan—the exchange of the black-square Bishop. Now he starts on the second stage, to get his Knight onto the weak f6 square. Black is threatened with check by the Queen from c3.

5. ... Qa5 6. Qe2!

With the same intention of transferring the Queen to the long diagonal.

6. ... f6 7. Qb2 Rf8 8. g4!

Not giving Black time to drive the Knight away with the move c6. There threatens 9. Nxf6.

8. ... h6 9. h4 g5 10. f4! gxh4 11. Nxf6

The second stage ends with the Knight's incursion on f6. Now the third stage: to take advantage of the Knight being on f6 and the shattered position of Black's King. There threatens 12. Nh5+ Kf7 13. Qf6+ and Rb8+.

11. ... Rf7 12. g5 Bc6 13. Rg1 Qa3 14. gxh6+ Kxh6 15. Rh2!

With the threat Rxh4++. In case of 15. ... Qf3+ White simply replies 16. Qg2.

15. ... Bxe4+

This sacrifice only postpones mate by several moves.

16. Nxe4 Qf3+ 17. Qg2 Qxg2+ 18. Rhxg2 Rxf4 19. Rg6+ Kh7 20. Nf6+. Black resigns.

"GOOD" AND "BAD" BISHOPS

When a closed Pawn position arises the question of "good" and "bad" Bishops acquires importance.

A Bishop whose movements are cramped by its own Pawns is a "bad" Bishop.

A Bishop having freedom of movement along squares of a different colour than those on which its own Pawns stand is a "good" Bishop.

A "good" Bishop defends a number of squares against incursions by opponent's pieces. A "bad" Bishop is entrapped in his own camp.

These differences are well brought out in the following game (Diagram 200) played by Alatortsev and Levenfish in the 10th USSR Championship in 1937.

Despite the complete material equality Black's position is a winning one. His Pawns stand on

Diagram 200

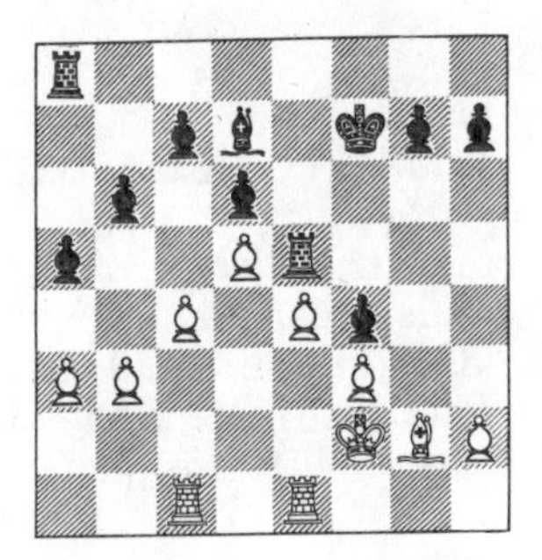

Black squares, while the Bishop on d7 (a "good" Bishop) defends white squares against incursion by the opponent's pieces. They supplement each other. The strongpoint e5 in the centre means a lot for Black.

The black squares in White's camp are irreparably weak, since both the Pawns and the Bishop stand on white squares. The Bishop on g2 is blocked by his own Pawn (a "bad" Bishop).

1. ... Kf6 2. Ke2 Rh5! 3. Rh1 Ke5! 4. Kd3 h6

Black plans to advance the g and h Pawns in order to form a passed Pawn along the f-file.

5. h3?

Weakens the g3-point. Black immediately takes advantage of this.

5. ... Rg5! 6. Rh2 Rg3 7. h4 Rg8 8. Ke2 g5 9. hxg5 hxg5 10. Kf2 g4! 11 Rh5+ Kd4 12. Rd1+?

A poor move that hastens defeat. However, Black also wins after 12. Rh7 gxf3 13. Bxf3 Bg4 14. Bxg4 Rxg4 15. Rxc7 Rh4!

12. ... Kc3 13. Rh7 gxf3 14. Bf1

If 14. Bxf3? there follows Rxf3+ 15. Kxf3 Bg4+ 16. Kxf4 Bxd1, etc.

14. ... Kc2! 15. Rd3

Or 15. Ra1 Bg4 16. Rxc7 Rh8!, with a decisive attack.

15. ... Bh3!

The final blow!

16. Rxf3 Rxf3+ 17. Kxf3 Bxf1 18. Rxc7 Rf8!

Black has an extra Bishop, and the outcome of the struggle is clear.

19. Rd7 Kd3 20. Rxd6 Be2+ 21. Kf2 f3 22. Rh6 Rg8 23. Rh2 Kxe4 24. Rh4+ Kd3 25. Rh2 Rg6 26. b4 axb4. White resigns.

HOW TO EXPLOIT MATERIAL ADVANTAGE

All other conditions being equal, the player with an extra Pawn or piece has greater chances of winning.

The example in Diagram 201, taken from the Spassky versus Tahl game in the 23rd USSR Championship in 1956 is instructive.

White, having two extra Pawns, sets out to simplify play by an exchange of pieces.

Diagram 201

Material advantage is usually exploited by carrying out exchanges and bringing the play into the endgame stage, where the presence of extra forces makes itself expecially telling.

1. Re7! Nxe7 2. Bxg7+ Kg8 3. Bxf8+ Kxf8 4. Rf1+ Kg8 5. Rd1 Rf8 6. a4 Rf2 7. Nc4!

The simplest of all. White has to win the Pawn on a7, after which his passed Pawns will go ahead unhampered.

7. ... Rxh2 8. Rd7 Nf5 9. Rxa7 Nd4 10. Rc7. Black resigns.

VIII. ENDGAME

KING AND PAWN VERSUS KING AND PAWN

1) *Passed Pawns on Different Flanks*

In such cases you have to calculate exactly whether you will be able to promote your Pawn or not. If you cannot promote it then you should hold up the opposing Pawn with your King.

Diagram 202

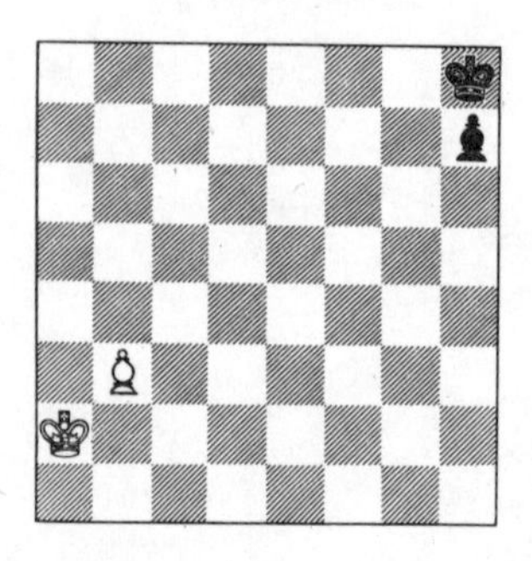

In Diagram 202 if White moves first he plays 1. b4! He advances the Pawn, queens it (Black's King cannot get there on time) and easily wins.

If Black moves first he wins. He should start with 1. ... Kh7! to get his King ready to block White's King. Only in reply to 2. Kb2 does

Black advance his Pawn, 2. ... h5! He wins easily, since White's King cannot prevent him from queening.

If both Pawns are held up (imagine that White's King is on h2 and Black's is on b8), the game ends in a draw.

Even in a simple King and Pawn versus King and Pawn ending there can arise positions containing various fine points.

Here, in Diagram 203, is an original endgame study by Réti.

Diagram 203

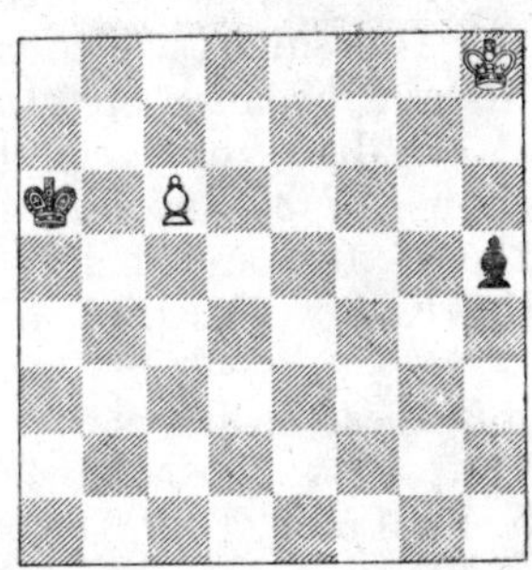

White's situation seems hopeless: his Pawn will perish while Black's irresistibly goes ahead to become a Queen. However, after 1. Kg7! h4 2. Kf6 Kb6 (or 2 ... h3 3. Ke6! h2 4. c7 Kb7 5. Kd7!) 3. Ke5! h3 (3 ... Kxc6 4. Kf4!) 4. Kd6 h2 5. c7 hlQ 6. c8Q the game ends in a draw.

The manoeuvres by White's King either to stop the opponent's Pawn or to give support to his passed Pawn are quite instructive.

2) *Blocked Pawns*

If in the position in Diagram 204 White moves first he wins by capturing the Pawn on d6. 1. Kf6! (White employs a method called *distant opposition*. This term means the opposition of Kings along a straight line or diagonal at a dis-

Diagram 204

tance of three or five squares. The move 1. Ke6? would be a mistake because of 1. ... Kc5, and Black wins.) 1. ... Kb7 (or 1. ... Kb5 2. Ke7! Kc5, etc.) 2. Ke6 Kc7 3. Ke7 Kc8 4. Kxd6 (the King is on the sixth rank before the Pawn!) 4. ... Kd8 5. Kc6 Kc8 6. d6 Kd8 7. d7, and White wins.

If Black moves first he plays 1. ... Kb5!, winning a Pawn, but after 2. Ke4 Kc4 3. Ke3 Kxd5 4. Kd3! Kc5 5. Kc3! d5 6. Kd3, the game ends in a draw.

In Diagram 205 you may see an interesting example of blocked R-Pawns.

Diagram 205

The game ends in a draw after the following moves:

1. Ke6 Kc3 2. Kd6? Kd4! 3. Kc6 Ke5 4. Kb7 Kd6 5. Kxa7 Kc7

However, if 1. Ke6 Kc3 2. Kd5! Kb4 3. Kc6 Kc4 4. Kb7, White makes it hard for Black's King to reach the c7-square on time. White then wins.

ENDINGS WITH SEVERAL PAWNS

Such endings vary a great deal. We shall limit ourselves to only a few examples here.

There are no passed Pawns in the position in Diagram 206. The Pawns are blocked and are located on different files. Whoever moves first wins.

Diagram 206

1. Ke2! (distant opposition) 1. ... Ke7 2. Ke3 Ke6 3. Ke4 Kf6 4. Kf4! (Kd5 is weaker because of Kf5) 4. .... Kg6 (or 4. ... Ke6 5. Kg5) 5. Ke5 Kg7 6. Kf5 Kh6 7. Kf6, and White wins.

Nor is 1. ... Kd8 of any help because of 2. Kf3! Ke7 3. Ke3!, etc.

If Black moves first, with 1. ... Ke7!, he wins. For instance, 2. Kd2 Kd6 3. Kd3 Kd5 4. Kc3 Ke4, etc.

In Pawn endings one of the sides often gains

superiority by setting up a remote passed Pawn.
White to play and win (see Diagram 207).

Diagram 207

1. h4! gxh4 2. gxh4 Ke5 3. Kf3 f4 4. h5 Kf5 5. h6! Kg6 6. Kxf4 Kxh6 7. Ke5

White wins by bringing the King closer to Black's Pawns.

Other moves by Black after 1. h4 will not help. For instance, 1. ... g4 2. Kf4 Ke6 3. h5 Kf6 4. h6! Kg6 5. h7 Kxh7 6. Kxf5, and White wins easily.

The relatively best reply by Black to 1. h4 is 1. ... f4+(!). Now White has to play with precision. 2. gxf4? is a mistake, since after 2. ... gxh4! Black gets a distant passed Pawn and after 3. Kf3 Kd5! 4. Kg4 Ke4 5. f5 h3 gains superiority.

Nonetheless, after 1. h4 f4+ 2. Kf3! gxh4 (or 2. ... fxg3 3. hxg5) 3. gxh4! Ke5 4. h5! Kf5 5. h6 Kg6 6. Kxf4 Kxh6 7. Ke5, White wins.

In Pawn endings a protected passed Pawn is important.

In the position in Diagram 208 White wins through 1. Kc3. White's King calmly sets off for the a-Pawn while Black's King has to guard the Pawn on f5.

Diagram 208

Exercises.

Diagram 209

White to play and win by forming a passed Pawn.

Diagram 210

White to play and win

Diagram 211

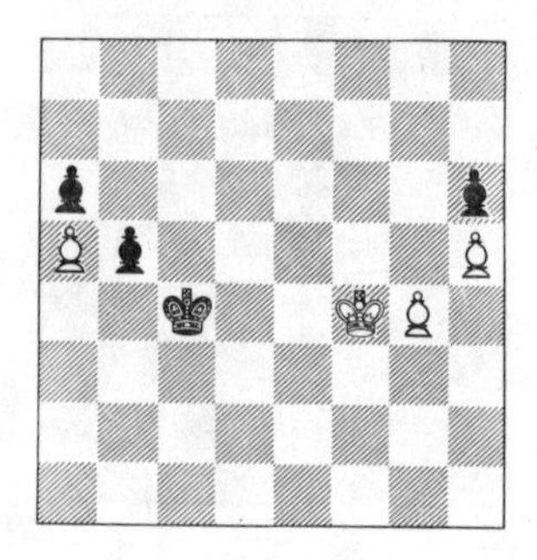

How can White bring home his Pawn while simultaneously holding back the opponent's Pawn?

Diagram 212

White to play and win

Diagram 213

White to play and win

Diagram 214

White to play and draw

KING AND QUEEN VERSUS KING AND PAWN

King and Queen easily win against King and a Pawn which is far away from promotion.

Diagram 215

In the position in Diagram 215 Black cannot be saved by the presence of the Pawn on the a3 square. 1. Qd4+ Kb1 (in the case of 1. ... Kb3 there will follow 2. Qa1, and if 1. ... Ka2, then 2. Qb4! immediately settles the issue) 2. Qb4+ Ka2 3. Kf2, and Black has to give up his Pawn.

White finds it more difficult when the opposing Pawn reaches the second rank, as in Diagram 216.

Diagram 216

White has to bring up his King and at the same time prevent Black from queening. Here is how he does it 1. Qf6+ Kg2 2. Qg5+ Kf1 3. Qf4+ Kg2 4. Qe3! Kf1 5. Qf3+ Ke1 6. Kd5! Kd2 7. Qf2 Kd1 (if Kd3, then 8. Qe1) 8. Qd4+ Kc1 9. Qe3+ Kd1 10. Qd3+ Ke1 11. Ke4! Kf2 12. Qf3+ Ke1 13. Kd3 Kd1 14. Qxe2+ Kc1 15. Qc2++.

This method is effective when the Pawn reaching the second or seventh rank stands on the b, d, e or g-file. As a rule, an R- or B-Pawn reaching the second or seventh rank enables the weaker side to get a draw.

Thus, for instance, in the positions in Diagrams 217 and 218 Black cannot win.

Diagram 217

Diagram 218

In the position in Diagram 217, after the moves 1. ... Qb5+ 2. Kc7 Qa6 3. Kb8 Qb6+ 4. Ka8 Black lacks, due to the threat of stalemate, a tempo for bringing up his King to the battle area.

In the position in Diagram 218, after the moves 1. ... Qg5+ 2. Kh7 Qf6 3. Kg8 Qg6+, White does not place himself in front of the Pawn but plays 4. Kh8!, and if Black takes the Pawn a stalemate results.

In some cases the King and Queen can win against the King and a B-Pawn or R-Pawn, if the King of the stronger side manages to come up nearer to create a mating threat. In the example in Diagram 219 White plays:

Diagram 219

1. Kc4 Ka1 (if 1. ... Kb1 there will also follow 2. Kb3!) 2. Kb3! Pc1N+ (or 2. ... Pc1Q 3. Qa2++) 3. Ka3, and White wins.

Sometimes the win against a R-Pawn located on the second rank may be achieved by the endgame study method. An old-time composition by G. B. Lolli (1763) is given in Diagram 220.

Exercises.

Diagram 220

White to play and win

Diagram 221

White to play and win

QUEEN AND PAWN VERSUS QUEEN

When the stronger side has a sufficiently advanced Pawn he usually wins, but great precision is needed to avoid perpetual check.

In his encounter with Minev at the 11th Olympiad in Amsterdam in 1954 Botvinnik, playing White, brought home his advantage.

Diagram 222

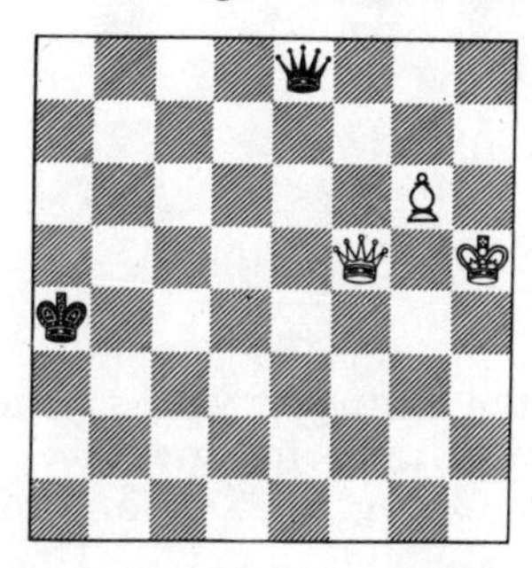

1. Qf4+ (it is useful to transfer the Queen to the central d4-square) 1. ... Ka5 2. Qd2+ Ka4

3. Qd4+ Ka5 4. Kg5 Qe7+ 5. Kf5! Qf8+ 6. Ke4! (A typical position! In reply to any check by the Queen, White blocks itself with a counter-check, forcing an exchange of Queens) 6. ... Qh6 7. Qe5+ Ka4 8. g7 Qh1+ 9. Kd4 Qd1+ 10. Kc5 Qc1+ 11. Kd6 (11. Kd5 is weaker because of 11. ... Qc8! Now, however, Black cannot reply 11. Qc8 because of 12. Qd4+ Kb3 13. Qd5+ Kb2 and 14. g8Q) 11. ... Qd2+ (or 11. ... Qh6+ 12. Kd5!) 12. Ke6 Qa2+ 13. Qd5 Qe2+ 14. Kd6 Qh2+ 15. Kc5! Black resigns.

Note the route of White's King: he should be on the same rank as Black's King, or on the neighbouring rank. Besides the threat of the Pawn's promotion White creates the threat of exchanging Queens.

It is easy to make a mistake in endings with Queens.

Diagram 223

Thus, in the Batuyev versus Simaghin game in Riga in 1954 there followed 1. ... e2??, after which came 2. Qg1+ Kd2 3. Qc1+ Kd3 4. Qc3++.

The simplest road to victory starts with 1. ... Kf2!

QUEEN ENDINGS WITH MANY PAWNS

Here a passed Pawn plays a big role.

In the Lisitsyn versus Suetin game at the 21st USSR Championship in 1954 White has an extra passed Pawn. Gradually moving it ahead, White realises his advantage.

Diagram 224

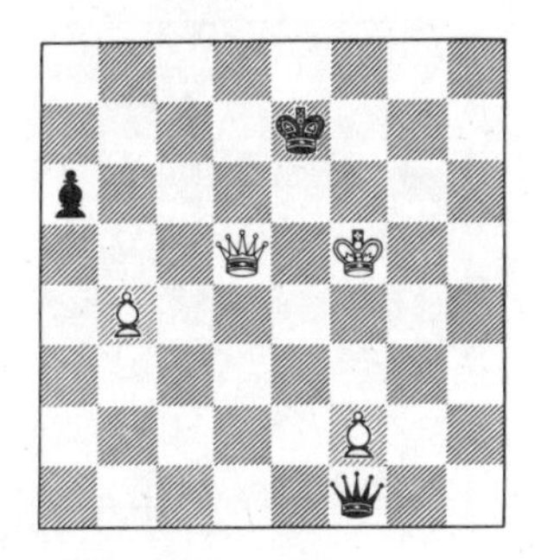

1. f4 Qh3+ (not, of course, 1. ... Qb1+ because of 2. Qe4+ with the exchange of Queens) 2. Kg6 Qa3 3. Qc5+ Kd7 4. f5 Qg3+ 5. Kf7 Qb3+ 6. Kf8 Qb2 7. Qa7+ Kd6 8. Qe7+! (8. Qxa6+ is weaker because of 8. ... Ke5!) 8. ... Kc6 9. f6 Qh2 10. Qc5+ Kd7 11. Qd5+ Kc7 12. Qd4! (Characteristic of a Queen ending! White places the Queen in the centre so as to defend his Pawns while at the same time limiting the mobility of the opponent's pieces) 12. ... Kb7 (also after 12. ... Qh8+ 13. Ke7 or 12. Qh6+ 13. Ke8 the White Pawn will reach the f7-square) 13. f7 Qh6+ 14 Ke7 Qg5+ (or 14. ... Qh7 15. Qg4!) 15. Qf6 Qe3+ 16. Qe6 Qg5+ 17. Ke8 Qh5 18. Kd8 Qh8+ 19. Qe8 Qh2 20. Qe7+ Kb6 21. Qc5+ Kb7 22. f8Q Qd2+ 23. Qd6. Black resigns.

When there is a large number of Pawns the side with a passed Pawn has greater chances of winning because it is harder for the opponent to declare a perpetual check.

In the Euwe versus Reshevsky game in Nottingham in 1936 White easily won by advancing the a-Pawn.

Diagram 225

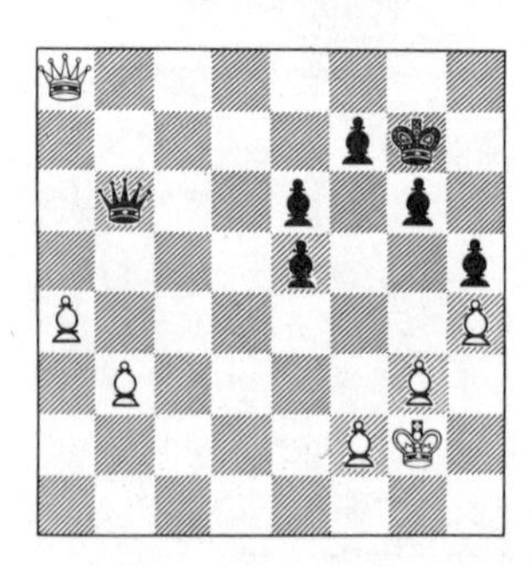

1. a5! Qxb3 2. a6 Qa3 3. a7 e4 4. Qb8! Qf3+ 5. Kg1 Qd1+ (or 5. ... e3 6. a8Q!, and neither 6. ... exf2+ 7. Kf1, nor 6. ... Qxf2+ 7. Kh1 Qf1+ 8. Kh2 Qf2+ 9. Qg2 cannot save Black) 6. Kh2 Qe2 7. Qe5+. Black resigns. In the case of 7. ... f6, there follows 8. Qc7+ Kh6 9. Qf4+ Kg7 10. a8Q. And if 7. ... Kh7, the move 8. Qf6 settles the issue.

In a Queen ending a far advanced passed Pawn frequently compensates for material inequality.

Exercises.

Solve this endgame study (see Dia. 227). Black has material advantage but White wins by taking advantage of the Black King's poor position.

Diagram 226

Black wins by an unexpected blow

Diagram 227

ROOK AND PAWN VERSUS ROOK

Since such endings are frequent it is useful to know typical positions and winning methods.

1) *The King of the weaker side is cut off from the passed Pawn* (see Diagram 228).

1. d6. (White pushes the Pawn ahead. Black's King is cut off from the e-file and cannot prevent that. All that remains for Black is to keep on checking with the Rook.)

Diagram 228

1. ... Rc2+ 2. Kb6 Kb2+ 3. Kc7 Rc2+ 4. Kd8 Kd2 5. d7 Rc2. Now there has arisen the position shown in Diagram 229.

Diagram 229

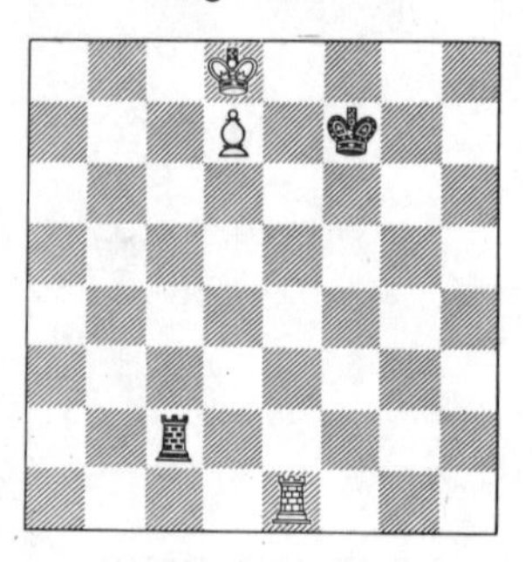

In this position White wins by the "bridge-building" manoeuvre. First he has to place his Rook on the fourth rank. 6. Re4! Rc1 7. Rf4+ Kg7 (if 7. ... Ke6 White replies 8. Ke8! and then d8Q) 8. Ke7 Re1+ 9. Kd6 Kd1+ 10. Ke6 Re1+ (or 10. ... Kg8 11. Rf5! and then Rd5) 11. Kd5 Rd1+ 12. Rd4!

The bridge is completed and the Pawn queens.

But victory is not always achieved when the King is cut off from the rest.

In the position in Diagram 230 White fails to push forward his passed Pawn still on the fourth rank. (Of course, the result is the same in the case of a Pawn on the second or third rank.)

Diagram 230

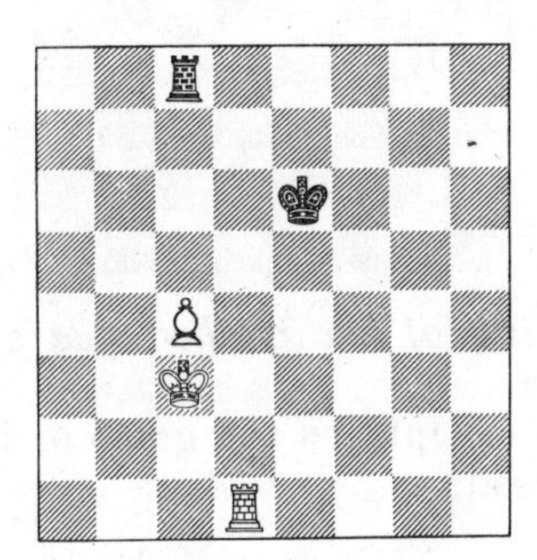

Black's Rook hampers advance of the Pawn and is ready to drive away White's King by checking it. All this enables Black to get a draw. For instance, 1. Rd5 Rc6 2. Kd4 (or 2. Kb4 Kc8 3. Rc5 Rb8+ 4. Rb5 Rc8 5. c5 Kd7! with a draw) 2. ... Rd6 3. Rxd6+ Kxd6, with a draw. Or 1. Kb4 Rb8+ 2. Ka5 Rc8! 3. Kb5 (neither 3. Rc1 Kd6!, nor 3. Rd4 Ke5! 4. Rd5+ Ke6 gives White anything) 3. ... Rb8+ 4. Kc6 Rc8+ 5. Kb5 Rb8+, etc.

If, however, the opposing King is far away, White wins. (Thus, if in the position in Diagram 230 Black's King is transferred to g7, and White's Rook to f1, then White wins by continuing 1. Kd4 Rd8+ 2. Ke5 Rc8 3. Rc1! Kf7 4. Kd6! Ke8 5. c5 Kd8 6. Rh1!.)

In Diagram 231 White has a R-Pawn. Though it is far advanced and the opposing King is cut off, there is no win because White's King has no freedom of manoeuvring.

Diagram 231

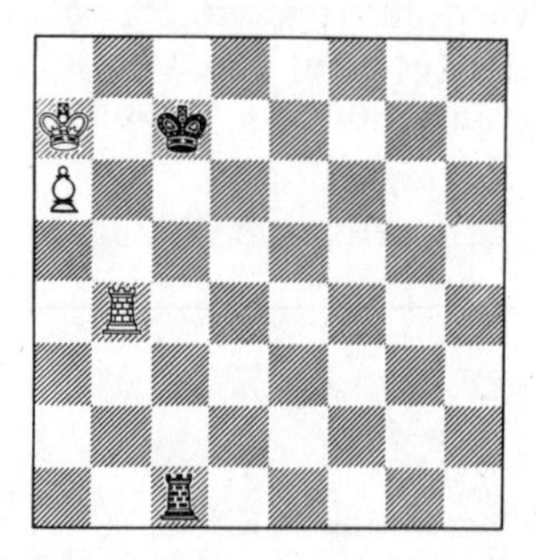

2) *The King of the weaker side stands ahead of the Pawn.*

With rare exceptions the game ends in a draw in such cases.

Diagram 232

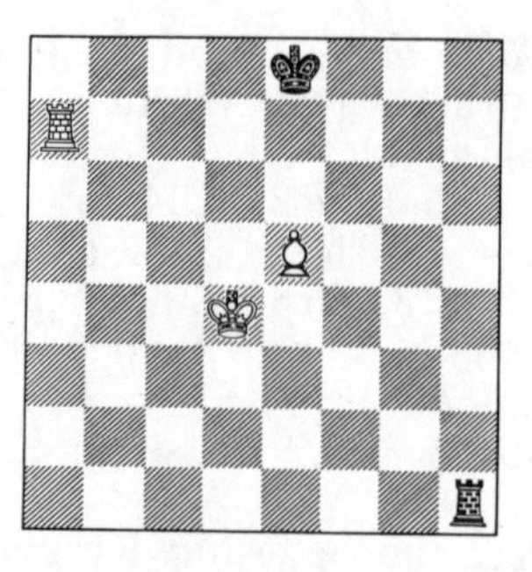

In the position in Diagram 232 Black's King stands on the file of the Pawn's promotion. The correct way for Black to bring about a draw is by transferring the Rook to the sixth rank so as prevent White's King from passing through. 1. ... Rh6! (it would be a mistake to keep on checking: 1. ... Rd1+ 2. Kc5 Rc1+ 3. Kd5 Rd1+ 4. Ke6! Kd8 5. Ra8+ Kc7 6. Ke7, and then 7. e6) 2. Kd5 Rg6! 3. e6 Rg1! (after the

Pawn reaches the sixth rank Black starts checking the King, thus attaining a draw) 4. Kd6 Rd1+ 5. Ke5 Re1+ 6. Kf6 Rf1+. A draw. White's King cannot hide from checks.

ROOK AND TWO PAWNS VERSUS ROOK

With Rooks on the board, two connected Pawns ensure the stronger side a win, as a rule.

The road to driving this advantage home can be clearly seen in the ending of the Blackburne versus Em. Lasker game in St. Petersburg in 1914 (Diagram 233).

Black has two extra Pawns standing in their initial positions. Gradually moving the Pawns and also the King, Lasker forces a win

Diagram 233

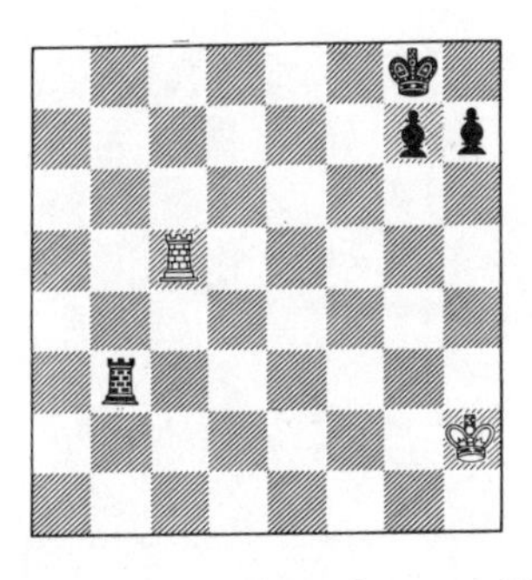

1. ... h6 (not, of course, 1. ... g6? because of 2. Rc7, cutting off Black's King) 2. Rc6 Kh7 3. Kg2 h5 4. Ra6 g6 5. Ra4 Kh6 6. Rc4 Rb5 (not 6. ... g5 because of 7. Rc6+ Kg7 8. Rc5 Kf6 9. Rc6+ Ke5 10. Rc5+ Kf4 11. Rc4+ Ke3 12. Rc5, etc.) 7. Kg3 Kg5 8. Rc3 (or 8. Ra4 h4+ 9. Rxh4 Rb3+) 8. ... h4+ 9. Kh3 Kh5 10. Rc4 Rb3+ 11. Kh2 g5 12. Ra4 Rb2+ 13.

Kh1 (after 13. Kh3? g4+! 14. Rxg4 Rb3+ White's Rook is lost) 13. ... h3 14. Rc4 g4 15. Kg1 g3 16. Rc5+ Kg6 17. Rc1 Kf5 18. Ra1 Rd2 19. Re1 Kf4! 20. Ra1 Ke3 21. Ra3+ (in the case of 21. Re1+, the simplest of all is 21. ... Kd3 22. Kh1 Kc2 and 23. ... Rd1) 21. ... Rd3 22. Ra1 Ke2. White resigns.

ROOK ENDINGS WITH MANY PAWNS

The Botvinnik versus Boleslavsky game in Moscow in 1941 (Diagram 234) offers a good example of how to exploit material advantage in a Rook ending.

White has an extra passed Pawn, which needs Rook support in order to advance.

Diagram 234

1. Rb1! The Rook gets behind the passed Pawn. In the case of other moves (for instance, 1. h3 or Kg1) Black could reply 1. ... Rb2!, making it difficult to advance the Pawn and gaining big chances of a draw. 1. ... Kf7 2. b5 Ke6 3. b6 Rc8 4. h3 (White must bring up the King. Premature is 4. b7 Rb8 5. Kg1 Kd6 6. Kf2 Kc7 7. Kg3 Rxb7 8. Rxb7+ Kxb7 9. Kf4 Kc6 10.

Ke5 Kd7, and White's King does not get through to the Pawns) 4. ... Rb8 5. Kh2 Kd5 6. Kg3 Kc6 7. Kg4 Kb7 (after 7. ... Rxb6 8. Rxb6+ Kxb6 9. Kf5 Kc6 10. Ke6 White wins easily) 8. Re1! Rg8 (there threatens 9. Re7+. The Pawn on b6 cannot be taken because of Rb1+, and after the exchange of Rooks, Kf5) 9. Re6 Ka6 10. Kg5 Kb7 11. h4 Ka6 12. h5 Kb7 13. g4 Ka6 14. Kh4 Kb7 15. h6 gxh6 16. Rxh6 Rg7 17. Kh5 Ka6 (If Black makes moves with the Rook to mark time, White transfers the King to h6, and, taking the Pawn on h7, easily wins.) 18. Rc6! Re7 19. Rc7 Re5+ 20. g5 Kxb6 21. Rxh7 Kc6 22. Kh6 Kd6 23. g6 Re1 24. Rf7 Ke6 25. Rf2 Ra1 (There now arises an endgame that was examined above. Black's King is cut off along the f-file, so that Black will have to give up the Rook for the Pawn.) 26. g7 Rh1+ 27. Kg6 Rg1+ 28. Kh7 Rh1+ 29. Kg8 Ke7 30. Re2+ Kd7 31. Re4! Rh2 32. Kf7. Black resigns.

No less instructive is the ending of the Botvinnik versus Najdorf game in the Alekhine Memorial Tournament in Moscow in 1956 (Diagram 235).

Diagram 235

White has an extra Pawn. Both the King and and Rook occupy active positions. Nonetheless, it isn't so simple to win because the Pawns are on the same flank. It is easier to push through a distant passed Pawn, as was shown in the preceding example. But Botvinnik finds an elegant road to victory.

1. e5 fxe5 2. fxe5 Ke7 3. e6 Ra4 (after 3. ... Rb7, there follows 4. Rd7+! Rxd7 5. exd7 Kxd7 6. Kg6, and White wins) 4. g5! hxg5 (Black can defend himself more tenaciously after 4. ... Ra7, but even then, continuing 5. e5! with the threat 6. Rg6 White should win) 5. Rd7+ Kf8 6. Rf7+ Kg8 7. Kg6! (Played with precision! Having prudently sacrificed the g-Pawn White gets on the g6-square, with no fear of checks along the g-file.) 7. ... g4 8. h6! gxh6 (or 8. ... Ra8 9. hxg7 g3 10. e7 g2 11. Rf8+, etc.) 9. e7! Ra8 (if 9. ... Ra6+ White covers with the Rook on f6) 10. Rf6! Black resigns since after 10. ... Re8 there will follow 11. Rd6!, and he is defenceless against the threat of Rd8.

Exercises.

Diagram 236

Solve this endgame study by Em. Lasker (Diagram 236). White to play and win. Having pushed away Black's King, White cedes the Rook for the Pawn on h2 and queens the Pawn.

Diagram 237

White also wins in the endgame study by N. Kopayev (Diagram 238). Sacrificing the Rook for a Pawn, he avoids a sacrifice by Black.

QUEEN VERSUS ROOK

Diagram 238

White's winning plan is simple: to push Black's King to the edge of the board, separate the King and the Rook, and employ checks to win the Rook or to ensure the decisive approach of his King.

1. Qe4+ Kd6 2. Kd4 Rc6 3. Qe5+ Kd7 4. Kd5 Rc7 5. Qe6+ Kd8 6. Qg8+ (But not 6.

Kd6? because of 6. ... Rc6+! 7. Kxc6, and stalemate. In such endings watch out sharply for such a possibility.) 6. ... Ke7 7. Qg7+ Kd8 8. Qf8+ Kd7 9. Qb8! Rc2! (or 9. ... Rc8 10. Qd6+ Ke8 11. Ke6) 10. Qb5+ Ke7 11. Qb4+ Kd8 (11. ... Kd7 12. Qa4+ or 11. ... Kf7 12. Qf4+, etc.) 12. Kd6, and White wins.

A Rook and Pawn versus a Queen can end in a draw in a number of cases.

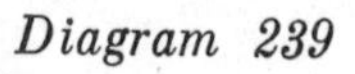

Diagram 239

In the position in Diagram 239 all White has to do is to keep on moving the Rook to a3 and back to c3 without letting Black's Queen through.

ROOK VERSUS MINOR PIECE

The Rook is considerably stronger than a Bishop or Knight. The difference in the strength between the Rook and a minor piece is called *Exchange*. If there are Pawns on the board in the ending, the extra Exchange usually proves sufficient for victory. If, however, the Pawns have been exchanged, the side having a Rook versus a Bishop or Knight rarely wins.

Diagram 240

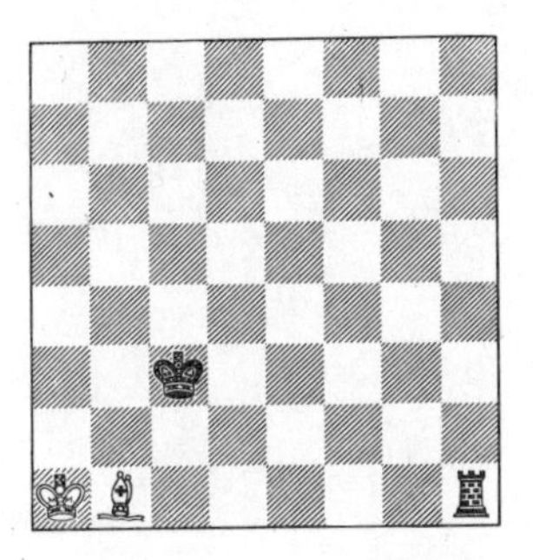

Black to play

White King stands on a corner square of a different colour than the one along which his Bishop moves. If Black plays 1. ... Kb3, a stalemate results.

In the case of 1. ... Rg1 White replies 2. Ka2. And if 1. ... Rh2, then White moves the Bishop. Black cannot strengthen the position.

All you have to do to get a draw when you have a Bishop versus a Rook is to keep the King in the centre or move him into a corner different in colour from the Bishop's square. If you have a Knight against a Rook you can bring matters to a draw by stationing it together with the King in the centre of the Board (it is dangerous to separate the King and the Knight) or on the extreme file in a position similar to the one shown in Diagram 241 (if it is your move).

This position leads to a draw only if White moves first.

Checking Black's King 1. Nh2+ Kg3 2. Nf1+ Kh3, White pushes away Black's King and then plays 3. Kh1, retaining the equilibrium. For instance: 3. ... Rf2 4. Kg1 Rg2+ 5. Kh1 Rg8 6. Nd2! Kg3 7. Kg1!, etc.

Diagram 241

BISHOP AND PAWN VERSUS BISHOP

In most cases such endings lead to a draw because the weaker side only has to give up the Bishop for a Pawn. In some cases, though, a win is possible. For instance, in the position in Diagram 242 White wins: 1. Bg7 Bd2 2. Bd4 Bh6 (though White's Bishop occupies the h6-f8 diagonal, Black's Bishop won't be able to stay on the short diagonal) 3. Be3! Bf8 4. Bd2 Bc5 5. g7.

Diagram 242

ENDINGS WITH BISHOPS AND SEVERAL PAWNS

In an ending with Bishops roaming along squares of the same colour much depends on where the Pawns stand.

A "bad" Bishop blocked by its own Pawns in the ending is a big liability. All other conditions being even, the side having a "good" Bishop versus a "bad" one has an advantage.

The Kashlyayev versus Zagoryansky game played in Moscow in 1949 illustrates that (Diagram 243).

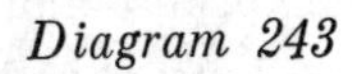
Diagram 243

Black threatens to play h5+ and then Kf6 and Kf5, with an easy win.

There follows 1. f5 h5+! 2. Kg5 Be7+ 3. Kf4 Kf6! 4. fxg6 Bd6+ 5. Kf3 Kxg6 6. Bf4 (or 6. Bg5 Kf5 7. Be3 Be7 8. Bf2 Bf6!, winning a Pawn) 6. ... Be7 7. Bg3 (There is a striking difference between the vigour of Black's "good" Bishop, which attacks White's Pawns and the passive role of White's Bishop, compelled to defend its own Pawns.) 7. ... Bf6 8. Bf2 Kf5. White resigns.

The following endgame study by Troitsky with Bishops on the white squares is interesting.

17-747

Diagram 244

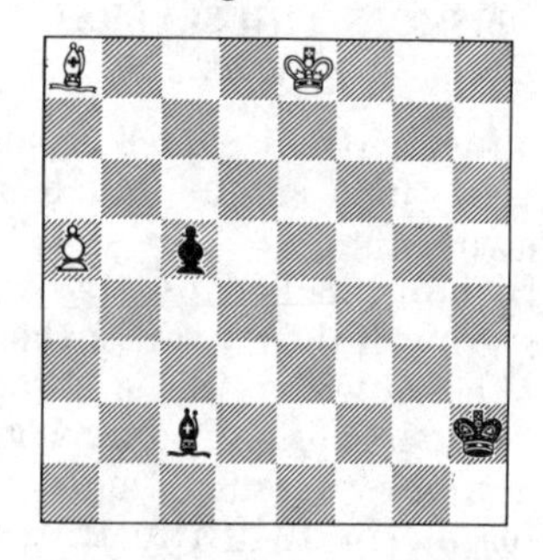

White to play and win

1. a6 c4 2. a7 c3 3. Bh1! (a beautiful winning move intended for the variation 3. ... Bg6+ 4. Ke7 c2 5. a8Q c1Q 6. Qg2++) 3. ... Ba4+ (not 3. ... Be4 in view of the simple reply 4. Bxe4 with a blow at c2) 4. Kf7! (the best retreat, as it soon becomes clear) 4. ... Bc6! 5. Bxc6 c2 6. a8Q c1Q 7. Qa2+ Kg3! 8. Qg2+ Kf4 (If 8. ... Kh4, there follows 9. Qf2+ Kg4 10. Bd7+ Kg5 11. Qg3+; if, however, 9. ... Kh5, then 10. Bf3+ Kg5, and now again 11. Qg3+.) 9. Qf3+ Kg5 (if 9. ... Ke5, then comes 10. Qf6++) 10. Qg3+ Kf5 11. Qg6+ Kf4 12. Qh6+, winning the Queen.

Diagram 245

Exercise.

Solve the endgame study by P. Vasilchikov (Diagram 245). White is to play and draw. At first sight White's position seems hopeless, but he saves himself by a stalemate.

ENDINGS WITH WHITE AND BLACK BISHOPS

With Bishops of opposite colour on the board the chances for a draw increase. Sometimes even an extra Pawn does not help to win. Only in some cases does one of the sides win.

Here, in Diagram 246, is an instructive example from a game between Fuchs and Kholmov in Dresden in 1956.

Diagram 246

With an equal number of Pawns and with Bishops of opposite colour on the board it looks like a draw and nothing else. Yet Black does have an advantage because of the King's active position and the possibility, if given a chance, of setting up a passed Pawn on the Q-side. Kholmov discovers a clever plan for forming a passed Pawn on the K-side: 1. ... f6! 2. Kd2 (Here, or somewhat later, White should cede a Pawn, playing d5! in order to improve the positions of the King and Bishop. White's passivity enables Black to carry out his plan.) 2. ... Kf5 3. Bf4 g5 4. Bc7 Kg4 5. Bd8 gxh4 6. gxh4 Kxh4 7. Bxf6+ Kg4 8. Ke3 Bd5! 9. Be7 b5. White resigns. White's passed Pawns on the d and f files are easily held up but White cannot stop Black's distant passed Pawns.

Botvinnik, playing Black against Kotov in the 22nd USSR Championship in 1955, won in endgame study style, with Bishop of opposite colour, an ending in that definitely appeared to be a draw.

Diagram 247

1. ... g5! (Botvinnik starts the combination.) 2. fxg5 (Also bad is 2. hxg5 h4 3. Bd6 Bf5 4. g6 Bxg6 5. f5 Bxf5 6. Kxb3 Kg2, and White has to give up the Bishop for the passed Pawn.) 2. ... d4+! (sacrifice of another Pawn) 3. exd4 (no better is 3. Bxd4) 3. ... Kg3 4. Ba3 (if 4. Be7 Kxh4 5. g6+ Kg4, White has to cede the Bishop for one of Black's Pawns) 4. ... Kxh4 5. Kd3 Kxg5 6. Ke4 h4 7. Kf3 (or 7. d5 Bxd5+) 7. ... Bd5+. White resigns.

KING, BISHOP AND R-PAWN VERSUS KING

Diagrams 248 and 249 show positions in which the stronger side has a R-Pawn and Bishop op-

Diagram 248

Diagram 249

posite to the colour of the Pawn's promotion. In such cases all the lone King has to do to get a draw is occupy the square in the corner ahead of the Pawn (Diagram 248). It is quite impossible to drive the King out of the corner.

In the position in Diagram 249, with White moving first there is a draw after 1. Kg1. If Black moves first he wins after 1. ... Bh2!, not allowing the King to get into the corner and then driving it away.

With a Bishop the colour of the Pawn's promotion the stranger side wins easily.

KNIGHT ENDINGS

In Knight endings the stronger side usually realises its material or positional advantage with comparative ease. A big role is played in such endings by a distant passed Pawn and also by the active position of the King and Knight.

The position in Diagram 250 arose in a game between Em. Lasker and Nimzovitch in Zurich in 1934. First of all Black pushes White's King out of the centre: 1. ... Nc6+ 2. Ke3 Kc5 3. Kd3 b4! 4. axb4+ Kxb4 5. Kc2 (otherwise there will follow 5. ... Kb3, winning the Pawn on

Diagram 250

b2) 5. ... Nd4+ 6. Kb1 (nor is 6. Kd3 Ne6 7. Kc2 Kc4! of any help, and Black captures the Pawn on e4) 6. ... Ne6 7. Ka2 Kc4! 8. Ka3 Kd4 9. Kxa4 Kxe4 (With material equality here—both sides have a Knight and Pawn—White nonetheless does not save his game. In Knight endings a R-Pawn is stronger than other Pawns, and in addition it is far advanced. Approaching White's Knight with his King, Black easily wins.) 10. b4 Kf3 11. b5 Kg2! White resigns.

Diagram 251

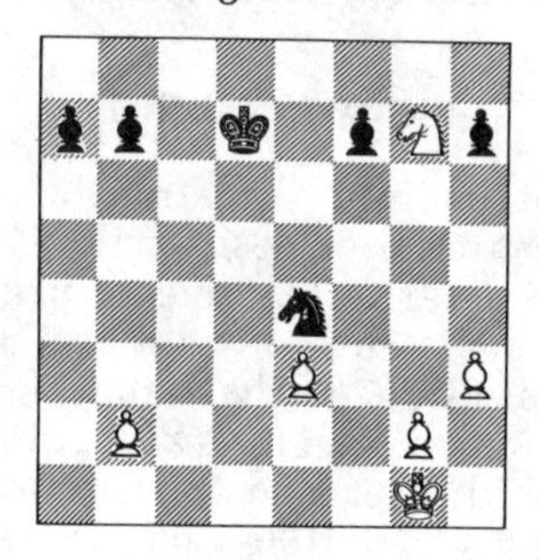

Diagram 251 shows a position from the Rabinovich versus Belavenets encounter at the 10th USSR Championship in 1937. Let us compare the distribution of the pieces and Pawns. Black's Knight, standing in the centre, hampers White's play while White's Knight stands aside. Black's King can get to the centre faster than White's. Black can form a distant passed Pawn on the a-file, whereas White cannot count on a passed Pawn. All this gives Black a positional advantage. The game continues thus: 1. Kf1 Kc6 2. Ke2 Kd5 3. Nf5 (After 3. Kd3 there follows 3. ... Nc5+ and then Ke4 or Kc4.) 3. ... Kc4 4. Nd4 a5 5. h4 a4 6. g4 b5 7. Kd1 (or 7. g5 b4 8. Kd1 Kd3, etc.) 7. ... Nf2+ 8. Kc2 Nxg4 9. Nf5 f6 10. Nd6+ Kc5 11. Ne4+ Kb4 12. Kd2 Kb3 13. Kc1 Kc4 14. Kd2 b4 15. Kc1 Kd5. White resigns.

Exercise.

Solve this endgame study by Gulyayev.

Diagram 252

White to play and draw

INTRICATE ENDINGS

Here are the main things to bear in mind in playing a complicated ending:

a) strive to create a passed Pawn backed up by pieces;

b) position your pieces as actively as you can;

c) bring your King closer to the centre to be able to help move your Pawns ahead or to hold up opposing Pawns.

In Diagram 253 note the finesse with which Levenfish (White) plays this ending against Flohr (Moscow, 1936).

Diagram 253

White has a small but clear advantage because his Rooks, Knight and Bishop occupy more active positions. By playing a5 his two Pawns can hold up Black's three Pawns on the Q-side. In the centre White can form a passed Pawn on the e-file.

Here is how the game proceeded: 1. f4! (Since White foresees an exchange of Rooks he wants to pave the way for his King to the centre.) 1. ... Nc4 2. Kf2 Rxd3 3. Rxd3 Rd8 4. Rxd8 Kxd8 5. Be4! (White transfers, with a tempo, the Bishop to a better position in order to keep both flanks under fire.) 5. ... h6 6. Bd3 Nb6 (better 6. ... Nb2) 7. e4! Na8 8. Ke3 Nc7 9. a5! Ke7 10. Bc4 Kd6 11. Kd4 Ne8 12. e5+ fxe5 13. fxe5+ Ke7 14. h4! Nc7 15. Ne4 Be6 (or 14. ... Ne8 15. Kc5 and the incursion of White's King settles the issue) 16. Nd6 Bxc4 17. Kxc4 Ke6 18. Nxb7. Black resigns. After 18. ... Kxe5 19. Kc5 Nd5 20. Nd8, White's victory is unquestionable.

IX. CHESS COMPOSITION

Chess composition is a fascinating sphere. Many fans are attracted by the absorbing creativity of composing and solving problems and endgame studies.

These are the two most popular subdivisions of chess composition.

Problems are contrived positions in which White or Black has to declare mate in a set number of moves. According to the number of moves required for the solution they are called twomovers, threemovers, etc.

Endgame studies are also invented positions in which White or Black has to find a way to win or to draw.

Among the most eminent pioneers in chess composition were Russia's A. Troitsky, M. and V. Platov, L. Kubbel, A. Galitsky and L. Isayev.

The Soviet Government conferred on A. Troitsky the title of Merited Art Worker in recognition of his outstanding contribution to endgame studies.

Currently Soviet chess composers are doing much to develop new problems and endgame studies, submitting them to national and international contests and publishing their compositions in magazines and newspapers. USSR team championships in chess composition are held.

Both in problems and in endgame studies the situation on the board must be realistic, in other words, the one that can in principle arise from the initial position in play according to the usual rules (for instance, a White Bishop on h1 with a White Pawn on g2 is impermissible). There must be only a single solution. There should not be any superfluous pieces on the board.

By solving problems and endgame studies you develop combinational abilities and learn to size up acute positions in the middle game. An acquaintance with endgame studies helps to improve your play in the ending, teaches you to assess the possibilities of the chessmen remaining on the board, to win economically and to work hard for a draw in what seems a lost position. Problems and endgame studies develop your imagination and show you original ideas.

PROBLEMS

In composing or solving a problem you should bear in mind the following five requirements:

1. The first move of the solution has to be a quiet one, without capturing a piece or declaring check.

2. The first move should not deprive Black's King of squares for retreat.

3. In twomovers the initial position should not contain any threat of checking White's King. Such a threat can only exist if White has a mating reply to it.

4. The larger the number of defences Black has the more interesting the problem. And the more defences there are the larger the number of the variations.

5. Both White's first move in the solution and his subsequent moves in each of the variations must be the only possible ones.

Diagram 254

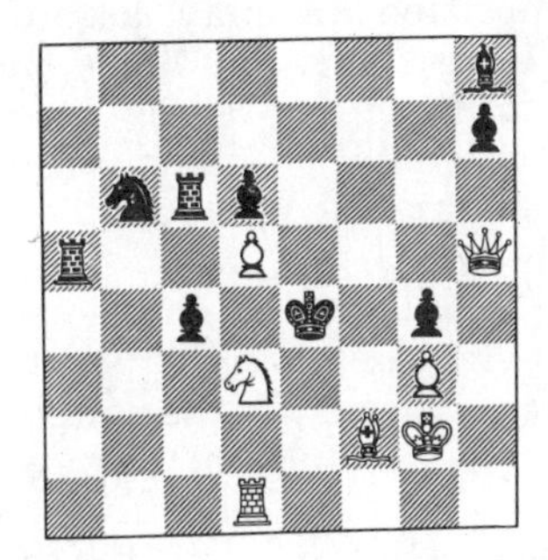

As an example let us look at V. Issarianov's problem in Diagram 254, in which White is to play and mate in two.

Before starting to solve the problem it is worthwhile noting that Black can capture White's Pawn on d5 and Knight on d3. If Black moves first he will take the Knight: 1. ... cxd3, then White will mate (2. Re1++), taking advantage of the circumstance that the d3 square is blocked and is inaccessible to Black's King. If 1. ... Rxd5 there follows 2. Qxg4++ (the d5-square is blocked). White replies to 1. ... Nxd5 with 2. Qxh7++ (the d5-square is blocked).

In solving the problem White plays 1. Ne5! (threatening 2. Rd4++), and after 1. ... Rxd5 there follows 2. Re1++ (the d5-square is blocked); in the case of 1. ... Bxe5, there comes mate: 2 Qxh7++ (the e5-square is blocked) and if 1. ... dxe5, then 2. Qxg4++ (again e5 is blocked).

Here are some problems that should interest you. The solutions are given at the end of the chapter. In problems we do not usually stated whose move it is because it is understood that White moves first (see Diagrams 255-258).

L. GALITSKY, 1892
Diagram 255

Mate in two

L. ISAYEV, 1928
Diagram 256

Mate in two

L. KUBBEL, 1928
Diagram 257

Mate in two

L. KUBBEL, 1936
Diagram 258

Mate in three

A. SOKOLSKY
Diagram 259

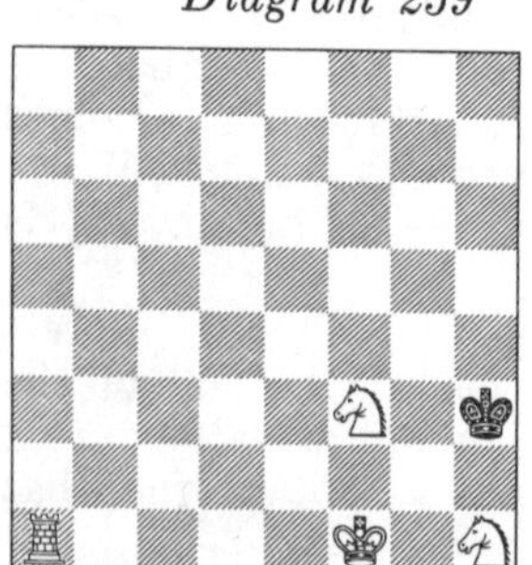

Mate in three

A. ALEKHINE, 1914
Diagram 260

Mate in three

V. GEBELT, 1965

Diagram 261

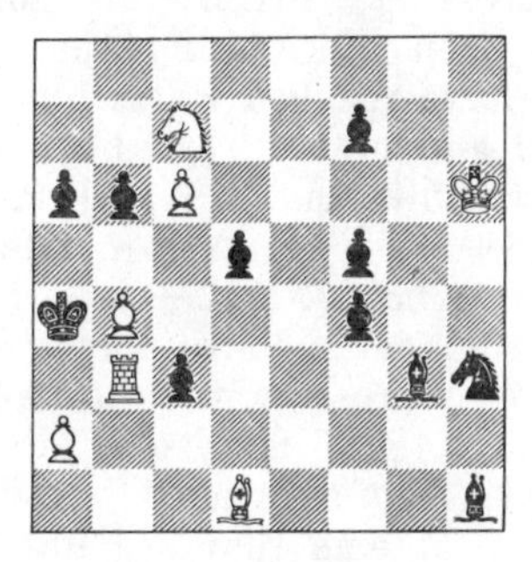

Mate in four

The problem in Diagram 262, composed by the famous Russian player A. D. Petrov in 1824, is entitled "Napoleon's Flight From Moscow to Paris".

Diagram 262

The a1-square is Moscow, and h8 is Paris. The a8-h1 diagonal is the river Berezina. Black's King is Napoleon, White's Knights are the Russian cavalry pursuing him. The solution of the problem is ingenious.

1. Nd2+ Ka2 2. Nc3+ Ka3 3. Ndb1+ Kb4 4. Na2+ Kb5 5. Nbc3+ Ka6 6. Nab4+ (here

Petrov, hinting at the failure to take advantage of the chance to capture Napoleon at the Berezina river crossing, writes: "Napoleon's road should have been blocked by the Queen, then he wouldn't have reached Paris but would have been checked and mated" (possibly 6. Qa8++) 6. ... Ka7 7. Nb5+ Kb8 8. Na6+ Kc8 9. Na7+ Kd7 10. Nb8+ Ke7 11. Nc8+ Kf8 12. Nd7+ Kg8 13. Ne7+ Kh8 14. Kg2++.

Napoleon, driven back to Paris, is mated.

I. Shumov's "Crossing the Balkans" problem (Diagram 263), 1878, is also interesting. Mate in eight moves. The solution is simple.

Humorous problems that are unusual in content or structure hold a special place in composition (see Diagrams 264, 265).

Diagram 263

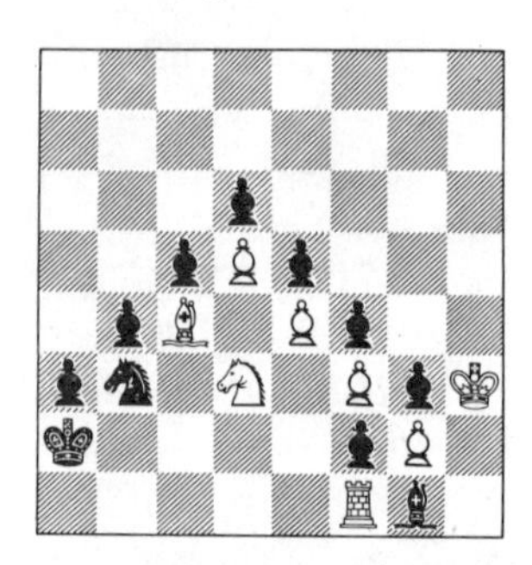

ENDGAME STUDIES

These are closer to actual play than problems are. They have no restrictions on the number of moves, and the solution can start with the capture of a Pawn or with a check.

Here are several original endgame studies.

"King in the Dungeon"
Diagram 264

Mate in four

"The Deposed King"
Diagram 265

Mate in eight

F. SAAVEDRA, 1895
Diagram 266

White to play and win

A. TROITSKY, 1916
Diagram 267

White to play and win

M. and V. PLATOV, 1909
Diagram 268

White to play and win

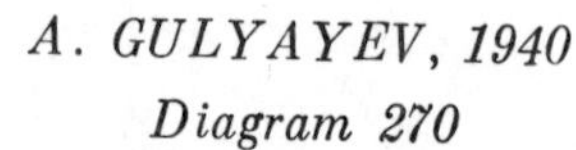

L. KUBBEL, 1935

Diagram 269

White to play and win

A. GULYAYEV, 1940

Diagram 270

White to play and win

G. KASPARYAN, 1937

Diagram 271

White to play and draw

A. TROITSKY, 1941

Diagram 272

White to play and draw

Solution of Problems

The solution of a twomover usually indicates only the first move. In a threemover it indicates the first two moves in each variation, and so on.

Diagram 255. 1. Ba4! An unexpected and spectacular move. White's Bishop goes "into ambush". An interesting variation is 1. ... Bxe4 2. Bd1++, with a blocking of the e4-square.

Diagram 256. 1. Rch5! (threatening 2. Qd5++) 1. ... Rg6 (unpinning the Knight in order to protect the d5-square). 2. Kf5++; 1. Bg6 2. Kg5++. Other moves by the Rooks do not achieve the aim: 1. Rg5? Bg6! Or 1. Rf5? Rg6!—his own Rook blocks the g5- or f5-square, to which White's King retreats in the main variations. Additional variations: 1. ... Nb4 2. Qc5++; 1. ... Nc3 2. Kxe3++; 1. bxc6 2. Qe5++.

Diagram 257. 1. Qc1! (threatening 2. Qf4++; Variations: 1. ... Rb4 2. Qc5++; 1. ... Nd3 2. e4++; 1. ... Bd6 2. Be6++; 1. ... g5 2. Bh7++. 1. Qe3? is refuted by 1. ... Nd3! (White's Queen covered up the e4-Pawn) and 1. e3? Rb4! (nor does 2. Qc5 produce mate because of the coverup).

Diagram 258. 1. f8N! There threatens 2. Qe2+ Kh6 3. Rg6++. Variations: 1. ... Bxf8 2. Qg1! and 3. Qh2++, (taking advantage of the diversion of the Black Bishop from the h4-d8 diagonal); 1. ... f5 2. Rh3+ Kg5 3. Qh4++ (the square f5 is blocked by a Black Pawn); 1. ... Kh6 2. Rg6+ Kh5 3. g4++ (Drawing Black's King to h6 to free the road to the g-Pawn with a tempo). The false spoor is refuted: 1. f8Q? f5!

Diagram 259. 1. Nh2! Kxh2 2. Ra3!; 1. ... Kh4 2. Ra5.

Diagram 260. The first move is spectacular: 1. Qf5!; 1. ... Bxf5 2. Ra7+!; 1. ... Bxd4 2. Kd7!

Diagram 261. 1. Be2! b5 2. Nxa6 Bf2 3. Nc7; 1. ... d4 2. Bb5+! axb5 3. Na8!; 1. ... f3 2. Nxd5! Bf4+ 3. Kh5.

Diagram 263. White's King sets out on the trip Kg4-f5-e6-d7-c6-b5-a4. At the same time

Black moves his Bishop: Bg1-h2-a1, etc. After that comes 8. Bxb3++.

Diagram 264. 1. Qc2! d3 2. Qc3+ d4 3. Qa5+ d5 4. Qc7++; 1. ... f3 2. Qh2+ f4 3. Qh5+; 1. ... e3 2. Nd3+ Ke4 3. Nc5+.

Diagram 265. 1. 0-0-0! Kxa7 2. Rd8! Kxa6 3. Rd7 Kxa5 4. Rd6 Kxa4 5. Rd5 Kxa3 6. Rd4 Kxa2 7. Rd3 Ka1 8. Ra3++.

Solution of Endgame Studies

Diagram 266. 1. c7! Rd6+ 2. Kb5!! Rd5+ 3. Kb4 Rd4+ 4. Kb3 Rd3+ 5. Kc2 Rd4! 6. c8R! (6. c8Q? Rc4+! 7. Qxc4. Stalemate) 6. ... Ra4 7. Kb3, and White wins.

Diagram 267. 1. Qd4+ Kg5 (not 1. ... Kf5 due to 2. Qd3+, winning the Queen) 2. Qf6+ Kg4 3. Qf3+ Kg5 4. Qg3+ Bg4 5. Qh4+!! Kxh4 6. Bf6++. A spectacular finale!

White also wins if Black does not take the Queen on the fifth move but draws his King back. For instance, 5. ... Kf4 6. Qf2+ or 5. ... Kf5 6. Qf6+ Ke4 7. Qd4+ Kf5 8. Qe5+ Kg6 9. Qf6++.

Diagram 268. 1. Bf6 d4 2. Ne2!! a1Q 3. Nc1!! (but not 3. Bxd4+ Qxd4 4. Nxd4 Kxd4 5. Kg4 Kxd3 6. Kg5 Ke4 7. Kh6 Kf5 8. Kxh7 Kf6 9. h6 Kf7 with a draw. Now threatening 4. Bg5++, and in case 3. ... h6, there follows 4. Be5 and 5. Bf4++. The Knight cannot be taken because of 4. Bg5+, and if 3. ... Kd2 there follows 4. Nb3+) 3. ... Qa5 (defending the g5-square) 4. Bxd4+, Kxd4 5. Nb3+, winning.

Diagram 269. 1. Qa1+ Kh7 2. Qb1+ Kh8 3. Qb2 (ladder) 3. ... Kh7 4. Qc2+ Kh8 5. Qc3+ Kh7 6. Qd3 (not 6. Qh3+ Kg6 7. Qg4+ Kf6 8. Qxg8 because of 8. ... Qxf2 with a draw) 6. ... Kh8 7. Qh3+ Bh7 8. Qc3+ Kg8 9. Qc8!!

(an unexpectedly beautiful move threatening a discovered check 10. Bc5+, winning the Queen) 9. ... Kf7 (or 9. ... Qf7 10. Bh6+! and mate on the next move) 10. Bc5!, and White wins the Queen.

Diagram 270. 1. g7! f2 2. Be7! f1Q 3. Bf6 Qxf6! 4. gxh8Q+ (not, of course, 4. exf7?, due to a stalemate) 4. ... Qxh8 5. d4! A rare position when Black, having a Queen against only two Pawns, loses. 5. ... Qg7 6. hxg7 h5 7. e6 h4 8. e7 h3 9. Kd7 h2 10. e8Q+, and White wins.

Diagram 271. White has two extra Pawns but his situation looks hopeless. Black's Pawn queens.

However, White obtains a stalemate.

1. Kd7 h5 (in the case of 1. ... Kb8? there will follow 2. Ke6, holding up the h-Pawn) 2. Kc7! h4 (not 2. ... Ka7? because of 3. b6+ Ka8 4. a4 h4 5. a5 h3 6. a6! and White wins) 3. Kb6 h3 4. Ka5 h2 (or 4. ... b6+ 5. Ka4! h2 6. a3 h1Q 7. b3, and no matter how Black moves White is stalemated) 5. b6! h1Q 6. b5! To carry out his plan White needs two more Pawn moves. Surprisingly, Black does not accomplish anything within these two moves. For instance, 6. ... Qb1 7. a4! Qe1+ (7. ... Qxb2, stalemate) 8. b4. A draw.

Diagram 272. Black has a Rook against White Pawns, but White gets a draw by perpetual check. 1. b6+! (enciting the Rook to the b6-square, where Black has to defend it with the King) 1. ... Rxb6 2. Bd6+! Nxd6 (the Knight covers the sixth rank. If 2. ... Rxd6 there follows 3. Nb5+ Kc6 4. Nxd6 Kxd6 5. b4! Nxb4. A draw). 3. Ne6+ Kc6 4. Nd4 Kc5 5. Ne6+ Kb5 6. Nd4+ Ka5 7. b4+! Nxb4 (not 7. ... Rxb4 because of 8. Nc6+) Now, however, the b-file is also cut off. White gives perpetual check with the Knight: 8. Nb3+ Kb5 9. Nd4+. A draw.

X. CHESS: PAST AND PRESENT

When and where did chess make its appearance? Although there is no exact information on this score and the name of its inventor is unknown, it is believed that the game originated in India 1,500 years ago. It was then called *chaturanga*.

The name *chaturanga* ("quadripartite") is connected with the four fighting arms in ancient India: elephants, cavalry, chariots and infantry. Later, probably outside India, in countries comprising the Arab caliphate, chaturanga was transformed into *shatranj*.

The rules of shatranj differed considerably from those of modern chess. The Queen moved only along a diagonal, one square at a time. The Bishop moved along a diagonal, jumping over one square at a time; the square over which it jumped could be occupied by its own or an enemy piece. Even from its initial position the Pawn moved only one square. Castling did not exist. Only the King, Rook and Knight moved according to the same rules as they do today. Play proceeded very slowly. This was improved a little by the creation of special opening positions, with which play usually started.

Chess penetrated into Western Europe in the eighth and ninth centuries through the Arabs.

Simultaneously, or perhaps earlier, chess appeared in Russia, which traded with India and the Middle Asia. Excavations by Soviet archaeologists reveal that the game was known in Kiev Rus and Novgorod in the 10th and 12th centuries.

The heroes of Russian epic tales—heroes Ilya Muromets, Dobrynya Nikitich and Alyosha Popovich—played chess. Trader Sadko, another character from Russian epic tales, took along with him to the bottom of Lake Ilmen a chessboard with golden pieces. Chess was widespread in medieval Georgia. Shotha Rusthveli mentions chess in his poem "The Knight in the Tiger's Skin" (12th century).

Chess underwent a new rise beginning with the 13th to 16th centuries thanks to the introduction of new rules which made the game lively and dynamic.

The first chess books appeared: a treatise by Luis Ramirez de Lucena (1497) and Damiano da Odemira (Rome, 1512). A book by the Spanish author Ruy Lopéz, *On Resourcefulness in Chess* (1561) created a big impression.

The Italians Giovanni Leonardo and Paolo Boi won renown in the 16th century. So, in the 17th century did another Italian, Gioacchino Greco, known as Il Calabrese. Greco's manuscript, first published in 1656, after his death, in an English translation gained wide popularity and was translated into several other languages.

The best player of the 18th century was the Frenchman Philidor (real name François André Danican). He was also an excellent chess composer. Philidor's book *Analysis of Chess* came out in a number of editions and was translated into many languages. There is an opening named after him: "Philidor's Defence".

International chess contests began in the 19th century. A series of matches between Mahé de Le Bourdonnais of France and Alexander Mac-

Donnel, the strongest British player, aroused general interest. The Frenchman emerged victorious, winning 45 games, losing 27 and drawing 13.

The first international tournament took place in London in 1851 in connection with an industrial exposition. The German master Adolph Anderssen of Breslau took first place. His beautiful combinations attracted the attention of contemporaries. One of the games, in which he carried out a brilliant combination with numerous sacrifices, was called immortal.

ANDERSSEN *KIESERITSKY*

London, 1851

King's Gambit. 1. e4 e5 2. f4 exf4 3. Bc4 Qh4+ 4. Kf1 b5 5. Bxb5 Nf6 6. Nf3 Qh6 7. d3 Nh5 8. Nh4! Qg5 9. Nf5 c6 10. g4! Nf6 11. Rg1! cxb5 12. h4 Qg6 13. h5 Qg5 14. Qf3 Ng8 15. Bxf4 Qf6 16. Nc3 Bc5 17. Nd5!? Qxb2 18. Bd6!!

An exceptional combination! White sacrifices two Rooks for an attack.

Diagram 273

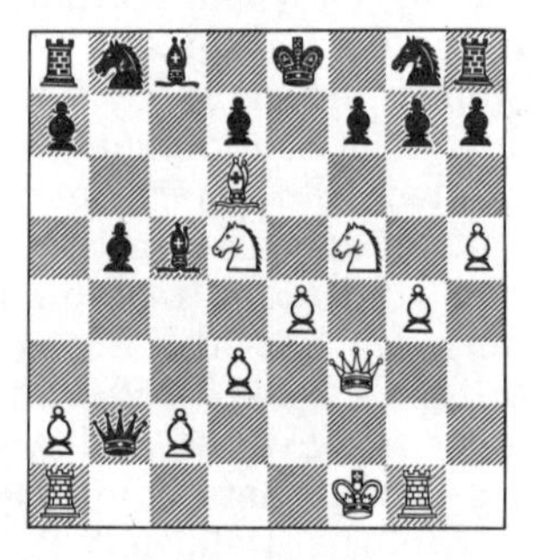

18. ... Bxg1 (the best chance is 18 ... Qxa1+ 19. Ke2 Qb2) 19. e5! (with this quiet move White excludes Black's Queen from defence of

the g7-point) 19. ... Qxa1+ 20. Ke2 Na6 (Tchigorin proved that even the better move 20. ... Ba6 was of no help) 21. Nxg7+ Kd8 22. Qf6+!! Nxf6 23. Be7++.

Among the participants of the first international tournament in London was Howard Staunton. His *The Chess Player's Handbook* (1847) was quite valuable at the time.

The American player Paul Charles Morphy was a star of the first magnitude in the chess world. He participated in contests only two years, 1857-59. He defeated the strongest players of Europe in matches. This included a victory over Anderssen with a score of 7 games, 2 lost and 2 drawn. The brilliant style of his victories, with their remarkable combinations, make a deep impression.

Here is one of his masterpieces (Paulsen versus Morphy, New York, 1857).

Diagram 274

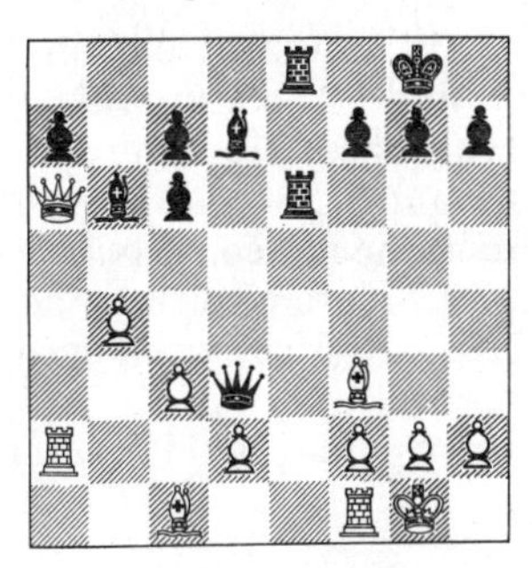

1. ... Qxf3!! (a brilliant sacrifice, after which White's position is indefensible) 2. gxf3 Rg6+ 3. Kh1 Bh3 (threatening 4. ... Bg2+ and 5. ... Bxf3++) 4. Rd1 Bg2+ 5. Kg1 Bxf3+ 6. Kf1 Bg2+ 7. Kg1 Bh3+ (Morphy passes over to a won ending) 8. Kh1 Bxf2 9. Qf1 Bxf1 10. Rxf1 Re2 11. Ra1 Rh6 12. d4? Bc3. White resigns.

Morphy's play was based on an excellent positional foundation. In positions of an open type he energetically took advantage of the edge in development. Harmoniously placing his pieces and Pawns in the centre of the board, he usually gained superiority in the early stage of the game and soon after he launched vigorous attacks. To say that someone "played in the Morphy style" is an accolade to this day. Unfortunately, Morphy stopped playing chess early due to the impairment of his health.

The second international tournament, held in London in 1862, ended in another victory for Anderssen.

Towards the end of the 19th century a contest was organised to name the world's best chess player. Wilhelm Steinitz (born in Prague) was officially recognised as the world champion after beating Johannes Zukertort in 1886, winning 10 games, losing 5 and drawing 5.

Steinitz laid the basis for the scientific theory of chess. He paid much attention to weak and strong points and the accumulation of small positional advantages. He regarded the appraisal of positions and the planning of play to be of paramount importance. Steinitz clearly revealed the flaws of premature attacks and made the most of the slightest weakening of a position.

The following game is characteristic of his style of play.

ZUKERTORT *STEINITZ*

Match, 1886

Queen's Gambit. 1. d4 d5 2. c4 e6 3. Nc3 Nf6 4. e3 c5 5. Nf3 Nc6 6. a3 dxc4 7. Bxc4 cxd4 8. exd4 Be7 9. 0-0 0-0 10. Be3 Bd7 11. Qd3 Rc8 12. Rac1 Qa5 13. Ba2 Rfd8 14. Rfe1 Be8 15. Bb1 g6 16. Qe2 Bf8 17. Red1 Bg7 18. Ba2 Ne7 19. Qd2 Qa6 20. Bg5 Nf5 21. g4? Nxd4! 22. Nxd4 e5 23. Nd5 Rxc1 24. Qxc1 exd4 25. Rxd4 Nxd5 26. Rxd5 Rxd5 27. Bxd5 Qe2 28. h3 h6 29. Bc4 Qf3 30. Qe3 Qd1+ 31. Kh2 Bc6 32. Be7 Be5+! 33. f4 Bxf4+ 34. Qxf4 Qh1+ 35. Kg3 Qg1+. White resigns.

Steinitz is the author of numerous studies dealing with chess theory. The Steinitz Defence in the Ruy Lopéz is widely known. His *Modern Chess Instructor* (1889) greatly influenced the further development of chess theory.

Russians have long been famed for their skill in chess. Ivan the Terrible played chess. Peter the Great introduced the game among his courtiers.

Nonetheless, the conditions in tsarist Russia were unfavourable for chess. For a long time no Russian masters played in international tournaments. The first famous Russian player was Alexander Petrov. He wrote an excellent manual *Systematised Chess Play* (1824). A copy of Petrov's book, with his autograph as a gift to the great Russian poet Alexander Pushkin, has survived to this day. Petrov was also widely known for the many excellent problems he composed.

Professor Karl Janisch of Russia was an eminent chess theoretician. His book *A New Analysis of Chess Openings* (1842) is a fundamental work in the theory of openings.

Among other Russian masters who made a noteworthy contribution to the national chess history were Ilya Shumov, the brothers Sergei and Dmitri Urusov and Emmanuil Schiffers.

Mikhail Tchigorin, founder of the Russian chess school, played an exceptional role in the development of the game in Russia. He competed successfully in international tournaments and also did much to popularise the game. In 1899 he organised the First All-Russia Tournament. The magazine *Shakhmatny Listok*, which Tchigorin published at his own expense, greatly influenced the game.

Tchigorin introduced many new features into the theory of chess. His defence in the Ruy Lopéz preserves its significance to this day. Tchigorin scored big successes in international contests. The prizes he took in major tournaments and his win over world champion Steinitz in a two-game cable match entitled him to play Steinitz for the world title in 1889 and 1892. Although Steinitz won both matches, a number of the games testified to the Russian master's high class.

Here is a game from the second match.

TCHIGORIN *STEINITZ*

Evans Gambit. 1. e4 e5 2. Nf3 Nc6 3. Bc4 Bc5 4. b4 Bxb4 5. c3 Ba5 6. 0-0 d6 7. d4 Bg4 8. Bb5 exd4 9. cxd4 Bd7 10. Bb2 Nce7 11. Bxd7+ Qxd7 12. Na3! Nh6 13. Nc4 Bb6 14. a4! c6 15. e5! d5 16. Nd6+ Kf8 17. Ba3 Kg8 18. Rb1! Nhf5 19. Nxf7!

Diagram 275

An unusual sacrifice based on intuition rather than on exact calculation. Black's King finds himself in the centre of the board. White is in a position to launch a devastating attack.

19. ... Kxf7 20. e6+! Kxe6 21. Ne5! Qc8 22. Re1 Kf6 23. Qh5 g6 24. Bxe7+ Kxe7 25. Nxg6+ Kf6 26. Nxh8 Bxd4 27. Rb3! Qd7 28. Rf3 Rxh8 29. g4 Rg8 30. Qh6+ Rg6 31. Rxf5+. Black resigns.

Emannuel Lasker (born in Berlinchen, now Barlinek, Poland) became the second world champion by defeating Steinitz in 1894, winning 10 games, losing 5 and drawing 4. He held the world crown for 27 years, defending it against rivals in a number of matches. Lasker, a man with doctorates in mathematics and philosophy, was a subtle psychologist and possessed exceptional competitive traits and will power. He retained his playing strength until old age. Taking part in the 1935 international tournament in Moscow at the age of 67, Lasker placed third without a single defeat. He came out ahead of many of the leading participants, including Capablanca, to whom he had earlier yielded the chess crown.

Lasker played the following game in the 1935 Moscow tournament with remarkable energy.

LASKER *PIRC*

Sicilian Defence.

1. e4 c5 2. Nf3 Nc6 3. d4 cxd4 4. Nxd4 Nf6 5. Nc3 d6 6. Be2 e6 7. 0-0 a6 8. Be3 Qc7 9. f4 Na5 (this is premature. 9. ... Be7 is better) 10. f5! Nc4 11. Bxc4 Qxc4 12. fxe6 fxe6 (see Dia. 276).

On the 13th move Lasker sacrifices the exchange and launches a crushing attack.

13. Bxf6! gxf6 14. Qh5+Kd8 5. Qf7 Bd7 (if 15. ... Be7 the issue is settled by 16. Nf5! Qc7 17. Kh1 with the threat Bb6) 16. Qxf6+ Kc7 17. Qxh8 Bh6 18. Nxe6+! Qxe6 19. Qxa8 Bxe3+ 20. Kh1. Black resigns.

Diagram 276

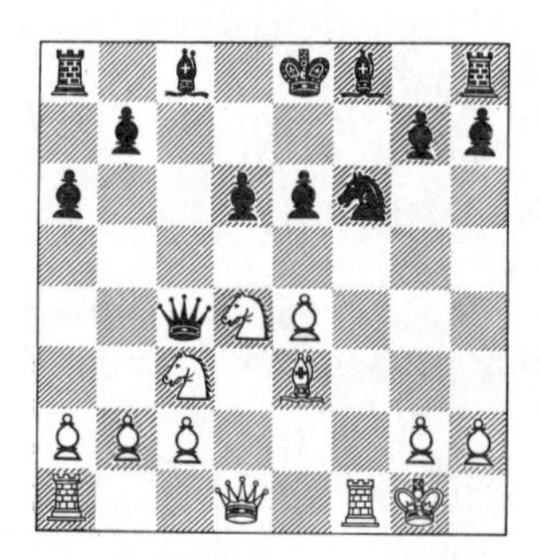

Lasker's books, *Common Sense in Chess* and *Chess Manual* were published in many languages, including Russian.

The Cuban master José Raoul Capablanca left a brilliant trail in the history of chess. By defeating Lasker in 1921 (he won 4 games, lost none and drew 10) he became the world's third chess champion. His play was distinguished by exceptional ease, speed and faultless technique. The peak of his success was the international tournament in New York in 1927, where he placed first. His brilliant victory over Spielmann won him the prize for the best game there. Here it is.

CAPABLANCA *SPIELMANN*

Queen's Gambit.

1. d4 d5 2. Nf3 e6 3. c4 Nd7 4. Nc3 Ngf6 5. Bg5 Bb4 6. cxd5 exd5 7. Qa4 Bxc3+ 8. bxc3 0-0 9. e3 c5 10. Bd3 c4 11. Bc2 Qe7 12. 0-0 a6 13. Rfe1 Qe6 14. Nd2! b5 15. Qa5 Ne4? (15 ... Bb7 is better) 16. Nxe4 dxe4 17. a4! Qd5.

Capablanca sacrifices a Bishop. He has calculated the combination exactly.

18. axb5!! Qxg5 19. Bxe4 Rb8 (or 19. ... Ra7 20. b6 Qxa5 21. bxa7! Qxa1 22. Rxa1 Nb6

Diagram 277

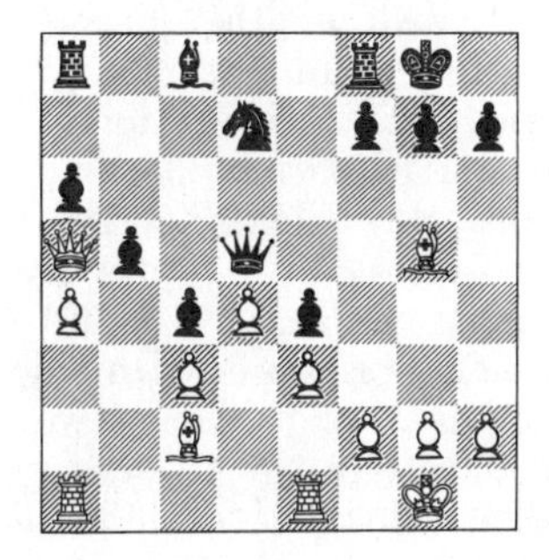

23. a8Q, and White wins) 20. bxa6 Rb5 21. Qc7 Nb6 22. a7 Bh3 23. Reb1! Rxb1+ 24. Rxb1 f5 25. Bf3 f4 26. exf4. Black resigns.

Capablanca's books *My Chess Career*, *Chess Fundamentals*, and *Chess Manual* have been published in Russian.

One of the most thrilling contests in chess annals was the world title match between Capablanca and Alekhine in Buenos Aires at the end of 1927. The battle lasted two and a half months. Alekhine won six games, Capablanca won three and 25 games ended in a draw. Alekhine was thus the first Russian to become the world champion.

Alexander Alekhine's inexhaustible imagination enabled him to carry out the most unexpected, far calculated combinations. He was unsurpassed in this sphere. Alekhine's victories in tournaments in Baden-Baden (1925), San Remo (1930) and Bled (1931), in which the world's strongest players competed, confirmed his fame. He made many valuable contributions to chess theory. There is an opening, Alekhine Defence, named after him. The collection of his best games is a manual for every lover of beautiful chess.

In 1935 Alekhine lost a match for the world title to Max Euwe of the Netherlands (Euwe won 9 games, lost 8 and drew 13). Grandmaster Euwe, a famed chess theoretician, holder of a doctorate in mathematics, became the world's fifth champion. But Alekhine regained the title in impressive fashion in a return match in 1937. Alekhine won 10 games, lost 4 and drew 11. He retained the world crown until his death in 1946.

From Alekhine's large legacy we present here his game with Réti in the tournament in Baden-Baden in 1925. Alekhine considered the combination in this game to be his best.

RÉTI *ALEKHINE*

Réti Opening. 1. g3 e5 2. Nf3 e4 3. Nd4 d5 4. d3 exd4 5. Qxd3 Nf6 6. Bg2 Bb4+ 7. Bd2 Bxd2+ 8. Nxd2 0-0 9. c4 Na6! 10. cxd5 Nb4 11. Qc4 Nbxd5 12. N2b3 c6 13. 0-0 Re8 14. Rfd1 Bg4 15. Rd2 Qc8 16. Nc5 Bh3! 17. Bf3 (not 17. Bxh3 Qxh3 18. Nxb7 because of 18. ... Ng4 19. Nf3 Nde3! with decisive threats) 17. ... Bg4 18. Bg2 Bh3 19. Bf3 Bg4 20. Bh1 (White unwisely refuses a draw) 20. ... h5! 21. b4 a6 22. Rc1 h4 23. a4 hxg3 24. hxg3 Qc7! 25. b5 axb5 26. axb5 Re3!!

Diagram 278

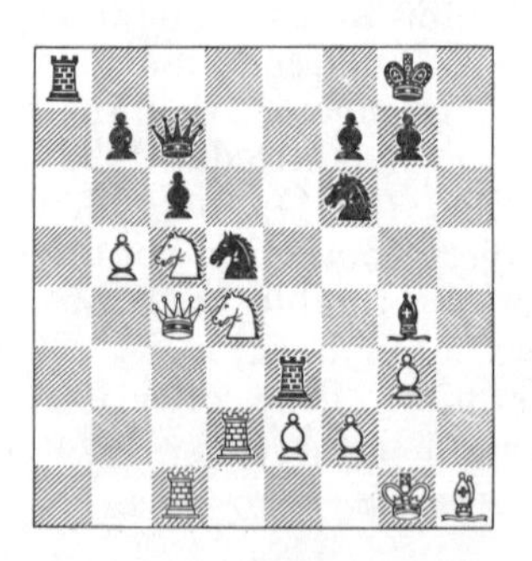

Alekhine launches a direct attack by a spectacular move. The Rook cannot be taken because of 27. ... Qxg3+ and 28. ... Nxe3. Black threatens to sacrifice the Rook on g3. Although Black's Rook remains a target for six moves White is unable to take it.

27. Nf3 cxb5 28. Qxb5 Nc3! 29. Qxb7 Qxb7 30. Nxb7 Nxe2+ 31. Kh2 (or 31. Kf1 Nxg3+! 32. fxg3 Bxf3, etc.) 31. ... Ne4!! 32. Rc4! (or 32. fxe3 Nxd2!, winning the Exchange) 32. ... Nxf2! 33. Bg2 Be6! 34. Rcc2 Ng4+ 35. Kh3 Ne5+ 36. Kh2 Rxf3! 37. Rxe2 Ng4+ 38. Kh3 Ne3+ 39. Kh2 Nxc2 40. Bxf3 Nd4! White resigns. If 41. Rf2 there will follow 41. ... Nxf3+ 42. Rxf3 Bd5!, winning a piece.

Two of the most eminent players in pre-revolutionary Russia, Grandmasters Akiba Rubinstein and Aron Nimzovitch, could not enter the battle for the world title owing to lack of funds. Rubinstein was distinguished by iron logic and consistency. Systems he developed live on in chess today.

A combination of rare beauty was implemented by Rubinstein, playing Black, in his game with Rotlewi in the Fifth All-Russia Tournament in 1907.

Diagram 279

Taking advantage of the strength of the Bishops on open diagonals, Rubinstein builds up mating threats.

22. ... Rxc3!! 23. gxh4 (or 23. Bxc3 Bxe4+ 24. Qxe4 Qxh2++) 23. ... Rd2!! (Deviation idea! Black gives up the Queen, and among the remaining five pieces four are under attack!) 24. Qxd2 Bxe4+ 25. Qg2 Rh3! White resigns.

An innovator to whom everything trite was alien, Nimzovitch was not only an outstanding player, but also a man of letters, author of the excellent books *Blockade*, *My System*, and *The Praxis of My System*. To this day the Nimzovitch Defence and the Nimzovitch Variation in the French Defence are popular openings.

"The Immortal Zugzwang Game" is how the Sämisch versus Nimzovitch encounter in Copenhagen in 1922 is called in chess literature.

Nimzoindian Defence 1. d4 Nf6 2. c4 e6 3. Nf3 b6 4. g3 Bb7 5. Bg2 Be7 6. Nc3 0-0 7. 0-0 d5 8. Ne5 c6 9. cxd5 cxd5 10. Bf4 a6! 11. Rc1 b5 12. Qc3 Nc6! 13. Nxc6 (otherwise there will follow Na5) 13. ... Bxc6 14. h3 Qd7 15. Kh2 Nh5 16. Bd2 f5! 17. Qd1 b4! 18. Nb1 Bb5 19. Rg1 Bd6 20. e4 fxe4!! (The sacrifice of a piece is designed to cramp White's play to the utmost.) 21. Qxh5 Rxf2 22. Qg5 Raf8 23. Kh1 R8f5 24. Qe3 Bd3 25. Rce1 h6!! (see Diagram 280).

White resigns in this position. Although almost all the pieces are on the board, he has no moves, finding himself in zugzwang. Any move he makes worsens his position or leads to material losses. Thus, for instance, 26. Kh2 or 26. g4 will be followed by 26. ... R5f3!

In the decades since the Great October Socialist Revolution of 1917 chess has reached unprecedented heights in the Soviet Union. All conditions for its development among the people at large have been created.

Diagram 280

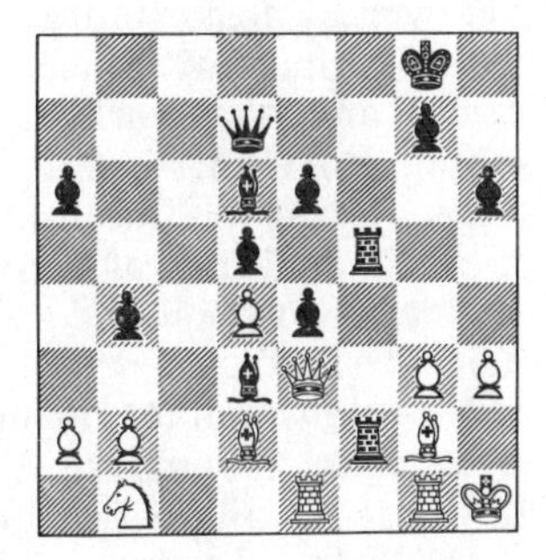

The creativity and achievements of Soviet players have won world-wide recognition.

Convincingly defeating all his rivals in the 1948 world title match-tournament played in the Hague and Moscow, Mikhail Botvinnik of the Soviet Union became the sixth world champion. Since then the world crown has been in the possession of Soviet players practically all the time.

Mikhail Botvinnik, long-standing leader of the Soviet players, is a profound connoisseur of chess theory. His approach to the game is scientific. His analysis of opening systems and middle game and ending positions is distinguished by utmost exactitude. Botvinnik is the author of a number of books and articles that are a valuable contribution to chess literature.

Defending his world title many times, Botvinnik held it with short intermissions, until 1963.

Besides chess Botvinnik is engaged in considerable scientific research. He holds a doctorate in technical science.

Vasili Smyslov, who became the seventh world champion, was Botvinnik's main rival for a long time. He encountered Botvinnik in three world title matches. The first, in 1954, wound up in a draw (7 won, 7 lost, 10 drawn). The second match brought Smyslov a victory (6 won, 3 lost, 13 drawn) and the world title. In the 1958 return match Botvinnik came out on top, winning 7 games, losing 5 and drawing 11.

The characteristic features of Smyslov are a rare comprehension of position and excellent endgame technique.

A number of Smyslov's games and endings have been included in chess manuals.

Mikhail Tahl scored a number of brilliant successes in 1957-1961. In addition to winning the USSR championships and international tournaments he defeated Botvinnik in a world title match in 1960, winning 6 games, losing 2 and drawning 13. However, Tahl lost the return match with a score of 5 games won, 10 lost and 6 drawn.

The eighth world champion, Mikhail Tahl is a player of a keenly combinational and uncompromising style. Attack is his element. His scintillating play has won him a big number of fans in the chess world.

One of the most interesting and representative tournaments of contenders for the world title took place in 1962 on the island of Curacao in the Caribbean Sea. In the course of a lengthy-tenacious struggle the Soviet player Tigran Petrosyan beat his revals. This was by no means easy. After all, among his opponents were such grandmasters as Keres, Geller, and Fischer.

Petrosyan faced an even more difficult problem a year later. In 1963 he met Botvinnik in a match, and came out on top with a score of 5 won, 2 lost and 15 drawn, became the ninth world champion.

The main thing in Petrosyan's play is his ability to wage a positional, manoeuvrable battle.

Harmoniously placing his pieces and Pawns, Petrosyan usually sets his opponent the difficult task of capturing the initiative. Parrying attempts to complicate the play, Petrosyan gradually intensifies the pressure.

Here is what Petrosyan said about one of the game in his 1966 match with Boris Spassky, which he won by the score of $12^1/_2$ to $11^1/_2$: "This game demonstrates my creative credo: limiting my opponent's possibilities, a strategy of play all over the board, encirclement and gradual tightening of a ring around the opposing King."

Boris Spassky, winner of the 1965 and 1968 tournaments of contenders for the world chess title, combines all-round play and an excellent background of chess theory with a creative approach.

The match with Petrosyan in 1966 did not end in Spassky's favour, but it showed how close he had come to his cherished goal, the world crown. Great interest was focussed on the match by the same two rivals in 1969, when Spassky emerged victorious and became the 10th world champion.

In 1972, the highly gifted American Grandmaster Robert Fischer became the world champion by winning a match against Spassky. It is to be regretted that Fischer stopped playing after gaining the world crown. In 1975, the title passed to the excellent Soviet player Anatoli Karpov. Karpov proved his unquestionable superiority over all his rivals not only in competition with challengers for the world title but also in the most representative international and USSR contests in the following years.

Soviet women players uphold our country's chess honour as well.

After the tragic death of the world's first woman champion, Vera Menchik, during a Luftwaffe raid on London in the Second World War a tournament of women claimants for the world title was arranged in 1949-50 by a decision of FIDE. The winner, Lyudmila Rudenko of the Soviet Union, was named world champion.

She lost the title in 1953 to her compatriot Yelizaveta Bykova, winner of a tournament of contenders, who became the third world champion. In 1956 Olga Rubtsova, also of the Soviet Union, emerged victorious in a three-cornered match-tournament (Rubtsova, Bykova and Rudenko) and captured the crown, but two years later Bykova wrested it from her.

A galaxy of talented young women players succeeded those illustrious champions. In 1962, at the age of 21, Nona Gaprindashvili from the Soviet Union's Georgian Republic defeated Bykova to became the fifth world champion. Nona's bold, energetic play brought her success both in women's and men's international tournaments. In 1978 Maya Ghiburdanidze, another young player from Georgia, became the sixth world champion.

XI. SOLUTIONS TO EXERCISES

No 3. h1, g3, h5, g7, e8, c7, a8, b6, a4, c3, e4, f6, d5, e3, c4, b2, d1, f2, h3, g5, h7, f8, d7, b8, a6, b4, a2, c1, e2 g1, f3, h4, g6, h8, f7, d8, b7, a5, b3, a1, c2, e1, g2, f4. e6, c5, d3, e5, g4, h6, g8, e7, c8, a7, c6, d4, f5, d6, b5, a3, b1, d2, f1, h2.

No 5. 1. a7, b7, c7, d7, e7, g7, h7, f4, f5, f6, f8, 2. f1, f2, f3.

No. 6. 1. a5, b6, c7, h4, g5, f6, e7, 2. d5, c6, b7, a8.

No 7. 1. g1, h2, h3, h4, h5, h6, g2, f3, e4, d5, c6, b7, a8. 2. No. The Pawn on h7 prevents that.

No. 9. 1. f4, e5, e7, f8, h8 2. The distance between all the neighbouring squares, according to the notations used, is one Knight move. That is one of the solutions of the Knight problem.

Nos. 10 and 11. b8, b7, c7, d7, d8; g8, g7, h7.

No 17. 1. Kxf2, 1. Rcxc4, 1. Bxd6, 1. Nxe4.

No. 18. 1. ... Rc2, 1. ... Cd4.

No. *25.* a) Nc5+; b) 1. ... Qd1+.

No. 26. a) Qe7++; b) ... Qg2++.

No. 32. a) Yes, 1. ... cxd3 or 1. exd3; 2. exd6 e.p.; b) No, pieces are not taken e.p.; c) No, the f-Pawn moved only one square.

No. 38. a) 1. Ra8++; b) 1. ... a1Q+ 2. Rxa1. Stalemate.

No. 41. 1. White: Kg1, Qe2, Ra1, e1, Bb2; Pawns: a2, b3, c4, f2, g2, h2 (11); Black: Kg8, Qh4, Ra8, d7, Ng4, Pawns: a7, b7, c6, f7, g6, h7 (11) 2. a) 1. Qe8+ Rxe8 2. Rxe8++; b) 1. ... Qxh2+ 2. Kf1 Qh1++.

No. 47. 1. Qf4 Kd8 2. Qf8++.
No. 52. 1. Kd6 Ke8 2. Rf1 Kd8 3. Rf8++; 1. ... Kc8 2. Rb1! Kd8 3. Rb8++.

No. 56. 1. Bc3! c4 2. Kf6! Kh8 3. Kg6++.

No. 75. A losing move. After 2. Nxc6 bxc6 White gets a remote passed Pawn ensuring him a win despite being a Pawn down, for instance: 3. a4 Kb7 4. Kc5 Kc7

5. a5 Kb7 6. a6+ Kxa6 7. Kxc6 Ka7 8. Kd7 Kb7 9. Ke7, etc.

No. 80. a) 1. ... Qxc6 (bxc6) 2. Qd8++; b) 1. Qd8+ Bxd8 2. Re8++.

No. 83. 1. ... Qxg5 2. Qxg5 Bxe3+ 3. Kd1 Rxf1+ 4. Rxf1 Bxg5.

No. 86. a) 1. Qxh7+ Kxh7 2. Rh3++; b) 1. ... Qa1+ 2. Kxa1 Bd4+ 3. Kb1 Ra1++.

No. 87. 1. e5 Bxb3 2. exf6!

No. 88. 1. Ne7+ Kh8 2. Ng6+! hxg6 3. hxg3+ Qh4 4. Rxh4++.

No. 89. 1. Qd8+! Kxd8 2. Ba5+ K~ 3. Rd8++.

No. 90. 1. ... Bb5!, winning (2. axb5 Qxe2++.)

No. 121. Black's position cannot be defended. For instance, a) 8. ... Nge7 9. Qxc7+ Ke8 10. Nd6+ Kf8 11. Qd8++; b) 8. ... Nh6 9. Nxc7 Rb8 10. Nd5, and there is no defence against the threats 11. Qc7+ or 11. Qe7++; c) 8. ... Qe7 9. Qxc7+ Ke8 10. Nd6+ Kf8 11. Nxc8; d) 8. ... Qe6 9. Nxc7; e) 8. ... Ng6 9. Bg5.

No. 128. 1. Qxd7+ (but not 1. Re8 Rd6, and Black defends himself) Rxd7 2. Re8+ Rd8 3. Rexd8++.

No. 130. 1. Bxd5+ cxd 2. Qxf8+ Kxf8 3. Rc8+

No. 132. 1. Nc5+ Kb8 2. Nd7+ Kc8 3. Nb6+ Kb8 4. Qc8+ Rxc8 5. Nd7++

No. 134. 1. Qxh5+ Nxh5 2. Rxh5+ Kg8 3. Bh7+ Kh8 4. Bxe4+ Kg8 5. Bh7+ Kh8 6. Bxd3+ Kg8 7. Bh7+ Kh8 8. Bxc2+ Kg8 9. Bh7+ Kh8 10. Bxb1+ Kg8 11. Bh7+ Kh8 12. Bb1+ Kg8 13. Bxa2, winning.

No. 137. 1. Qh8+! Kxh8 2. Nxf7+ Kg7 3. Nxg5, winning.

No. 140. 1. Qa7!! Qa5 2. Qxa6 Qc7 3. Qa7.

No. 143. 1. ... Qf1+ 2. Bg1 Qf3+ 3. Bxf3 Bxf3++.

No. 145. 1. Bd5! exd5 2. Qxc6+ Kd8 3. Qxa8+ Kd7 4. Qb7+ (but not 4. Qxd5+? because of 4. ... Qxd5 5. Nxd5 Bf3) 4. ... Ke6 5. Qc6+ Bd6 6. Bf4! Black resigned.

No. 147. 1. Qxb8+! Rxb8 2. Bxb5++.

No. 149. 1. Rf8+ Kxf8 2. Qf7++.

No. 151. Rc5! Qxc5 2. Rxh7+ and 3. Qg7++.

No. 154. 1. f8R! Kh6 2. Rh8++.

No. 159. 1. ... Rg6+! 2. Kh5 Rg5+, etc.

No. 175. 1. Rh8+! Black resigned (1. ... Kxh8 2. Qh7++).

No. 176. 1. Qh6! Qxe1+ 2. Bf1 Re8 3. Qg7++.

No. 177. 1. Rxc5! Black resigns. If 1. ... bxc5 (Qxc5), then 2. Qh4 and wins.

No. 178. 1. Nf6+ gxf6 2. exf6 and there is no defence against the threats 3. Qxf8+ and also 4. Rd8++ or 3. Qg3+ and 4. Qg7++.

No. 179. 1. ... Bh2+ 2. Kh1 Bg1! White resigns.

No. 180. 1. Qf3!! Qxf3 2. Rg1+ Kh8 3. Bg7+ Kg8 4. Bxf6+ Q∽ 5. RxQ++.

No. 181. 1. g6! f5 2. Rb8! Black resigns. If 2. ... Qxb8, then comes 3. Qxh4 followed by 4. Qh7+ and 5. Qh8++.

No. 182. 1. ... Rxe4! 2. Qxe4 Ng3 3. Qxd4 (3. Qxh7 Ne2++) 3. ... Nge2+ 4. Kh1 Qxh2+ 5. Kxh2 Rh8+ 6. Qh4 Rxh4++.

No. 186. 1. ... Nxf2! 2. Kxf2 Qh4+ 3. Ke2 Qxh2+ 4. Kd3 Nb4++ (4. Kf1 Bg3 and mate is inevitable).

No. 187. 1. Bxg6! e5 (1. ... hxg6 2. Rh2 with an irresistible attack) 2. Qh2 hxg6 3. Rxg6! Qxg6 4. Nf7+ Kg8 5. Qh8++.

No. 188. 1. ... Bxh2+ 2. Kxh2 Ng4+ 3. Kh3 Rd6 4. Bxe4 Rh6+ 5. Kg3 Qh4+ 6. Kf4 Qh2+. White resigns for mate is inevitable.

No. 189. 1. Bxh6 gxh6 2. Rd7! Nxd7 (2. ... Qxd7 3. Nf6+) 3. Qxg6+ Kf8 4. Qh7! Black resigns.

No. 191. 1. Bxh7+! Kxh7 2. Rh3+ Kg8 3. Bxg7+! Black resigns. In the case of 3. ... f6, there follows 4. Bh6! Qh7 5. Qh5 Bf8 6. Qg4+ Kh8 7. Bxf8.

No. 209. 1. b6! axb6 2. c6! bxc6 3. a6, and the a-file Pawn queens. 1. ... cxb6 2. a6! bxa6 3. c6, and the e-file Pawn queens.

No. 210. 1. a6 bxa6 2. bxa6 f3 3. a7 f2 4. a8Q f1Q 5. Qe8+ Kf5 6. Qf8+, and White wins. 1. ... b6+ 2. Kc6! f3 3. a7 f2 4. a8Q f1Q 5. Qe8+ Kf5 6. Qf8+, and White wins.

No. 211. 1. g5! hxg5+ (or 1. ... b4 2. g6! b3 3. g7 b2 4. g8Q+, etc.) 2. Ke3! b4 3. h6 b3 4. Kd2!, and White wins.

No. 212. 1. Kb1! (but not 1. Kc3? because of 1. ... a3! 2. b4 Ke6 3. Kb3 Kd6 4. Kxa3 Kc6 5. Ka4 Kb6, and a draw) 1. ... a3 2. b3! Ke6 3. Ka2 Kd6 4. Kxa3 Kc6 5. Ka4! Kb6 6. Kb4! Kc6 7. Ka5, and White wins.

No 213. 1. Kd5! (remote opposition!) 1. ... Kh6 (or 1. ... Kh4 2. Ke6! Kg4 3. Ke5) 2. Ke6 Kg6 3. Ke5 Kg7 4. Kxf5 Kf7 5. Ke5 Ke7 6. Kd5! Kf6 7. Kc5 Kf5 8. Kxb5 Kxf4 9. Kc6, and White wins.

No. 214. 1. Kh1! (that's the only right way! It is easy to see that after 1. Kg3 Ke1! 2. Kg4 Kf2 3. Kxg5 Kxf3, or 1. Kf1 Kd2 2. Kf2 Kd3! 3. Kg3 Ke3 4. Kg2 Ke2 5. Kg3 Kf1 6. Kg4 Kf2, and White loses) 1. ... Kd2 2. Kh2! Kd3 3. Kh3! Ke2 4. Kg2, White maintains the opposition, achieving a draw.

No. 220. 1. Kb6! Kb2 2. Ka5+ Kc1 (or 2. ... Ka1 3. Kb4, etc.) 3. Qh1+ Kb2 4. Qg2+ Kb1 5. Ka5 (or 5. Kb4) 5. ... a1Q+ 6. Kb3, and White wins.

No. 221. 1. b5 axb5 2. a5! h3 3. a6 h2 4. a7 Kg2 (or 4. ... h1Q+ 5. a8Q+ and White wins) 5. a8Q+ Kg1 6. Qg8+ Kh1 7. Qg3! b4 8. Qf2 b3 9. Qf1++; 1. ... a5 2. b6 h3 3. b7 h2 4. b8Q Kg2 (or 4. ... h1Q 5. Qb7+) 5. Qa8+ Kg1 6. Qxa5 h1Q 7. Qe1+, and White wins.

No. 226. 1. ... f5+! 2. gxf6 (or 2. Kh4 Qh1++) 2. .. Qf5+ 3. Kh4 Qh5++.

No. 227. 1. Qe4+ Kh5 2. Qh7+ Qh6 (2. ... Kg4 3. Qh3+, winning the Queen) 3. Qf5! c5 4. e6 c4 5. e7 Qc6+ 6. Qf3+, and White wins.

No. 236. 1. Kb7 Rb2+ 2. Ka7 Rc2 3. Rh5+ Ka4 (3. ... Kb4 4. Kb7!) 4. Kb7 Rb2+ 5. Ka6! Rc2 6. Rh4+ Ka3 7. Kb6 (threatening 8. Rxh2!) 7. ... Rb2+ 8. Ka5! Rc2 9. Rh3+ Ka2 10. Rxh2!, and White wins.

No. 237. 1. d6 g2 2. Rdg2! Rxg2 3. d7 rg3+ 4. Kd2! (but not 4. Ke4 Rg4+ 5. Ke5 Rg5+ 6. Ke6 Rg6+ 7. Ke7 Rg1! 8. D8Q Re+ and a draw) 4. ...Rg2+ 5. Kc3 Rg3+ 6. Kc4 Rg4+ 7. Kc5 Rg5+ 8. Kc6 Rg6+ 9. Kc7, and White wins.

No. 245. 1. g6 a3 2. Be7 a2 3. Bxd6+! Bxd6 4. g7 a1Q 5. g8Q Qa2+ 6. Kd7 Qxg8. Stalemate.

No. 252. 1. Nd3 Ke2 2. Ne5 Kf1! (or 2. ... Kxf2 3. Kxg4+! Nxg4. Stalemate) 3. Nxg4! Nxg4 4. f4! Nf2+ 5. Kh2 g4 (or 5. ... gxf4. Stalemate!) 6. Kg3, with a draw.